Living Well in a Down Economy

2nd Edition

by the Experts at Dummies

A Wiley Brand

Living Well in a Down Economy For Dummies®, 2nd Edition

Published by: **John Wiley & Sons, Inc.**, 111 River Street, Hoboken, NJ 07030-5774, www.wiley.com

Copyright © 2023 by John Wiley & Sons, Inc., Hoboken, New Jersey

Published simultaneously in Canada

For general information on our other products and services, please contact our Customer Care Department within the U.S. at 877-762-2974, outside the U.S. at 317-572-3993, or fax 317-572-4002. For technical support, please visit https://hub.wiley.com/community/support/dummies.

Wiley publishes in a variety of print and electronic formats and by print-on-demand. Some material included with standard print versions of this book may not be included in e-books or in print-on-demand. If this book refers to media such as a CD or DVD that is not included in the version you purchased, you may download this material at http://booksupport.wiley.com. For more information about Wiley products, visit www.wiley.com.

Library of Congress Control Number: 2022950998

ISBN 978-1-394-15964-2 (pbk); ISBN 978-1-394-19542-8 (ebk); ISBN 978-1-394-15965-9 (ebk)

SKY10040657 122822

Table of Contents

Introduction

Ask an economist what a *recession* is, and you'll likely get the answer "a decline in gross domestic product lasting two or more consecutive quarters." (*Gross domestic product*, or *GDP*, is the total value of goods and services produced in a country.) At the time of this writing, the United States isn't officially in a recession, but the economy is definitely in a downturn.

This isn't good news. Fortunately, you can do more than cross your fingers and hope for good luck. During a downturn, you have the following main objectives:

>> **Prepare yourself in case you lose your job.** Companies are always looking for ways to save money. Unfortunately, payroll reduction (read "layoffs and firings") is a way to save. Fortunately, by preparing a resume and seeing this as an opportunity to explore alternative careers and ways to work, you can be proactive in protecting yourself in case you find yourself on the job market.

>> **Take control of your finances.** Figure out what you have and what you spend and then make deliberate decisions about ways to rein in your spending. Your goal should be to live within your means (if you're not already), to preserve your long-term financial goals, and to save enough to see you through a period of unemployment in case you lose your job.

>> **Continue to live and enjoy your life while maintaining control of your finances.** The key isn't just to scale back but to do so in a way that you don't feel deprived. You can save a lot just by being a savvier consumer and by spending your money a little differently.

>> **Have a plan to follow if the worst happens.** In uncertain times, you may find yourself, despite your best efforts, facing a financial catastrophe like a bankruptcy or foreclosure. Even in these circumstances, you still have options — maybe not many, and maybe not pleasant ones, but options that can help you weather even these storms.

Bottom line: In a stumbling economy, you have to tread carefully, but you can still move forward. This book helps you one step at a time.

Within this book, you may note that some web addresses break across two lines of text. If you're reading this book in print and want to visit one of these web pages, simply key in the web address exactly as it's noted in the text, pretending as though the line break doesn't exist. If you're reading this as an e-book, you've got it easy — just click the web address to be taken directly to the web page.

About This Book

Living Well in a Down Economy For Dummies, 2nd Edition, contains 175 tips and suggestions to help you through tough economic times. How can you scale back on celebrations without sacrificing the fun? How can you continue to save for retirement when you need all your income to make ends meet now? What do you do when college loans — or tuition — come due and money is tight? How can you save money on household expenses?

This book answers these and other questions for people looking to save money without sacrificing quality of life.

Each part of this book is divided into tips containing information relevant to that part's theme. The great thing about this book is that you decide where to start and what to read. It's a reference you can jump into and out of at will. Thumb through to glance at a variety of tips, or go to the Table of Contents to find the different categories of tips.

Foolish Assumptions

In writing this book, we made some assumptions about you:

>> You feel uneasy about the economy and want to get yourself and your family in a better financial position.

>> You worry about losing your job, or you've already lost your job, and you need advice on finding work and cutting your expenses.

>> You want to know how you can continue to plan for long-term financial goals like retirement and college savings when money's tight.

>> You want to be a savvier, more thoughtful consumer so you can continue to enjoy life's pleasures without spending too much.

Icons Used in This Book

Many people, when facing stressful times, become very focused. In addition to myriad tips, this book uses the following icons to highlight information:

REMEMBER

This icon appears beside especially important information: stuff that you absolutely need to know to make informed, wise decisions.

TIP

This icon highlights especially clever advice about living well when the economy is in a downturn.

WARNING

When times are tough and money is tight, mistakes are especially dangerous. This icon warns you about things that may have serious negative consequences.

Beyond the Book

In addition to the material in the print or e-book you're reading right now, this product comes with some access-anywhere goodies on the web. To get this free Cheat Sheet, simply go to www.dummies.com and search for "Living Well in a Down Economy For Dummies Cheat Sheet" in the Search box.

Where to Go from Here

Whether you read this book from front to back or jump in and out as the need arises, you're certain to find a variety of ways to cut your expenses and stabilize your finances. Look at the Table of Contents to find general categories of tips, search the index to find specific tips, or just flip through until something catches your eye.

1

Facing Off Against a Recession

Take hold of your own finances and your attitude, even amid rising costs, falling income, uncertain employment, and no real idea how long the downturn will last. Harbingers like these can make anyone feel that economic stability is slipping beyond his grasp, but you can control how you respond.

Try out some useful relaxation tips — because everyone deserves a break during stressful times.

#1
Determining Your Net Worth

Your *net worth statement* is simply a listing of all that you *own* and all that you *owe*. The difference between the two is your *net worth*. Your net worth is like a financial report card and reveals a lot about you. One glance at a net worth statement and you have a pretty good idea whether a person has made a lot of financial mistakes, has had terrible misfortune, has been a fantastic money manager, or has been just darn lucky.

TIP

Figure out your net worth now using the following table and update it each and every year, shortly after year-end, because that's when you receive the previous year's year-end statements on your mortgage, retirement accounts, pension, investments, bank accounts, and a slew of tax-related documents. That's an excellent time to update your net worth statement.

REMEMBER

Don't beat yourself up over your current financial situation. It does no good; in fact, it's actually very harmful. You may not like what you see on your net worth statement, but consider this step the beginning of your quest for financial freedom. The only things that matter are the decisions you make in the present and the future. You can't change the past, but you can learn from your successes and failures. Focus on what you can gain from the exercise in the following table and then use that knowledge to help stay on track going forward.

Assets	Value	Liabilities	Balance
Cash Accounts	$ _____	**Home Mortgage**	$ _____
Checking	$ _____		
Savings	$ _____		
Money Market	$ _____		
Cash on Hand	$ _____		
Personal Use Assets	$ _____	**Home Equity Loan/ Line of Credit**	$ _____
Residence	$ _____	**Auto Loans**	$ _____
Personal Property	$ _____		
Auto(s)	$ _____		
Boat(s)	$ _____		
Vacation Home	$ _____		
Other	$ _____		
Investment Assets	$ _____	**Investment Loans**	$ _____
Brokerage Accounts	$ _____	**Margin Account**	$ _____
Mutual Funds	$ _____	**Loans against 401(k), 403(b)**	$ _____
IRAs	$ _____		
401(k), 403(b)	$ _____		
Other retirement plans	$ _____		
Cash Value of Life Insurance Policies	$ _____	**Loans against Life Insurance**	$ _____

Assets	Value	Liabilities	Balance
Loans / Accounts Receivable	$ _____	Loans / Accounts Payable	$ _____
Deferred Compensation	$ _____	Salary Advances	$ _____
Total Assets	$ _____	Total Liabilities	$ _____
		Total Assets Minus Total Liabilities = Net Worth	$ _____

#2
Calculating Spendable Income

So you make $20,000, $40,000, or even $120,000 per year. Don't be lured into the common misunderstanding that you have $20,000, $40,000, or $120,000 per year to spend any way that you want. After you pay income, Social Security, and Medicare taxes on your gross earnings, your earnings likely decrease by a third or more. Then you need to account for the costs related to earning these wages, such as commuting, dry cleaning, and childcare, just to name a few. You may also eat out more often and take a vacation periodically or treat yourself to regular massage therapy to decompress from the stresses of your job. These are job-related costs, even if they're not deductible as such on your tax return. You wouldn't have these expenses if you didn't have the job.

What you have left after you take out all your must-pays (like taxes) is your *net, net income,* or *spendable income.* To figure out your net income, gather the last month's worth of paycheck stubs and complete the following table with information you take directly from your paycheck stubs.

REMEMBER

Some deductions occur monthly rather than per pay period, so two to four consecutive paychecks should reveal all deductions. For example, if you receive two paychecks per month but your medical insurance deduction is only taken out of the first paycheck of each month, divide this amount by 2 when completing the worksheet.

TIP

The next time you consider making a purchase and you tell yourself, "Ah, it's only 20 bucks," calculate how long you'd have to work to net $20. For example, netting $20 takes nearly three hours of work for some people. Stop and ask yourself whether the purchase is worth three hours of your work life and energy.

1. Gross Income Per Pay Period	$_____
Minus:	
Taxes	
Federal	$_____
State	$_____
Local/City	$_____
Social Security (FICA)	$_____
Medicare	$_____
2. Total Taxes Withheld	$_____
Automatic Payroll Deductions	
Medical Insurance	$_____
Life Insurance	$_____
Disability Insurance	$_____
Dental Insurance	$_____
Charitable Contributions	$_____
Retirement Plan 401(k), 403(b), and so on	$_____
Retirement Plan Loan Repayment	$_____
Deferred Compensation Plan	$_____
Employee Stock Purchase Plan	$_____

Flexible Spending Acct FSA (Section 125)	$_____
U.S. Savings Bonds	$_____
Other Automatic Drafts for Investments	$_____
Other Automatic Drafts for Expenses	$_____
3. Total Payroll Deductions (Excluding Taxes)	$_____
4. Net Income Per Pay Period (Line 1 – [Line 2 + Line 3])	$_____
5. How Many Times Are You Paid Per Year?	$_____
a. Weekly = 52	
b. Every Other Week = 26	
c. Twice a Month = 24	
d. Monthly = 12	
6. Multiply Line 4 times Line 5 for Annual Net Income	$_____
7. List Traditional Job-Related Expenses (Annual)	

Expense	Annual Cost
Commuting Costs	$_____
Clothing and Clothing Maintenance	$_____
Child Care	$_____
Unreimbursed Business Expenses	$_____

8. List Nontraditional Job-Related Expenses (Annual)

You may incur these expenses due to the stress of your job, long hours, or working conditions. Examples include dining out frequently because you're working long hours, going out for lunch instead of preparing them at home, treating yourself to much-needed massage therapy or vacations to help decompress from the stresses of your job, and so on.

Expense	Annual Cost
_____	$_____
_____	$_____
_____	$_____
_____	$_____
_____	$_____
_____	$_____
_____	$_____
_____	$_____
_____	$_____
_____	$_____
_____	$_____
9. Total Annual Expenses on Lines 7 and 8	$_____
10. Subtract Line 9 from Line 6 for Annual Spendable Income	$_____
11. Divide Line 10 by Number of Hours Worked Per Year (Traditional Full-Time Work Equals 2,000 Hours)	
Equals Your Net Hourly Spendable Income	$_____

#3
Calculating Required Expenses

Your required expenses, or *needs*, must come first. To figure out what your required expenses are, fill out the following table by entering the total amount you're personally responsible for or the total for the household, whichever is easier. (Sorry, your needs don't include cellphones, cable or satellite TV, streaming TV services, or high-speed Internet, unless they're required for employment. These aren't necessary to sustain life, and therefore, you must classify them as wants.)

Shelter:	
Mortgage or rent	$_____
Home maintenance	$_____
Utilities:	
Electric	$_____
Gas	$_____
Water, sewer, and trash pickup	$_____
Basic phone service	$_____

Protection: Include the things you can't afford to be without.	
Life insurance	$_____
Disability insurance	$_____
Homeowner's or renter's insurance	$_____
Health insurance	$_____
Auto insurance	$_____
Healthcare/medical and dental care	$_____
Prescription drugs	$_____
Childcare	$_____
Rainy-day fund (minimum of 10 percent of gross income)	$_____
Food: This category doesn't include dining out.	
Groceries (basic essentials only)	$_____
Clothing and Clothing Maintenance: Presuming that you have some clothes now, ask yourself what else you really need.	$_____
Basic Hygiene:	
Personal: toothbrush, deodorant, soap (for example)	$_____
Household: laundry detergent, toilet paper, and so on	$_____
Transportation: Only list required expenses. List any additional transportation costs in the *wants* category.	
Automobile loan or lease payments	$_____
Auto maintenance	$_____
Gasoline	$_____
Other: tolls, parking, public transportation	$_____

Legal Requirements:	
Real estate and property taxes	$_____
Child support	$_____
Alimony	$_____
Required Debt Payments Not Listed Elsewhere:	
School loans	$_____
Personal loans	$_____
Credit cards	$_____
Other debt	$_____
Total Required Monthly Expenses (Needs)	$_____
After-Tax Income	$_____
Note: If you include all expenses for the household, add the after-tax income of both spouses/partners.	
Surplus or Shortfall (After-Tax Income – Total Needs)	$_____

So where do you go after figuring out what you're spending on needs? If you have a surplus after meeting your required living expenses, check out Tip #4, which covers using your excess money for wants. However, if your income comes up short (negative or close) after figuring out your needs, check out the nearby sidebar.

If you don't already do so, set up automatic monthly withdrawals from your paycheck or your checking account to pay for or fund each of the required expenditures from the preceding table (just make sure you keep track if the values fluctuate). That way, you meet your requirements automatically each and every month, and whatever's left over is yours to spend on your most important wants.

#4
Calculating Discretionary Spending

Hopefully you find yourself with some extra money after determining and paying for your needs (see Tip #3, "Calculating Required Expenses"), and you can begin to use some of that money for the items or services you want most. Use the following table to list your desired expenditures and to figure out how much you can justify spending on them.

REMEMBER

When determining what to do with your surplus, just remember not to exceed that amount when prioritizing your wants.

Shelter:	
Home renovations or remodeling	$_____
Home furnishings	$_____
Utilities:	
Cellphone(s)	$_____
Streaming TV services	$_____
Cable or satellite TV	$_____
Internet	$_____

Shelter:	
Additional Savings:	
Children's college	$_____
Retirement (minimum of 10 percent of gross income)	$_____
Vehicle replacement fund	$_____
Other financial goals	$_____
Food:	
Groceries (beyond basic essentials)	$_____
Dining out	$_____
Meals purchased at school or work	$_____
Snacks and drinks purchased at school or work	$_____
Clothing and Clothing Maintenance (beyond basic essentials):	$_____
Personal:	
Haircuts, perms, manicures, massages	$_____
Gifts: birthday, anniversary, wedding, holiday	$_____
Charitable donations	$_____
Entertainment:	
Health club or other club membership(s)	$_____
Movies, plays, concerts	$_____
Vacations	$_____
Summer camp, sports, lessons, hobbies	$_____
Books and print subscriptions	$_____
Parties: holiday, birthday, social	$_____
Household:	
Home maintenance: lawn care, exterminators, painters	$_____

Shelter:	
Domestic help: housecleaning, baby sitters, pet sitters	$_____
Transportation (beyond basic essentials included in needs):	
Automobile loan or lease payments	$_____
Vehicles and related expenses for children	$_____
Auto maintenance	$_____
Gasoline	$_____
Other: tolls, parking, public transportation	$_____
Other:	
_____	$_____
_____	$_____
_____	$_____
_____	$_____
Total Desired Additional Monthly Expenses (Wants)	$_____
After-Tax Income	$_____
Surplus or Shortfall (After-Tax Income – [Total Needs + Total Wants])	$_____

After you add all your needs from Tip #3 together with your wants from the preceding table, you'll likely discover that you have little or no surplus cash flow. If you have negative cash flow, you should revisit the preceding table and prioritize and/or reduce your expenditures so you don't plan to spend more than you bring in.

#5
Tracking Expenses

Tracking your cash flow is especially useful when your out-flow exceeds your income. Fortunately, you don't need to go back and tally up months' worth of checking account register entries, credit- and debit-card statement amounts, and cash withdrawals. This is a very time-consuming and painful exercise, and it doesn't yield the desired results. What has happened in the past is behind you; all you can and should focus on is the present and the future.

TIP

Monitor your spending for the next couple of months. The hassle of tracking all expenditures is a deterrent to spending money unnecessarily. This activity helps raise your consciousness about each expenditure, which helps your budgeting immensely. The Weight Watchers organization has a very effective mantra: "If you bite it, you write it!" The same concept applies to expenses, and it works!

If you're looking for a simpler method of tracking your expenses, carry a pocket notebook to track every cent of your surplus money or use the Notes app (or an app devoted to tracking expenses) on your smartphone. Record every occasion you spend your surplus money, whether you purchase a drink at work, buy gasoline on the way home, or go to the movies. Account for every cent. Also, track whether you paid by cash, check, or debit or credit card; who you paid; and whether the expenditure falls into the need or want category.

Use one log for each pay period or month, whichever works best for you. Note at the top of the worksheet (or in the Note) how much your beginning surplus is and subtract each expenditure from that amount.

By keeping your eye on the magic number (your surplus cash flow after meeting your required expenses), you can simply spend your money any way that best meets your priorities (your wants) so long as you don't exceed the magic number. No more detailed budget keeping is required.

#6
Setting Spending Practices

Sometime throughout your life, you may have had someone encourage you to "dream big" or "reach for the stars." But have you ever taken the time to really examine what your visions or dreams are and how you can actually turn your aspirations into reality? Well, now's your chance to do more than just daydream about that island vacation, about starting your own business, or about funding your child's college education. The time has come to turn your dreams into realities.

This section is designed to help you convert the dreams that matter most to you into measurable goals. After you can measure your goals, you can manage them, take action, and achieve them.

REMEMBER

Financial planning involves channeling your resources — all of them — to best accomplish *what matters most* in your life. You need to consider not only your financial assets and liabilities but also your personal assets and liabilities, dreams, goals, and fears. Financial instruments (investments, insurance, retirement plans, savings, and so on) are just tools that you utilize along your financial journey through life. However, first things first: What matters most in your life?

Delve into Your Dreams

No matter what you want to call it — brainstorming or brain dumping — it's time to dream big without holding back and to get those dreams written in stone. (Paper or a Note on your smartphone will have to do for now.) Think of all the things you want to do and see and who you want to become. Then list the dreams that are most important to you at this time.

Write down the following column headings: What?, When?, What's Required?, What Are You Willing to Do?, and Revised Priority. Then follow these steps:

1. In the What? column, quickly list the first 30 goals that come to mind when responding to the question, "What 30 things would you most like to do, see, accomplish, or experience in your life?"

Dig deep and list 30 goals — no more, no less. The first 5 or 10 may come to you easily. However, if you get stuck, consider all the possibilities, including:

- What do you want to do? (activities/hobbies/interests, home improvements, assist aging parents)

- What or who do you want to see? (travel, cultural events, family, friends)

- Who do you want to be? (personal or career development, community involvement, activism, philanthropy)

- What experiences do you want to have? (spend more quality time with family, vacation with spouse, continue your education, provide a legacy for your children or favorite cause)

2. Review your list of goals and rank them by their priority.

Indicate in the left column how important achieving each item is to you by selecting from the following Priority list:

A = Must achieve (no choice or would cause regret)

B = Would love to achieve (but will live if you don't)

C = Would really be nice to achieve, but not at the cost of A or B goals

3. **Indicate in the When? column approximately when you want to, or when you must, achieve each of your stated goals.**

Be as specific as possible. If an actual date or deadline is involved, use that date. If you have no deadline, provide yourself with as much guidance as possible.

4. **In the What's Required? column, try to list the resources you need to accomplish the stated goal.**

Do you need time, energy, labor, money, or help? Be as specific as possible. Say, for example, that you want to remodel your kitchen this year. You may need to do some research and gather specific details regarding exactly what's involved in your remodeling project. Consider these questions:

- How much of the work can you complete yourself, compared to how much of the work licensed professionals must perform?

- Do you have friends or family members who are willing, able, and available to assist you, and if so, will compensation be appropriate or necessary?

- How much time and energy do you anticipate needing to invest personally?

- How much will purchasing the materials and supplies cost?

- How much will the licensed professionals cost?

- Do you need to finance any or all of these costs?

- What are your options for paying for this project?

5. **In the What Are You Willing to Do? column, write what you're willing to do to achieve this goal.**

The achievement of goals often involves much more than just money. Some goals may be so important to you that you're willing to forgo or postpone many of your other dreams to ensure that you achieve your most important goals. You must make the call.

To help you determine how you plan to allocate your time, energy, and money to accomplish your goals, ask the following questions:

- What are you willing to sacrifice to achieve specific goals?

- Is achieving a certain goal so important that you're willing and able to earn more money if that's what's needed?

- Can you adjust the desired time frame for achieving this goal?

- Are you willing and able to sell something to raise the money needed to achieve the goal?

- Are you willing and able to do more of the work yourself to reduce your out-of-pocket costs?

- Are you willing and able to dedicate the time and energy necessary to achieve this goal?

- Do your spouse/partner and family support your efforts for the goals in which they're involved?

6. **For now, leave the Revised Priority column blank; you can fill it in after going through the exercises in the next section.**

TIP

If you're in a relationship, have your spouse or partner complete the exercise, too. They should complete the list separately. After Step 5 is completed, compare your list with your partner's and then move on to Step 6. It's amazing just how much you can discover about yourself and your significant other when you really dig deep into your life goals. Plus, you want to make sure that you're both fully aware of each other's priorities.

It's unlikely that you'll come up with most of the same goals, and that's okay. You're an individual, and you may also be part of a couple. You have individual goals, and you also have goals you want to achieve with your partner. And your goals and priorities will be different — frequently. There's nothing wrong with differences. The only thing that can go wrong is not exploring what matters most to you and sharing that with your partner.

Determine Which Dreams Matter Most

So you may know what your dreams are, but do you know which ones are most important to you? How do you know which ones to focus on as you begin to shape your goals? (See the next section for more on establishing goals.) In this section, approach the same subject — your visions or dreams — from a markedly different perspective.

Work through the following questions. (If you haven't created your wish list, you may find it easier to do the exercise in the preceding section first.) Be sure to invest thoughtful time and energy as you ponder the questions. If you really devote yourself to this task, you may begin to develop a realization and level of clarity about your dreams that you may not have had before. You may discover that some things no longer have the importance they once had, while other ambitions have now become most important in your life.

TIP

You can also have your spouse or partner answer these questions on their own and then compare notes. What you discover may raise your level of commitment and motivation to achieve certain dreams tremendously, and you're more likely to pursue and achieve the dreams to which you're most committed.

After you answer the preceding questions, go back to the exercise in the previous section and revisit the Revised Priority column with the three questions in mind. You may want to revise your priority ranking at this stage. Use the Revised Priority field to record any changes.

Develop an Action Plan

After you figure out your wish list and prioritize what matters most, you can then create and structure an action plan for these dreams to become goals. And with that action plan, your goals can become realities.

Each goal must be measurable and must be a top priority, something you have the desire and capacity to achieve. First, review your revised priority rankings in the exercise in the earlier section "Delve into Your Dream" and list your top priorities in order of importance. Note each goal's what and when. Then, sort your priorities by time period and action items involved. Don't worry if you don't know some of the "Hows" at this time. The rest of this book can help you address those.

#7
Creating a Budget

D oes the word *budget* send chills up your spine? It shouldn't. Budgets allow you to be organized and have some control over what you spend. They help you decide how to spend your money, plan for your future, pay off existing debt, and save a few pennies each month by reducing wasteful and impulsive purchases.

Step 1: Categorize Your Expenses

When you begin setting up a monthly budget, start with big categories before breaking your budget down into smaller expense categories. A good list of basic budget categories to begin with includes the following:

» **Housing:** Mortgage/rent, repairs, property taxes, cleaning supplies, homeowner's/renter's insurance, utilities, furnishings, decor

» **Food:** Groceries, meals out, food delivery, snacks and beverages at work

» **Transportation:** Car payments, insurance, gas, oil changes, parking, repairs and maintenance, public transportation fees

>> **Medical:** Insurance, out-of-pocket expenses such as deductibles and non-insurance covered medical services, pharmacy, eye care, dental

>> **Clothing:** New purchases, dry cleaning, repair

>> **Personal:** Cosmetics, haircuts, cleansers

>> **Insurance:** Life insurance and any other insurance not covered under home, transportation, or medical expenses

>> **Education:** Tuition, dues/fees, school pictures, yearbooks, school supplies, books

>> **Credit accounts:** Major credit cards, department store cards, lines of credit through your bank or other lender, any other outstanding debt

>> **Gifts:** Holidays, birthdays, graduations, weddings, showers

>> **Recreation:** Vacations, movies, books, magazines, TV (cable, satellite, and/or streaming services), restaurants, sporting events, sports equipment

>> **Savings:** Long-term and short-term goals, as well as retirement

>> **Taxes:** Property and excise tax, for example

>> **Donations:** Charities, religious groups, and so on

REMEMBER

Be sure to set aside money each month for those yearly and quarterly payments that often sneak up on you when you least expect them. If you spend $1,200 on your yearly property taxes (and that payment isn't included in your mortgage payment), divide that number by 12 and set aside $100 per month so you aren't caught off guard by your property taxes, insurance payments, or any other periodic bills.

Within each general budget category, some items are essential (the mortgage or rent payment, electric bill, and groceries); others are extra (new furniture, gifts, and food delivery). From your first list of general budget items, develop two separate budget lists, one for essentials and the other for extras. Then look through these lists to find flexible budget expenses where you can cut back by using the tips and advice throughout this book. Put a star next to these flexible items so you can identify them.

Step 2: Estimate What You Spend

Go through your checking account and any other receipts or records (paper and/or online) you've kept over the past few months so you can track how much you actually spend on essentials. Then for one month, keep a detailed diary of all your extra purchases, even for cheap things like coffee at your favorite café or snacks from the vending machine at work. Little expenses quickly add up to big money when they're made on a daily basis. These smaller, out-of-pocket purchases are frequently made with cash, so they usually don't show up in your check register; writing them down makes you aware of where the cash is dribbling out of your life.

Step 3: Calculate and Adjust

Are your spending habits keeping you in the red? To find out, add up the essentials list and the extras list separately. Subtract the essentials total from your monthly income. If you have money left over, subtract the extras total from that amount. If you still have money left over, great! Look into a savings or investing plan (talk to your bank or a certified financial planner for help setting up a plan).

If your extras list takes you into negative numbers, start looking for places to cut back (for example, eat out once a month instead of once a week). You can also trim from the extras list to put more money toward debt repayment if that's a high priority in your financial picture.

#8
Breathing Away Tension

As the economy heads south and you tighten your budget to keep spending under control, stress and tension creep into your life. You can't control the economy, but that's okay — truly living well is about far more than money. On the other hand, no matter how good things get, stress always leeches the fun out of the good life.

Breathing properly is one of the simplest and best ways to drain your tension and relieve your stress. Simply by changing your breathing patterns, you can rapidly induce a state of greater relaxation. If you control the way you breathe, you have a powerful tool in reducing bodily tension and increasing your joie de vivre.

Change the Way You Breathe

Altering the way you breathe can change the way you feel. Here's one of the best and simplest ways of introducing yourself to stress-relieving breathing:

1. **Either lying or sitting comfortably, put one hand on your belly and the other hand on your chest.**

2. **Inhale through your nose, making sure that the hand on your belly rises and the hand on your chest moves hardly at all.**

3. As you inhale slowly, count silently to three.

4. As you exhale through your parted lips slowly, count silently to four, feeling the hand on your belly falling gently.

   Pause slightly before your next breath. Continue to breathe like this until you feel completely relaxed.

Breathe through an Emergency

Breathing properly is no big deal when you're lying on your bed or vegging out in front of the TV. But what's your breathing like when you're caught in gridlock, when you're facing down a deadline, or when the stock market drops 20 percent? You're now in a crisis mode. You need another form of breathing. Here's what to do:

1. Inhale slowly through your nostrils, taking in a very deep diaphragmatic breath, filling your lungs and filling your cheeks.

2. Hold that breath for about six seconds.

3. Exhale slowly through your slightly parted lips, releasing all the air in your lungs.

   Pause at the end of this exhalation. Now take a few "normal" breaths.

   Repeat Steps 1 through 3 two or three times and then return to what you were doing. This form of deep breathing should put you in a more relaxed state.

#9
Tensing Your Way to Relaxation

The uncertainty of a faltering economy can tie anyone in knots, despite even the best of efforts to keep things in per-spective, set priorities, and take control. Fortunately, one of the better relaxation techniques actually uses tense muscles to your benefit. It derives from a method called *progressive relaxation,* or deep muscle relaxation.

This method is based on the notion that you aren't aware of what your muscles feel like when they're tensed. By purposely tensing your muscles, you're able to recognize what tension feels like and identify which muscles are creating that tension. This technique is highly effective and has been proven to be a valuable tool for quickly reducing muscle tension and promoting relaxation.

Relax Your Body, Part by Part

When you have 10 to 15 minutes, follow these steps for progressive relaxation:

1. **Lie down or sit, as comfortably as you can, and close your eyes.**

   Find a quiet, dimly lit place that gives you some privacy, at least for a while.

2. **Tense the muscles of a particular body part.**

   To practice, start by tensing your right hand and arm. Begin by simply making a fist. As you clench your fist, notice the tension and strain in your hand and forearm. Without releasing that tension, bend your right arm and flex your bicep, making a muscle the way you might to impress the kids in the schoolyard.

   REMEMBER

   Don't overdo it and strain yourself in any of these muscle-tensing maneuvers. When you tense a muscle group, don't tense as hard as you can. Tense to about 75 percent of what you can do. If you feel pain or soreness, ease up on the tension, and if you still hurt, defer your practice until another time.

3. **Hold the tension in the body part for about seven seconds.**

4. **Release the tension quickly, letting the muscles go limp.**

   Notice the difference in the way your hand and arm feel. Notice the difference between the sensations of tension and those of relaxation. Let these feelings of relaxation deepen for about 30 seconds.

5. **Repeat Steps 1 through 4, using the same muscle group.**

6. **Move to another muscle group.**

   Simply repeat Steps 1 through 4, substituting a different muscle group each time. Continue with your left hand and arm and then work your way through the major muscle groups: face, head, neck, shoulders, back, legs, feet, buttocks, and stomach.

Use the Quickie Method

When pressed for time, you can use a quickie version of the progressive relaxation exercise explained in the preceding section. This technique compresses all the muscle tensing and relaxing sequences into one. Think of it as one gigantic scrunch.

In order to do this, you have to master the gradual version first. The success of this rapid form of relaxation depends on your ability to create and release muscle tension quickly, skills you master by slowly working through all the muscle groups individually.

To start, sit or lie comfortably in a room that is quiet and relatively free of distractions. Now, tense all of the muscle groups listed here, simultaneously:

>> Clench both fists, bend both arms, and tense your biceps.

>> Lift both legs until you notice a moderate degree of tension and discomfort.

>> Tense the muscles in your buttocks and hold that tension.

>> Scrunch up your face, closing your eyes, furrowing your brow, clenching your jaws, and pursing your lips.

>> Bring your shoulders as close as you can to your ears.

>> Tense your stomach muscles.

Hold this "total scrunch" for about five seconds and then release, letting go of any and all tension. Allow your legs to fall to the floor or bed and let your arms fall to your sides. Allow the rest of your body to return to a relaxed position. Repeat this sequence at various points throughout your day.

#10
Stretching Away Your Stress

Stretching is one of the ways your body naturally discharges excess bodily tension. You may notice that you automatically feel the need to stretch after waking up in the morning or just before retiring at night. But a good stretch can drain away much of your body's tension at other times, too. You may be desk-bound or otherwise required to sit for long periods of time during the day, causing your muscles to tense and tighten. Consider adopting one or more basic stretches and taking a stretch break at various points throughout the day. Cats do, dogs do, why not you?

Following are two tension-relieving stretches that are wonderful ways of draining a lot of excess tension. They're simple and shouldn't evoke much comment or ridicule from friends or coworkers:

>> **The Twist:** This stretch is great for your upper body. Sitting or standing, put both your hands behind the back of your head, locking your fingers together. Move your elbows toward each other until you feel some moderate tension. Now twist your body slightly, first to the right for a few seconds and then slowly to the left. When you finish, let your arms fall to your sides.

>> **The Leg Lift:** This stretch is good for your lower body. Sitting in your chair, raise both your legs until you feel a comfortable level of tightness in them. Maintaining that tension, flex and point your toes toward your head. Hold that tension for about ten seconds and then let your legs fall to the floor. If doing this with both legs together is a wee bit uncomfortable, try it one leg at a time.

Stretch slowly and don't overdo it. You're trying to relax your muscles, not punish them.

REMEMBER

#11
Practicing Habits of Effective Stress Managers

The following qualities are important skills and behaviors for reducing stress and creating stress resilience. How many of these describe you? If you can't check off all (or any!) of the items, don't worry — you can change old habits and learn new ones:

Managing your stress isn't a magical process. It's about mastering new behaviors and finding new ways of looking at yourself and your world.

>> **Know how to relax.** You need to know how to let go of tension, relax your body, and quiet your mind. There is no one right way to relax. For some people, meditation, focused breathing, and imagery may be the favored path. Others may prefer a more active approach, with techniques such as progressive muscle relaxation.

Attaining a state of greater relaxation need not be limited to formal approaches. Any activity that distracts you from the stressors of your world can be relaxing. It can take the form of a hot bath, a stroll in the park, a cup of coffee

REMEMBER

(decaffeinated), or a good book or favorite TV program. All can provide a relaxing escape from stress.

>> **Eat right and exercise often.** The foods you eat can play an important role in controlling your stress levels — or making them worse. When you're under stress, you tend to be far less vigilant about what goes into your mouth. You should be eating foods that reduce your stress. Unfortunately, you're probably craving foods that aren't on anybody's list of healthy choices — sugary foods, fatty foods, and salty foods (not to mention caffeine and alcohol). And even if you manage to eat healthy foods, chances are, if you're under stress you'll overeat or, at times, undereat.

Eating the wrong foods can affect how well you deal with stress. Your body needs a balanced, healthy diet to maximize your ability to cope. That means giving your body the right nutrients that supply you with adequate reserves of vitamins, minerals, and other essential elements. And don't forget the liquids. Your body needs to be adequately hydrated.

And don't forget about exercise. Engage in some form of physical activity regularly — at least twice a week and, when possible, more often. It can be participating in a sport or working the treadmill. Your exercise regime doesn't have to be fancy or overdone. Walking whenever you can is one of the more overlooked forms of exercise. If you belong to a health club or gym, even better. The secret of exercise is building it into your life — scheduling it. And make it convenient. If you can find a gym near your home or where you work (or even *at* work), that's great. The chances of your showing up there are now far greater. Just do it!

>> **Get enough sleep.** Sleeping enough is a key element in managing your stress. Too little sleep can leave you tired and drained of energy. Your body and mind aren't prepared to tackle stress. Most people do well on seven or eight hours per night, but individual needs vary. You can usually tell if you're getting enough sleep if you wake up rested and can get through the day without feeling tired. If you're unsure about how much sleep you need, experiment on the weekend or on vacation, gradually lengthening your sleep time and seeing how much better you feel. By the way, getting *too much* sleep (more than eight hours) may not be so good for you, either.

Basic sleep hygiene can help. Try to get to bed at a consistent time, leaving you enough hours of sleep before you hear your alarm. Before bed, don't get overstimulated by exercise, your smartphone or tablet, or an argument with your partner or spouse. Keep the room dark and cool. Stay away from large meals just before bedtime. Avoid stimulants like smoking or caffeinated drinks. Reserve the bedroom for sleep (and sex) if at all feasible.

For many, getting to bed isn't too difficult. It's the "falling asleep" part that's problematic. And while sleeping pills and alcohol may work in the short run, they're *not* recommended as part of a long-term solution.

WARNING

>> **Don't worry about the unimportant stuff**. Know the difference between what's truly important and what isn't. Put things into perspective. Many — if not most — of life's stressors are relatively inconsequential.

One good way of putting things into perspective is asking yourself, "On a scale of one to ten, how would I rate the relative importance of my stressor?" Remember that eights, nines, and tens are the "biggies" — major life problems such as a serious illness, the loss of a loved one, a major financial loss, and so on. Your fours, fives, sixes, and sevens are problems of moderate Importance — a lost wallet, an unreliable car, or a broken water heater. Your ones, twos, and threes are your minor worries or stressors — you forget your wallet or you get a bad haircut.

Now, rate the level of worry and distress you feel *about* that stressor. Again, use a similar ten-point scale, where ten represents "a great deal of distress" and one is "only a very small amount of distress."

Compare the two numbers. If the amount of stress you're experiencing is larger than the importance of the stressor, you're probably overreacting.

>> **Don't get angry often.** Anger is a stress emotion you can largely do without. Knowing how to avoid becoming angry and losing your temper is a skill well worth mastering. Learning how to control the expression of your anger can also spare you a lot of grief and regret. Much of your anger comes from various forms of distorted thinking. You may have unrealistic expectations of others (and of yourself!) that trigger anger when they aren't met. Your anger may arise

from low frustration tolerance, where you exaggerate your inability to cope with discomfort. You may be "catastrophizing and awfulizing" or creating some "can't-stand-it-itis."

>> **Be organized.** Feeling a sense of control over your environment is important. A cluttered and disorganized life leads to a stressed life. Getting organized means developing effective organizational strategies and tools. For many, clutter is the prime culprit. For others, the lack of an organizational strategy becomes the roadblock — where did I file that file? Fortunately, many useful ideas can help you reverse disorganization challenges.

>> **Manage time efficiently.** Know how you spend your time and how you waste your time. Learn to use time effectively. Be in control of your schedule. A good place to start is creating and using organizational lists. By combining to-do lists and your calendar (paper or digital), you have a powerful organizational tool to help you gain control over your time. To know where your time goes, you may try keeping a simple log, tracking how you use your time. Doing this for even a few days gives you a good picture of what needs to be changed.

>> **Have a strong support system.** Don't neglect the meaningful people in your life. Spend time with your family and friends. Have people in your life who listen to you and care for you. If you find that your social support system is a little thin, consider ways of meeting others. These days, you have no shortage of places to meet others who want to meet you. The activities can include joining a book group, playing a sport, hiking, walking, or biking, to suggest but a few. Going online can make this process much easier. Your local house of worship can also bring you into contact with people who share your values and goals. And don't rule out a volunteer experience; you can help others and meet new friends.

>> **Live according to your values.** Examine your values and goals, assessing whether they truly represent who you are and where you want to go in life. Pursuing values that aren't reflective of the kind of life you want can lead you to an unhappy and stressful place. Ask yourself, "What do I want to get out of my life? What is truly important to me?"

>> **Have a good sense of humor.** Laugh at life's hassles and annoyances. Be able to laugh at yourself, and don't take yourself too seriously.

2

Bumping Up Your Bring-Home

Find out your options if you're thinking of ways to bring more money home. Perhaps you've been laid off or down-sized, you're facing the possibility of being laid off or downsized, or you just want to build a nest egg in case your financial situation goes south.

Examine opportunities for finding other work — whether it's a new job to replace an old one or a part-time job to supplement what you earn now.

Get tips on how to create and update a resume that'll get you a second look from prospective employers.

Increase your income by changing *the way* you work. Working from home, for example, is a viable option for many people.

#12
Updating Your Resume

When you see a job that you hope has your name on it, you won't have time to start from scratch and write a targeted resume that shows why you're the one to interview. The answer is to begin building a *core resume* — a basic resume that you customize — before the pressure hits. Use this resume as a base to spin off targeted editions when you need to move quickly. Constructing a targeted resume is easier when you follow this three-step game plan.

Here are the essential parts that make up a resume:

REMEMBER

>> Contact Information

>> Summary

>> Key Skills

>> Education and Training

>> Experience

>> Activities and Affiliations

>> Honors and Awards

You may also include the following:

>> Certifications and Licenses (also frequently grouped with Education)

>> Endorsements

>> Work Samples (not actually included, but listed as available)

The current trend is not to include an objective statement (see #14 Making Your Resume Stand Out).

Step 1: Prepare Your Core Resume

Easy resume writing involves starting with the right information in front of you. That way you don't get stuck staring at a blank screen. Before you sit down to write, take the time to gather the following:

>> **Resumes:** Gather any resumes you've written in the past ten years.

>> **Employment records:** Collect any written evaluations, job descriptions, or other previous employment records.

>> **Training records:** Gather certificates or lists of training, continuing education, degrees, and licenses.

>> **Recommendations:** Amass letters of recommendations, thank-you letters, emails, or cards from bosses, customers, or other related persons.

>> **Projects:** Accumulate copies of any major projects or abstracts/details about them.

>> **Awards:** Collect copies of any awards received professionally or personally.

>> **Publications:** List publications written such as books or articles.

>> **Presentations:** List presentations made, topics, and where presented.

>> **Affiliations:** Create a list of all voluntary roles held (business, board level, social, civic, academic). Be sure to gather any details, such as recognitions or awards received, projects chaired and outcomes, hours contributed, and so on.

» **For new graduates or those with a new major certification that is the job target:** Major course textbooks or material, course syllabi, and school's course descriptions (usually in the catalog).

When all your data is staring you in the face, it's time to make it work for you. With your core resume, don't target a specific job advertisement, but rather focus on making all the skills, accomplishments, and experience you've accrued shine for you toward the type of job you desire (think "I am a chemical engineer" or "I am a receptionist"). That way you can pick and choose among the diamonds when you pull from your core resume into your targeted one to fit a specific job opening.

You can rapidly create the bones of your resume with a few easy steps:

1. **Set up your contact information.**

Lay out your brief contact information at the top of the page.

2. **Create section headers.**

Although these sections and their titles are subject to change as you format, you probably have a good idea of what your main sections are going to be for your resume so you can put them in as placeholders: objective header statement, summary, key skills, experience, education, professional affiliations, and so on.

3. **Fill in the straightforward content.**

Sections such as education are going to be presented in black-and-white fashion. The most selling you do is to list an honor or GPA.

TIP

The summary section doesn't get a title. It's meant to complement the job target with your requisite expertise and skill. Listing the word *summary* as a placeholder right now in your document will help you remember to go back and create it.

Another list-like section is the keyword skills, which is near the top of your resume (following your summary) in one to three columns of bullets. This list highlights the key skills you possess for your profession. You'll likely have anywhere from 9 to 21 bullets for your core resume after you go through the content you've collected.

Step 2: Study the Job Description

To spoon-feed a prospective employer directly what they are seeking in a position, take a look at the job description. If you find the description to be vague, search online for that job title and look at other descriptions to get a deeper sense of what is desired.

REMEMBER

Read the job description to determine exactly what the employer needs. Mirror back what you find in each section of your targeted resume. Tweak your header statement and the contents of your summary, keywords, and employment history

Step 3: Customize Each Spinoff Resume

After you read the job description, you can start transforming your core resume by doing the following:

1. **Cut irrelevant content from each section.**

Keeping this content won't make you look better; instead it makes you look like you're overqualified and not likely to stay — or uncommitted and likely to leave.

2. **Tweak wording to speak directly to the targeted position.**

This step may require crossover language if, for example, you're working with physicians and surgeons as your clients in the healthcare industry to executives in the IT industry.

Crossover language is easy to apply when you've looked at the job description for your target position. Does the employer refer to clients as "patients"? Are their customers called "members" or "key decision-makers"? Do they "sell" or "consult"? Are their products "cardiothoracic medical devices" or "high-tech equipment"? After you have a feel for this language, you can begin changing the wording in your core resume to reflect the target for your new targeted resume.

#13
Choosing the Right Resume Format

Resume format refers not to the design or look of your resume but to how you organize and emphasize your information. Different format styles flatter different histories. At root, formats come in three styles:

>> The *reverse-chronological format* (or traditional format), which lists employment beginning with the most recent and working backward

>> The *chrono-functional format,* which most frequently emphasizes skills and accomplishments first and chronology timeline second

>> The *hybrid format,* which lets you customize how you emphasize both the functional skills and the chronology depending on your unique needs

WARNING

Yes, a functional resume can focus primarily on skills and leave out company names and dates where the work was performed. However, this format presents a big red flag for prospective employers, so don't be tempted to use it under any circumstances.

The following table gives you a breakdown of which of the three formats enhances your personal curb appeal.

Your Situation	Suggested Formats
Perfect career progression	Reverse chronological
New graduate	Chrono-functional
Seasoned ace	Reverse chronological; hybrid when old jobs are most relevant
Military transition	Reverse chronological or chrono-functional
Job history gaps	Chrono-functional or hybrid
Career change	Hybrid; sometimes reverse chronological
Special issues	Hybrid or chrono-functional
Multitrack job history	Chrono-functional
Demotions	Any

REMEMBER

The big question to ask yourself when you're considering different formats is: "Does this format maximize my qualifications for the job I want?" The format you choose should promote your top qualifications, so make sure to select a format that helps you present your top-pick value.

#14
Making Your Resume Stand Out

Think your resume could sparkle with a few tweaks? Feeling like you've busted your chops and still are on the outside looking in? Close but no cigar? Here are some easy fixes to power up your resume.

Don't Tell It — Sell It

Forget sticking to the old naming-your-previous-responsibilities routine. Merely listing "Responsible for XYZ" doesn't assure the prospective employer that you met your responsibility or that the result of your efforts was worth the money someone paid you. Plus, this kind of generic overview won't make you stand out from all the other qualified applicants.

By contrast, read over your resume and make sure you have answered that pesky "So what?" question, which is lying in ambush for each bit of information you mention. Try to imagine what's running through a prospective employer's mind when you relate that you were responsible for XYZ: *So what? Who cares? What's in it for me?* Anticipate those questions and answer them by including the challenge you faced, the actions you took, and the results you attained.

Reach Out with Strength

Highlight the qualifications and past job activities that speak to the kind of job you want and the skills you want to use. If, for instance, you want to transition from military training to civilian training, remain riveted to your training skills without diluting your message by mentioning your ability to keyboard 80 words per minute.

REMEMBER

Don't muddle your resume's message with minor skills or skills you no longer want to use or need for the position for which you are applying; stay on message and ruthlessly delete what doesn't qualify you for your target job.

Use Keywords

In the long-ago 1990s, recruiters and employers used keywords to search computer databases for qualified candidates. Today they type keywords into search engines to scour the entire Internet for the best people to select for a candidate pool. Employers allow powerful computer systems to search the resumes they receive as well.

That's why, when you're looking for a job, you can't afford to ignore search engines. Take pains to feed those wooly-mammoth software creatures with effective keywords that shoot your resume to the top of recruiting search results. (In techie talk, the concept is called *search engine optimization,* or SEO.) Keywords are the magnets that draw junior screeners and nonhuman eyes to your talents.

In computerized job searches, keywords describe not only your knowledge base and skills but also such things as well-known companies, big-name colleges and universities, degrees, licensure, and professional affiliations. Keywords identify your experience and education in these categories:

>> Skills

>> Technical and professional areas of expertise

>> Accomplishments and achievements

>> Professional licenses and certifications

>> Other distinguishing features of your work history

>> Prestigious schools or former employers

Employers identify keywords, often including industry jargon, that they think represent essential qualifications necessary for high performance in a given position. They specify those keywords when they search for resumes.

TIP

Keywords are arbitrary and specific to the employer and each employer search. So the keywords (qualifications) — starting with the job title — in each job ad are the place to start as you customize your resume for the position. Make educated guesses when you're not responding to advertised jobs but are merely warehousing your resume online on a job search site.

Action verbs are a prelude for keywords in stating your accomplishments. You managed *what?* You organized *what?* You developed *what?* Applicant software looks for the *whats*, and the whats are usually nouns.

Discover the Art of Lost Articles

Although using articles — *a, an,* and *the* — in your resume isn't *wrong,* they also aren't common. Delete them for a crisper and snappier end result. Recruiters and employers expect to read resumes in compact phrases, not fully developed sentences. The first person *I* is another word that your resume doesn't need. Look at the following examples:

With Articles	Without Articles
I reported to the plant manager of the largest manufacturer of silicone-based waxes and polishes.	Reported to plant manager of largest manufacturer of silicone-based waxes and polishes.
I worked as the only administrative person on a large construction site.	Worked as only administrative person on large construction site.

Delete the Leave-Outs

Eliminate clutter by removing useless information that doesn't support the reasons why you're a qualified candidate. Here's a short list of the worst offenders:

>> The title word, "Objective." It's understood that the top line under your contact info will be your job target.

>> "References available on request." Listing the references on your resume is even worse.

>> Your Social Security number or driver's license number.

>> The date your resume was prepared.

>> Your company's telephone number.

>> Your high school or grammar school.

>> Dates you spent involved in college extracurricular activities.

>> Dates you were involved with professional or civic organizations, unless you're using them to fill in gaps or add heft to your claims.

>> Names of (human) past employers; put these on your reference sheet with contact information.

>> Most jobs older than 10 to 15 years ago to avoid showing your age or over qualifications.

>> Any content that doesn't qualify you for the position or emphasizes that your heart and skills lie elsewhere (jobs, volunteer work, affiliations, education).

>> Activities not related to your job target that could be considered inflammatory or might cause discrimination, such as religious or political affiliation, age, race, and dangerous sports.

#15
Preparing for a Job Interview

I f you overprepare for a job interview, you'll be tight. Especially don't memorize any answers. Many candidates script answers to such questions as "Tell me about yourself." But usually, even if the interviewer asks such a question, it's often a variant, and the memorized answer can seem nonresponsive. Plus, under the pressure of an interview, you can easily get thrown off your script and become tongue-tied. And even if you stay on-script, you'll sound scripted. That doesn't build credibility.

TIP

Sure, if you need to, script your answer to help flesh it out, but then reduce it to a few signpost words. Practice using those few words as your cheat sheet, and then going without it. Don't over-practice, or your recitation could resemble high school students reciting the Pledge of Allegiance.

Focus only on the following tactics for your interview and you'll likely be ahead of the pack:

>> **Wear appropriate attire.** Dress one notch above what you'd wear if you were hired for that position. Not sure? Call the employer's office and ask.

>> **Prepare answers to the two or three questions you're most afraid to be asked.** Perhaps it's the wide open statement "Tell me about yourself." *Hint:* Don't start from when you were born. Start with the first moment you thought you might like a career or job like this one, and then walk the interviewer, in about a minute, through the key moment that made you eager to apply for the job. Here's an example:

- "I thought I wanted to be a doctor, but after reading a medical textbook, I too often found myself thinking, 'Do I have this disease?' That bit of hypochondria made me pivot to hospital administration. I took a course in that and liked it, did some job shadowing and liked that, and now that I've graduated, I'm excited about launching my career in hospital administration. That's why I applied for this job."

>> **Get technical-minded.** Ever more jobs require one or more technical skills — for example, coding — and so interviews may include a technical test. Take the time to bone up.

>> **Prepare a few talking points.** These illustrate attributes you bring to the table that might give you an edge over other candidates. For example, if you wrote a paper in school on a topic related to the job, look for an opportunity to briefly describe it. Or say that your relative suffered from a disease that the company's device helps; explain how that situation moves you to want the job. Or maybe you just attended a boot camp on using Spark with Python and are excited to get to use it on a real-life project on artificial intelligence.

>> **Have three PAR stories ready.** These are 30- to 60-second stories of a *P*roblem you faced, the clever or dogged *A*pproach you used to resolve it, and the positive *R*esult. No surprise: Pick three stories that would impress your target employer. If you can't think of three from work, volunteering, or school, even consider something from your extracurricular life, as in this example:

- "When I was co-captain of my school's lacrosse team, we had one guy who played dirty. Everyone was scared of him. Even the coach seemed to look the other way. But it bothered me that he would do things like poke opponents in the eye intentionally! So I figured I'd give it a try. I asked if he'd go out for ice cream with me — I knew he liked ice cream. After some small talk, to avoid sounding like his father, I told a little lie. I said, 'My father told me that he'd rather see me lose honestly than win by cutting corners.' I saw his face get angry and then his eyes dropped. I felt I didn't need to say any more and changed the topic to the upcoming game. I can't tell you that turned him into a saint, but he seemed to play a little cleaner after that. That sort of experience is motivating me to have a career in people management, which is why I applied for this job."

TIP

Tell your stories at the right level of technicality. People like to feel good about themselves, so if you're talking tech, tell your story in a way that's technical enough to impress but not so technical that the person doesn't understand. Generally, unless the interviewer is a specialist in your area, it's wise to use the grandparent rule: Tell it so simply that your grandparent would understand it.

>> **Show, don't tell.** Be prepared to demonstrate what you can do. Of course, that works especially well in sales positions: Offer to show how you'd sell the product. But demonstrating can be useful for many other jobs. You might bring in work samples that would be relevant to the job. You might offer to go to the whiteboard to lay out how you'd structure your planning for a problem they say you'd be tackling. Or you might offer to role-play. Say you're applying for a job in child protective services. You might role-play how you'd try to convince a reluctant parent to allow you to come to their home. If your job would include teaching, training, or explaining and by the end of the interview they don't ask you to do a demo, offer to do one.

>> **Be prepared to discuss salary.** Better for you to preempt the question "What's your salary requirement?" than to answer it. Answering it risks stating too high or low a number. Right after you've given your first good answer in the interview, say, "By the way, what salary range has been budgeted for the position?" If the interviewer refuses to answer and instead asks for the amount you're looking for, it's best to say, "I'm confident that if we both want each other, we'll come to a fair agreement." If they push for a number, give a wide range — for example, "$65,000 to $80,000 depending on the nature of the position, the benefits, and so on."

» **Prepare emotionally.** Even if you're dying for the job, remind yourself that you can always find other jobs, and that this one may not be as good as it sounds. Also note that if you're rejected, it may well mean that the job wasn't a sufficiently good fit or that some factor beyond your control made them choose another candidate. Yes, *prefer* to get the job, and do well in the interview, but be yourself and let the chips fall as they may. If it's not meant to be, it's not.

For many people, such advice helps but is insufficient to keep you calm enough in the interview. It may additionally help to physiologically tire yourself out: Exercise before your interview, leaving enough time to shower and get there, including a little cushion for the unexpected: traffic, parking problems, and even getting a bit lost.

Immediately before entering the building, review an index card with key words reminding you of your PAR stories and answers to tough questions.

REMEMBER

The dating mindset: Just before opening the door to the interview, remind yourself one more time that although you might prefer to get the job, perhaps in learning about it in the interview, you won't. And even if you do want it but don't get it, there are always other jobs, probably ones that are a better fit. This is a date — you're both checking each other out.

#16
Standing Out during an Interview

I f the job interview takes place in person, stride in, stand straight with good posture, hold your chin just slightly above 90 degrees, and wear a slight, pleasant smile that doesn't appear forced. Shake the interviewer's hand (or interviewers' hands), and wait to be invited to sit down.

Again, don't focus so much on yourself that you forget it's a date — you're both checking each other out. Listen intently to the questions while maintaining eye contact most of the time. Get in touch with how you're feeling about that boss. How are you feeling about the job as the questioning reveals it? Such thoughts can help you avoid a bad job *and* keep you relaxed because you're not obsessing about the nanodetails of how you're coming across.

TIP

Follow the traffic light rule: During the first 30 seconds of an utterance, the light is green: They're listening. All's good. During the second 30 seconds, the light is yellow: The chance is increasing that they've heard enough. After 1 minute, the light is red: You probably should stop or ask a question. If they want more information, they can ask.

Following the traffic light rule ensures that you're leaving your interviewers enough time to talk. If you end up talking more than about three-quarters of the interview, it tends to deenergize the interviewers and can make you seem too eager or even desperate. In contrast, when they talk, they gain investment in you.

TIP

The free video "Interview Simulation" (at `https://www.youtube.com/watch?v=2zKsBfsrxrs`) may be helpful. It shows an interviewer asking typical interview questions, allowing you 60 seconds to answer each one. That can help you get a sense of pacing — 30 to 60 seconds is about the right length for answering most interview questions.

When answering, if you're facing more than one interviewer, try to do this: Begin answering the question while looking the questioner in the eye for a second or two. Then talk to the person to the questioner's right. Continue moving right until you reach the last person, and then reverse directions. Eye contact makes people feel valued.

TIP

Applicants who are asked a question that's difficult to answer, such as "Why have you been unemployed so long?" or "Why should we hire you when you have no experience in this field?," tend to give long answers to dig themselves out of trouble. Usually, it's wiser to do the opposite: Give short answers to difficult questions and longer answers to easy questions so that more of the interview is spent in areas you'd like to talk about.

Many interviews contain simulation or case questions: "How would you handle this issue?" Often, there's no single correct answer. The interviewers are looking to see how you structure your thinking. So take a moment to think, and then describe how you'd tackle the problem, step by step. Don't be afraid to say, "I'd like to take a moment to reflect."

For legal reasons, some interviews must be identical for all candidates. In such cases, you're not allowed to ask questions until the end. If you're permitted to, it's wise to ask two or three during the interview. That shows enthusiasm and helps you decide how much you want the job. The best questions tend to build on something the interviewer discussed or asked about, though a canned question or two may be okay. Here are some examples:

> **»** If I turned out to be an excellent employee, what would you hope I'd accomplish in the first week or month?

>> Every office culture is different. What would you say differentiates yours?

>> Every boss has a different style. How would you describe yours?

>> What should I know about the organization (or workgroup) that might not appear in the employee handbook?

TIP

Early in your career, you're likely to have less relevant experience than do other candidates. In such cases, shift the conversation from the past to the future. The interviewer may focus on what you've done, for example, by walking you through your resume, but that won't help you. So talk about what you would do if hired. Make it impressive enough, and it may trump your lack of background.

If you're good at thinking on your feet, try to convert the interview into a conversation about the challenges your prospective boss or the organization are facing. Ask questions, listen carefully and perhaps tactfully offer suggestions, all in a relaxed, conversational and even slightly playful manner. Even if the job you're interviewing for is tactical — for example as a graphic artist or administrative assistant — asking bigger-picture questions and, if it feels right, offering an idea or two can make the employer think *the* most important thought: "This is a person I'd like on my team."

At the end of most interviews, you're asked, "Do you have any questions?" Here are a couple of canned ones to consider if you think you want the job:

>> "I am more interested in the position than ever, and I'm wondering whether you think I'm a good fit?"

That gives you a chance to counter any objections.

>> "Do you have a sense of when you'll be getting back to me?"

If no one contacts you when promised, you have a basis for following up with a phone call. That gives you a chance to not only connect again but also, if they're hesitant to hire you, to ask whether there's a concern that you may be able to address.

#17
Dealing with Video Interviews

Video interviewing, as the name implies, is a live, two-way electronic communication that permits two or more people in different geographic locations to engage in face-to-face visual and audio exchange. Miles separate them: sometimes few, sometimes many, and sometimes oceans. As companies look to trim expenses associated with interviewing and hiring, video interviewing is becoming more common.

The content of a video interview is much the same as that of an in-person interview, but the execution differs. For example, lag time occurs when data is compressed and sent from one location to another. Be sure to allow for the delay and not step on the interviewer's lines, and don't be surprised if the interviewer inadvertently cuts you off in mid-sentence. In addition, you may feel performance pressure. When it's your turn to speak, you have very little time to look away, down, up, or sideways to process your thoughts. The pressure on you is somewhat like that on a contestant at a quiz show: talk or walk.

Here are some tips to help you gracefully navigate your way through a video interview:

>> Send materials for show-and-tell in advance if the interviewer wants to ask questions about an updated resume or project.

>> Run a technical check to make sure all video equipment is functioning properly.

>> Position the webcam so that it's a head-and-shoulders shot and none of the frame is in shadows.

>> Keep your movements calm.

>> When the interview begins, ask your interviewer whether the video and audio are okay.

>> Introduce yourself simply and remember the sound delay.

>> Pretend that your interviewer is an inch above the lens. Looking at that spot raises your chin slightly so that you look more confident and have better eye contact.

>> Let the interviewer end the interview.

>> Sign off with a *virtual handshake.* You can say something as simple as "Thank you for interviewing me. I enjoyed it. Let's talk face to face very soon." When you're in a professional setting, push the mute button and leave the room. When you're at home, mute the mic and close the camera.

Increasingly, interviews are conducted asynchronously: The interviewer has prerecorded the questions, and you answer them, clicking a key when you're done. Why do employers do that? It enables you and the interviewer to complete the interview when convenient. It also ensures that all applicants see the same questions and interviewer body language. If the employer wants to ask follow-up questions later, they can.

#**18**

Employing Post-Interview Tactics

J obs are often won or lost after the interview. The following sections look at ways you can make a win more likely.

Write an Influencing Letter

Writing a thank-you letter won't distinguish you from many other applicants. Also, it can make you seem toady: Do you really want to thank them for putting you through the wringer with no guarantee that it will pay off?

Instead, write an *influencing letter.* Yes, you can begin with "Thanks for the opportunity to meet with you to discuss the position. I'm more interested than ever because [*insert something said in the interview that makes the job more appealing*]." But instead of going right to the phrase "Hoping to hear from you," you have opportunities to do the following:

>> **Present new information:** For example, in light of the interview, you might realize that a key factor in the hiring

decision is to pick a candidate who's good at streamlining office processes. If so, you might say something like this: "I've reflected on your comment that you'd like the candidate to streamline some of the office's processes. I hadn't stressed that in my interview, so I thought I'd mention my relevant experience." Or, "I had a thought about how you might make more efficient the linkages between the salespeople, warehouse, and office. I could well be off-base about this because there's so much I don't know about the way you do things, but it at least offers a window into the way I think."

>> **Take a second swing at a question:** If you flubbed a question, your influencing letter gives you a second chance at answering it. You might write, "I've reflected on your question about such-and-such, and here's my new-and-improved answer."

>> **Include new collateral material:** Consider attaching a piece of collateral material that might be impressive, even if it's only someone else's article that you know would interest the employer. Or send a list of actions you'd take to get off to a good start on the job. Or include a reference letter, custom tailored to the position, that highlights how you'd be a good fit, particularly with regard to a factor that the interviewers said would be important.

Follow Up

At the end of the interview, ask when you'll get the employer's decision. If the employer doesn't keep the promise, send an email or, better, phone. Whether you get the person or the voicemail, say something like this: "You had mentioned that you'd be getting back to me before now, so, like any good employee, I figured I'd follow up. I'm enthusiastic about the position, and although I have other irons in the fire, I wanted to check back with you."

TIP

Yes, you're eager, but it's usually wise to wait a few days beyond when you feel like following up. When you reach out first, it can feel too eager, even desperate. People like to feel that they have to chase you.

#19
Trying Quick Ways to Find Good Jobs

The approaches outlined in this section could help you avoid a long job-search slog.

Call-Email-Call

Walking in may be the fastest way to get hired for an entry-level job. The *call-email-call* tactic may be the fastest route to a not-so-entry-level job: After hours, you leave voicemail for, say, a dozen target employers, immediately email them, and three days later, phone to follow up. You select those employers without regard to whether they're advertising an appropriate opening.

REMEMBER

Starting to get cold feet? You're imposing no more than if you asked a stranger on the street for directions. If the person doesn't want to help you, they can (and often will) say no. Nor should you let your fear of sounding stupid stop you. In the worst case, you flub — there are *so* many other employers. Just start with your least desirable employers so that if you do blow it, you've lost only your worst prospect. It may also help to remember that many sales reps make 50 to 100 sales calls a day and are usually selling something they care less about than about themselves. You, the job seeker, are selling yourself, and if you close just one sale, you make thousands of dollars.

So, can you suck it up? Call-email-call 10 or 20 target employers in one shot so you can get your job search over with. Don't know who those people might be? Search LinkedIn on those places of employment.

TIP

Look for people with a job title who might hire someone at your level. For example, if you're looking to be an individual contributor, you might look for people in a large company with the title of *manager*. If it's a small company, *director* might also be an appropriate title. Do prefer someone from the desired division rather than HR. For example, if you're looking for an analyst position, you might look for a title like *director of research* rather than *HR director*.

Phone a Friend (Okay, Ten Friends)

Reach out. Your friends may even welcome the chance to help.

TIP

Phoning is more powerful than email or text. It's harder for even your marginal friends to turn down the sound of your voice than to ignore the disembodied bits and bytes of an email or text message.

So list a dozen or two people who like you who could possibly hire you or refer you to a potential employer — everyone knows people. Sure, each person is unlikely to have something for you, but if you phone a bunch, you put the numbers game in your favor. Then call them all in one (okay, two) sittings, leaving voicemail as necessary. Here's an example:

> "Hi, this is Greg Michaels. I'm trying to find a first job in database management, but because job searches these days can take months, and because I could use the income and structure, I'm open even to interim jobs of whatever sort. As you know, I like work that requires good reasoning skills. By any chance, might you know someone who might want to

hire someone like me or refer me to someone who could? If so, I'd love to hear from you. Actually, I'd like hearing from you, even if it's just to chat; it's been awhile. My phone number is 510-555-2368."

This method may yield only an interim job. That's okay. You wouldn't be reading a section on ultrafast ways to land a job if you wanted to hold out for the dream position. Many people would be wise to take such a job. Just don't work there so long that it vitiates your motivation and energy to look for something better.

If you have to take a low-level job but aspire to something loftier, start developing relationships with higher-ups at your workplace and perhaps at headquarters — after all, many employers give employees a directory of internal phone numbers. Plus, continue networking and answering ads for good positions elsewhere.

Blast Your Social Media

An even faster and wider-reaching version of the phone-a-friend tactic from the preceding section is simply to send that email to all your LinkedIn connections and Facebook friends — you'll see how good these friends really are. If you're on Twitter, post a few-sentence version. If your friends are on Instagram or follow you on YouTube, you might even make your pitch on video.

TIP

Need to expand your social media network and fast? On LinkedIn and Twitter, follow ten or more organizations that interest you and individuals there who could hire you. In inviting to connect with someone on LinkedIn, don't use the standard invitation. Rather, in a sentence or two, explain what you like about the person or organization: for example, "I am an avid user of Evernote and would certainly consider working there. Might you add me to your LinkedIn connections?" Over the next week, post a few smart, occasionally flattering comments and questions on the Evernote feed. Then ask for an interview as described in the previous paragraphs. That should add some fresh folks to that blasted email blast.

#20
Looking into Federal Jobs

Unless you're a born entrepreneur, consider a government job. With companies and nonprofits converting ever more full-time jobs into freelance gigs, government is the major source of stable, full-time, benefited careers (with paid holidays and vacations) requiring only a 40-hour work week.

TIP

The number-one way to spot a federal job that may interest you is to visit the official USAJOBS website (www.usajobs.gov). You can search by keyword and location (or remote).

#21
Checking Out Best Career-Changing Tips

As companies trim their workforces and more and more jobs are farmed out to contractors or sent offshore, even once stable and reliable positions are no longer so stable or reliable. If you've built your career in a field that's vanishing and now find yourself in the market for a job, the answer may be to change careers. Making a career change isn't the easiest thing to do, but it may be the smartest. To make the change, follow the advice in the following sections.

Change by Retraining

If you have the time and money, retraining gives you the most options. For example, have you been in corporate America and want to become a teacher? Many colleges offer teacher training programs, and school districts may offer alternative certifications, learning mainly on the job.

Or vice versa: You've been a teacher and you want to leverage that experience by becoming a manager in an educational technology company, preparing with an MBA or an MS in educational technology development.

Or you've worked for an environmental nonprofit and you love the cause but not the pay and you want to leverage your fundraising skills. So you take one or more sales training courses and do "ride-alongs" with excellent and ethical salespeople. That training gives you a shot at a well-paying career selling big-ticket environmental products to businesses.

TIP

A side benefit of taking career-preparatory courses is that it provides the opportunity to make career-door-opening connections. Your instructor, fellow students, and fieldwork and internship supervisor can pave the way.

Use Your Network

Especially for people who lack the time and money for a long retraining effort, the best chance of making a successful career change is to invoke and, if necessary, build your network.

You see, if you rely only on answering ads, you'll probably fail. Few employers would go through the hassle of screening oodles of applicants if they wanted to hire someone with no experience. Someone who wanted to do that would simply hired his wayward cousin.

So with, and especially without, solid training in your next career, you really boost your odds of landing a good launchpad job if you fully invoke your network and, if it has too few people likely to refer you to an employer, to build your network. Don't worry. That can be fun, sort of — well, if you're an extrovert. Otherwise, it can still be tolerable and worth the effort.

Work Up from the Bottom

Sometimes people try to change careers by working their way up from the bottom. Perhaps they tried for a higher-level job to no avail. Or their self-esteem is in the toilet. Or as a beginner, they prefer to do their learning concretely, on the job.

Here's an example: A former corporate drone and aspiring tradesperson took a job handing nails to a kitchen countertop installer. He watched, asked questions, learned, and soon got to be in charge of simple jobs in which someone handed *him* the nails. Then his boss gave him more complicated jobs, and, finally, he opened up his own shop.

#22
Figuring Out Whether You Should Change Your Career Course

Sometimes a career tweak just won't do, not only because a career is a misfit but also because, sometimes, a career misery's cause lies within the person. In those cases, a person brings the cause of their unhappiness to their new career, having expended a lot of time and, usually, money for nothing. These questions can help you decide whether you need a career change:

>> **True or false:** You're confident that your unhappiness in this career is unfixable — it won't help to simply change your employer, adjust your job responsibilities, or gain a new skill or attitude. For example, a psychologist gets consistently poor results despite being well-mentored. Or a salesperson gets more and more call-reluctant, even though the product is a good one. Or a journalist finds it impossible to make a living because of all the "citizen journalists" willing to write for free.

>> **True or false:** After sufficient reflection, Internet research, and perhaps informational interviewing, you're confident that you'd be happier and more successful in a particular new career.

>> **True or false:** You have the time and money to afford retraining and, often, a pay cut.

>> **True or false:** You're confident that with (or even without much) training, you'd be employable in your new career. For example, you know that the job market is good for people newly trained in this field, or you know someone who'd likely hire you whether the job market is good or not.

>> **True or false:** You're confident that if you made the aforementioned career change, you'd be happier and more successful.

#23

Telecommuting as an Alternative to Traditional Work

With the proliferation of technology — both at work and at home — and the availability of fast and inexpensive Internet hookups and communications software, telecommuting is becoming a common arrangement with many benefits. The Covid-19 pandemic also showed that some jobs can be performed remotely.

According to studies, employee productivity can increase by 30 percent, less time is lost as people sit in cars or mass transit to and from work, workers are more satisfied with their jobs, and society (and our lungs) benefits from fewer cars on the road every rush hour.

You need to consider some pros and cons when your thoughts turn to the idea of telecommuting.

Here are some advantages to telecommuting:

>> Depending on the job, employees can set their own schedules.

- Employees can spend more time with customers.

- Distracting office politics are often reduced.

- Employees can conduct more work because everything is there where they need it.

- You may be able to save money by downsizing your facilities.

- Costs of electricity, water, and other overhead are reduced.

- Employee morale is enhanced because people have the opportunity to experience the freedom of working from their own homes or other locations of their choice.

And here are some of the disadvantages to telecommuting:

- Monitoring employee performance is more difficult.

- Scheduling meetings can be problematic.

- Organizations may have to pay to set up employees with the equipment they need to telecommute.

- Employees can lose their feelings of being connected to the organization.

- Managers must be more organized in making assignments.

For many employees, the prospect of being able to work out of their own homes is much more appealing than merging onto the freeway each morning. For example, one telecommuter still gets out of bed at about the same time they did when they worked at a large corporate publisher, but now their commute is a few steps down the hall instead of an hour and 15 minutes of bumper-to-bumper, smog-filled, Los Angeles stop-and-go traffic. By 9:30 a.m. (15 minutes before their old starting time), they've already made several calls to East Coast clients, contacted publishing contacts overseas, and created a sales presentation.

However, telecommuting isn't just a plus for a company's current employees. It can be a powerful recruiting tool when you're on the hunt for new people to supplement your workforce. As Baby Boomers retire and move on to greener pastures (or golf courses), the younger generations (Gen X, millennials, and Gen Z) will have fewer people to replace them. Long story short, a shortage of good workers is going to arise. Anything you can do to attract and retain good employees in the future will become not just a nicety, but a necessity.

#24
Persuading Your Organization to Let You Work from Home

Telecommuting can mean big savings. Consider the expenses associated with a typical workday that would either vanish or be greatly reduced if you worked from home: commuting costs (including gas, tolls, and so on), dining expenses (breakfast from a drive-thru, coffee during your break, lunch, trips to the snack machine), and other expenses like dry-cleaning for your work clothes. This is, admittedly, a most unscientific guesstimate. But if you're currently working outside your home, track just one week's worth of your own *in-office* expenses and add them up on Saturday. The total may surprise you.

The big hitch, of course, is getting permission to stay home. You may have the perfect job for telecommuting. You may have the perfect home-office setup. The benefits to your company may be impossible to deny. And you may still wind up with a non-negotiable *no* for an answer. You can, however, stack the deck in your favor. Working from home, without a doubt, is a win–win arrangement, in which both employer and employee benefit.

A corporation has human characteristics. Before it makes a major change, it wants to know, "What's in it for me?" Don't expect to get anywhere if your only answer is "a happier employee." Fortunately, that doesn't have to be your only answer. One survey found that each telecommuting employee saved their respective employer an average of more than $10,000 a year by reducing absenteeism rates, saving the business money on recruitment and replacement, lowering facilities costs, and increasing productivity.

Although this general information is a big help when you set out to sell your boss on the benefits of telecommuting, you ultimately need to show how telecommuting can benefit your particular company, department, and job:

» **Examine how you working from home can help your organization reach its specific goals.** For example, if part of your company's mission is to provide excellence in serving its customers, working at home may enable you to deal with customer queries and complaints at unusual hours. This ability can be especially useful if your firm has overseas clients whose workday differs from yours.

» **Do a cost/benefit analysis to compare what your organization will spend with what it'll save by allowing you to work from home.** The idea is to quantify some of those soft numbers and to demonstrate to your boss (and possibly upper management) exactly why telecommuting is good for business.

» **Demonstrate that telecommuting will work for your job.** When you can demonstrate that telecommuting will benefit your organization, your next task is to prove that it can be done by someone in your job — in other words, you. Begin by researching your own company's history with telecommuting. Your company may already have a telecommuting policy in place, in which case you simply have to demonstrate that you fit within its parameters. Then look outside your company to your main competitors and other companies in your field to see whether they allow telecommuting among their employees. Finally, find out whether others in your particular profession are telecommuting.

#25
Considering Self-Employment

Perhaps you've always wanted to be self-employed. Or maybe you've always preferred to be employed by an organization but haven't been able to land something good. In either case, self-employment can be an attractive option — but only if you succeed.

Here are the core attributes of the successfully self-employed. The more of these that describe you, the better your chances:

REMEMBER

>> **You're a self-starter.** It's the key because, unlike when you're an employee, no one will push you to keep working.

>> **You're money-motivated yet ethical.** Most successfully self-employed people are motivated by money but manage to stay ethical, even though they have no boss to monitor them. These people have the strength of character to resist cutting ethical corners, even at the risk of losing money. That's a high bar, but it's the right one.

>> **You're smart about spending.** Successful people husband their money so that they maximize their chances of surviving long enough to become profitable. For example, they may often comparison-shop while remaining aware of when the

lowest-priced product or supplier isn't the wisest choice. They may remain as a one-person operation they run from home. Are you reluctant to start your business by yourself? Rather than take a partner, you can hire a consultant short-term, or a trusted friend ongoing, and part-time if possible.

>> **Getting yeses comes naturally to you.** If you're a business owner, you need lots of yeses: people willing to work for you for stock and little or no cash, vendors willing to sell to you on credit, people willing to let you share their space or equipment for little or no money, and customers willing to buy your product at a price with a good profit margin. The successfully self-employed person has the ability to get people to say yes without exerting undue pressure. Look back at your track record, not just professionally but also personally. Do people tend to agree with you, to say yes to your requests?

>> **You can handle diverse problems on the fly.** Time is money, and you can't afford to hire help for too many tasks.

>> **You're resilient.** Even if they're well-run, most businesses suffer setbacks. Successfully self-employed people see whether there's a lesson to be learned and then, rather than wallow, move forward. Yet they're objective enough to know when a wiser use of further time and money is to replace their business with one of greater potential or to resume looking to be employed by others.

Honestly, to what extent do the qualities in this list describe you?

#26
Getting Acquainted with Home-Based Businesses

If employment options look bleak outside your home, maybe the answer is inside your home: Consider a home-based business. Owning your own home-based business may be the most rewarding experience of your entire life. And not just in a financial sense (although many home-based businesspeople find the financial rewards to be significant) but also rewarding in the sense of doing the work you love and having control over your own life.

Starting and running your own home-based business offers these advantages:

- **You're the boss.** For many owners of home-based businesses, this reason is enough to justify making the move out of the 9-to-5.

- **You get all the benefits of your hard work.** When you make a profit, it's all yours. No one else is going to try to take it away from you (except, perhaps, Uncle Sam).

- **You have the flexibility to work when and where you want.** Perhaps your most productive times don't coincide with the standard 9-to-5 work schedule that most regular businesses require their employees to adhere to.

- **You get to choose your clients and customers.** When you own your own business, you can fire the clients you don't want to work with. Sounds like fun, doesn't it?

>> **You can put as much or as little time into your business as you like.** You can decide whether you work for only a few hours a day or week or on a full-time schedule.

Don't forget to consider some of the potential pitfalls:

>> **The business is in your home.** Depending on your domestic situation, working in your own home — a home filled with any number of distractions, including busy children, whining partners, televisions, loaded refrigerators, and more — can be a difficult proposition at best.

>> **You're the boss.** Yes, being the boss has its drawbacks, too. When you're the boss, you're the one who has to motivate yourself to work hard every day — no one's standing over your shoulder (except maybe your cat) watching your every move. For some people, focusing on work is very difficult when *they* are put in the position of being the boss.

>> **Health insurance may be unavailable or unaffordable.** If you've ever been without health insurance for a period of time, or if you've been underinsured and had to make large medical or dental payments, you know just how important affordable health insurance is to your health and financial well-being. Unfortunately, when you work for yourself, finding good health insurance can be a challenge.

>> **A home-based business is (usually) a very small business.** As a small business, you're likely more exposed to the ups and downs of fickle customers than larger businesses are. And a customer's decision not to pay could be devastating to you and your business.

>> **You may fail or not like it.** No one can guarantee that your business is going to be a success or that you're going to like the business you start. Failure may cost you dearly, including financial ruin (no small number of business owners have had to declare bankruptcy when their businesses failed), destruction of personal relationships, and worse.

Admittedly, starting a home–based business isn't for everyone. In fact, for some individuals, it can be a big mistake. If, however, you have an entrepreneurial spirit and you thrive on being independent and in charge of your life, a home–based business may be just the thing for you.

#27
Setting Up Your Home-Based Business

The following sections go through exactly what you need to do to start up your own home-based business.

Develop a Business Plan

Despite what you may read on many small business websites or blogs, many home-based business owners can get by without drafting a business plan. Indeed, just the thought of having to draft a 50-page tabbed and annotated, multipart business plan is enough to scare many potential home-based business owners away from their dreams. Truth be told, most business owners today use their business plans to obtain financing from third parties, such as banks or investors, and many successful businesses — home based or not — have been started without one.

That said, the process of drafting a business plan can be very beneficial — both to you as a business owner and to your business. Taking the time to draft a plan helps you do the right things at the right time to get your business off the ground; plus, it forces you to think through what the challenges will be and what you can do about them before they overwhelm you.

In essence, a good business plan

>> Clearly establishes your goals for the business

>> Analyzes the feasibility of a new business and its likelihood of being profitable over the long haul

>> Explores the expansion of an existing business

>> Defines your customers and competitors (very important people to know!) and points out your strengths and weaknesses

>> Details your plans for the future

REMEMBER

Even if you think your business is too small to have a business plan, it's really worth your time to see what it's all about — the process of developing the plan for your business will produce a clarity of thought that you can't find any other way.

Consult Outside Professionals

As a new home-based businessperson, you need to consider establishing relationships with a number of *outside professionals* — trained and experienced people who can help you with the aspects of your business in which you may have little or no experience. By no means do you have to hire someone from each category in this section. But if you run into questions that you can't easily answer yourself, don't hesitate to call on outside professionals for help as you go through the business startup process.

REMEMBER

Any professional advice you get at the beginning of your business may well save you heartache and potentially expensive extra work down the road.

Here are just some of the outside professionals you may choose to consult as you start your home-based business:

>> Lawyer

>> Accountant

>> Banker

>> Business consultant

>> Insurance agent/broker

REMEMBER

The relationships you establish with outside professionals during the startup phase of your business can last for years and can be of tremendous benefit to your firm. Be sure to choose your relationships wisely. In the case of outside professionals, you often get what you pay for, so be penny-wise but don't suffer a poor-quality outside professional simply to save a dollar or two.

Choose a Legal Structure

Most home-based businesses begin as either sole proprietorships or partnerships because they're the easiest business structures to run and the least expensive. But as these businesses grow, many explore the transition to another kind of legal entity. Before you decide what kind of business you want yours to be, consider the following legal structures:

>> **Sole proprietorship:** A *sole proprietorship* is the simplest and least regulated form of organization. It also has minimal legal startup costs, making it the most popular choice for new home-based businesses. In a sole proprietorship, one person owns and operates the business and is responsible for seeking and obtaining financing. The sole proprietor (likely you) has total control and receives all profits, which are taxed as personal income.

>> **Partnership:** A *partnership* is relatively easy to form and can provide additional financial resources. Each partner is an *agent* for the partnership and can borrow money, hire employees, and operate the business. Profits are taxed as personal income, and the partners are still personally liable for debts and taxes. Personal assets can be attached if the partnership can't satisfy creditors' claims.

REMEMBER

When entering into any partnership, consult a lawyer, and insist on a written agreement that clearly describes a process for dissolving the partnership as cleanly and fairly as possible.

>> **Limited liability company:** A *limited liability company* (LLC) is often the preferred choice for new operations and joint ventures because LLCs have the advantage of being treated as partnerships for U.S. income tax purposes while also providing the limited liability of corporations. Owners of limited liability companies, called *members,* are comparable to stockholders in a corporation or limited partners in a limited partnership.

>> **Corporation:** As the most complex of business organizations, the *corporation* (also known as a *C corporation*) acts as a legal entity that exists separately from its owners. Although this separation limits the owners from personal liability, it also creates a double taxation on earnings (corporate tax and personal tax).

A special type of corporation, an *S corporation,* allows owners to overcome the double tax and shareholders to offset business losses with personal income; however, if you offset losses for an S corporation against regular income, you basically guarantee that you'll be audited.

REMEMBER

As you set up your new home-based business, take time to carefully think through the ramifications of your business's legal structure. Each option has many potential advantages and disadvantages for your firm, and each can make a big difference in how you run your business. If you have any questions about which kind of legal structure is right for your business, talk to an accountant or seek advice from an attorney who specializes in small businesses.

Decide on a Name

Naming your business may well be one of the most enjoyable steps in the process of starting up your own home-based business. Everyone can get in on the action: your friends, your family, and especially your clients-to-be.

WARNING

Consider your business name carefully — you have to live with it for a long time. Your business name should give people some idea of the nature of your business, it should project the image you want to have, and it should be easy to visualize. Names can be simple, sophisticated, or even silly. Try to pick one that can grow with your business and not limit you in the future.

TIP

Along with a name, many businesses develop a logo, which provides a graphic symbol for the business. As with your name, your logo needs to project the image you want, so develop it carefully. Spend a few extra dollars to have a professional graphic artist design your logo for you.

After you come up with a name, register it with your local government to make sure it isn't already in use. If you don't check first, you may have to throw out your stationery and business cards and redesign your logo and website when you eventually find out that another company has your name — and registered it 15 years before you did!

Take Care of the Red Tape

Handling all the local, state, and federal government legal requirements of starting up a business is something that too many budding home-based entrepreneurs put off or ignore. Unfortunately, ignoring the many legal requirements of going into business may put you and your business at risk.

Getting through the maze of government regulations can certainly be one of the most confusing aspects of starting up and running a business. But even though this process can be intimidating, you have to do it — and do it correctly — because noncompliance can result in costly penalties and perhaps even the loss of your business. Consider this step as one that fortifies the professionalism of your business at the same time that it helps you rest easy at night, knowing that you're following the rules. Do you want people to take you seriously? Then you need to establish your business in a professional way.

WARNING

Even very small or part-time businesses have certain requirements. It's your responsibility to adhere to any and all regulations that apply to your business. Fortunately, a lot of people and organizations — government small business development centers, chambers of commerce, and sometimes lawyers and certified public accountants — are willing and eager to answer questions and help you with this task. For your sake — and the sake of your business — don't hesitate to ask someone for help when you need it.

Get the Insurance You Need

In today's expensive, litigious world of business, insurance isn't really an option — it's essential. Without it, all your years of hard work can be lost in a minute because of a catastrophic loss.

So what kinds of insurance do you need for your business? Talk to an insurance agent and discuss your business and its needs with them. Some of the most common kinds of business insurance include the following:

>> Health insurance

>> Basic fire insurance

>> Extended coverage

>> Liability insurance

>> Product liability coverage

>> Professional liability and/or errors-and-omissions insurance

>> Vandalism and malicious mischief coverage

>> Theft coverage

>> Vehicle insurance

>> Business interruption insurance

>> Workers' compensation

WARNING

A homeowner's policy isn't usually enough insurance for a home-based business for a couple of reasons. First, your typical homeowner's policy provides only limited coverage for business equipment and doesn't insure you against risks of liability or lost income. Second, your homeowner's policy may not cover your business activities at all.

REMEMBER

Insurance is the kind of thing you don't think about until you need it. And in the case of insurance, when you need it, chances are you *really* need it! Take time to set up proper coverage now — before it's too late.

Decide on an Accounting System

Accounting is one of those topics that makes people nervous (with visions of IRS audits dancing in their heads), but keeping books doesn't have to be complicated. In fact, simplicity is the key to a good system for home-based businesses. Keep in mind that your records need to be complete and up-to-date so that you have the information you need for business decisions and taxes.

TIP

When you establish an accounting system, pick up one of the excellent computer software programs dedicated to this purpose. Programs such as Quicken, QuickBooks, and Sage 50cloud do everything your home-based business will ever need — and more.

The two basic bookkeeping methods are *single entry* and *double entry:*

>> **Single entry:** It's simpler, with only one entry required per transaction. This method is preferred for most home-based businesses, and the vast majority can operate very well with the single-entry system.

>> **Double entry:** It requires two entries per transaction and provides cross-checks and decreases errors. Consider going with a double-entry system if someone else manages your books, if you use your accounting system for inventory management, or if you want more sophisticated reporting for analyzing your business.

You can also choose between two methods to keep track of the money coming in and going out of your business:

>> **Cash:** Most small businesses use the cash method, in which income is reported in the year it's received and expenses are deducted in the year they're paid.

>> **Accrual:** Under the accrual method, income is reported when it's earned, and expenses are deducted when they're incurred, whether money has changed hands yet or not.

REMEMBER

The accounting methods you use depend on your business. You may want to talk to an accountant for help in setting up your system. Even with the support of a professional, however, you need to understand your own system thoroughly.

Develop a Marketing Plan

If you want to be successful, you can't just start a business and then patiently wait for customers to walk in your door. You have to let potential customers know about your new business, get them in to have a look, and then encourage them to buy your product or service. Marketing is all of this and more. Your specific approach to marketing depends on your business, your finances, your potential client or customer base, and your goals.

Marketing sells your products and services, which brings in the cash you need to run your business. Marketing is so important to the survival (and success) of your business that it deserves a plan of its own. A *marketing plan* helps evaluate where your business currently is, where you want it to go, and how you can get there. Your marketing plan should also spell out the specific strategies and costs involved in reaching your goals.

TIP

You can integrate it into your business plan as one comprehensive section. As with the business plan, you should refer to it regularly and update it as necessary.

#28
Taking a Few Steps Before Leaving Your Job

As soon as you're consistently earning enough income from a part-time business to cover your bare-minimum living and business expenses, you're ready to make a full-time commitment to your business. Before you turn in your resignation, however, take the following steps:

>> **Check when any company benefit plans you have will vest or increase in value.** If you have a 401(k) or other retirement plan to which your employer has been contributing, it may not be fully available to you until you've completed a particular number of years of service. Checking this information may help you determine the best time to resign. It'd truly be a shame, for example, if you quit two weeks before the value of your retirement benefits was set to jump from 80 to 100 percent.

>> **Find out when you can expect to receive any bonus money or profit sharing.** You may, for example, be slated to receive an annual performance bonus or profit sharing a month after the end of the company fiscal year. This information can help with the financial planning for your business.

>> **Get all annual health exams and routine procedures done, and fill all prescriptions, while you and your family are still covered by your medical/dental/vision insurance.** Check to see whether your group coverage can be converted to an individual policy at favorable rates or what other health coverage options are open to you.

Don't forget that if you work in the United States, you're likely covered by COBRA (the Consolidated Omnibus Budget Reconciliation Act); visit www.dol.gov/general/topic/health-plans/cobra for the latest information.

>> **Pay off or pay down the balance on your credit cards while you still have a steady job.** This helps your credit rating (always a good thing) and provides you with another source of potential funds to help you finance various startup costs (and depending on the nature of your business, you may have plenty of those!).

Don't make your announcement or submit your resignation until you're really, actually, for sure ready to go. Some companies are (sometimes justifiably) paranoid about soon-to-be former employees' stealing ideas, proprietary data, or clients. This can make for a very hasty exit, with a personal escort, when you do resign.

#29
Getting the Cash Flowing

Every new business starts at the beginning. No matter how much experience you have in your current job or how many other businesses you may have started in the past, when you create a new home-based business, you're starting from scratch. In the beginning, every sale counts, and your primary goal quickly becomes building financial momentum. The faster you get the cash flowing into your new business, the sooner you can leave your 9-to-5 job behind and dedicate yourself fully to your home-based business. Consider these approaches to getting the cash flowing as you start your business:

>> **Begin part-time with your new business.** When you start your own business, you usually have a choice to make: Keep your day job or quit. Keep your regular job for as long as you can while building your own business part-time. That way you still have your regular job to fall back on if your own business fails for whatever reason in its early stages. At some point — after your own business has built up a sufficient clientele — you can leave your regular job and devote yourself fully to your home-based business.

>> **Work part-time at your old job.** If you have enough work in your home-based business to keep you fairly busy, but not enough to make it your full-time vocation, consider working part-time in your regular job. Depending on your particular

situation, your current employer may be willing to be flexible with your schedule. For many employers, keeping a good employee part-time is better than losing them altogether.

» **Turn your employer into your first client.** If you're really good at what you do, what better way to get your business off the ground than to do work for your current employer on a contract basis? Not only do you give your employer the benefit of your expertise while contracting with a known entity, but you also develop your business while working with people you already know, using systems and procedures you're already familiar with.

WARNING

Take care, however, to clearly separate yourself from your former employer as an independent contractor rather than continuing to work in the role of an employee. If you don't make this distinction clear, the IRS may disallow any tax deductions you take for your home-based business.

» **Take business with you (ethically, of course!).** Although stealing clients away from a previous employer is unethical (and may very well land you in court, forcing you to pay an attorney a lot of money to get you out of trouble), you may be able to get your employer's blessing if you let them know exactly what you want to do. The advantage of taking clients with you to your new business is that you maintain the strong working relationship you already have in place — which greatly benefits both your new business and your new clients.

» **Finance your business with startup funds.** You need money to start a business — any business. By lining up sources of startup funds, you can ease the financial entry into owning your own home-based business.

» **Piggyback with your partner.** If you're married or living with a partner, they can continue to work their regular job, providing a steady paycheck, benefits, and more, while you start your own home-based business. Although your overall income will be reduced until you're able to crank up your sales, you have the shelter of a secure job and benefits. Such a shelter can save you a lot of sleepless nights, allowing you to focus your attention where it's most needed — on building your business.

#30
Surveying Tax Deductions Available to Home-Based Businesses

Home-based businesses pay self-employment tax (the government's way of collecting payments for Social Security and Medicare from the self-employed), state and federal income taxes, excise and property taxes, and miscellaneous local taxes or assessments. With all these taxes, you can easily be turning over 30 to 50 percent or more of your business's revenues to the government. Fortunately, you can take a number of deductions — some significant — for your home-based business.

Home-Office Deduction

For many, the home-office deduction is a major financial incentive to start businesses at home, and it can have a significant and positive effect on a home-based business's financial position (as well as the personal financial situation of the owner). For many home-based business owners, the ability to take the home-office deduction literally means the difference between success and failure.

The beauty of the home-office deduction is that it allows you to deduct the costs of operating and maintaining the part of your home that you use for business. And it doesn't matter what kind of home you live in. Whether you live in a single-family home, a condominium, a commercial building, or even a houseboat, if you meet the IRS's criteria for the home-office deduction, you're eligible to take it.

REMEMBER

Consult with an accountant, tax planner, or other tax professional before you take the home-office deduction. The rules are complicated, and the penalties for doing the wrong thing can be significant. For more information on deductions for your home-based business, check out *IRS Publication 587: Business Use of Your Home* at www.irs.gov/pub/irs-pdf/p587.pdf.

Other Important Tax Deductions

Aside from the home-office tax deduction, home-based businesses are allowed to deduct a variety of other business expenses. As you may imagine, a home-based business owner can legally deduct lots of different things from their taxes. Examples of legal deductions include postage, auto expenses, Internet access, business meals and entertainment, interest payments on business credit cards, health insurance, and office supplies and furniture.

REMEMBER

To be deductible, the Internal Revenue Code specifies that expenses must be *ordinary and necessary* for the operation of your business. So although the purchase of a vintage 1959 sunburst Gibson Les Paul electric guitar for $150,000 may be ordinary and necessary (and thus an allowable deduction) for a professional musician, it likely wouldn't fly for a home-based software designer — in fact, it'd surely sink like a lead balloon.

#31
Recognizing Often Overlooked Ways to Save on Your Taxes

As you're probably well aware, the rules that govern income taxes and the deductions you're allowed to take are complex. But despite appearances to the contrary, you're not required to pay any more tax than is necessary. In fact, you shouldn't pay any more tax than you're legally required to pay.

REMEMBER

Because of the complexity of the tax rules and the fact that they change — sometimes substantially — every year, hiring a professional tax lawyer or accountant can really pay off, and it's deductible, too.

However, it's understandable if you'd prefer not to spend a lot of money paying for a tax lawyer or accountant just yet. You can still employ a variety of strategies to reduce your tax burden. Consider the following ways to save on your taxes that sometimes get overlooked:

> » **Maximize your vehicle deduction.** You can choose between the standard mileage deduction or the actual

costs of operating your vehicle, which includes fuel, mainte-nance, taxes, and license fees. Where you live can determine whether choosing to use the standard deduction will save you more money than reporting actual costs.

Note, however, that if you use the actual cost method in the first year you use a vehicle, you must stick with this method ever after. And unless you use a vehicle 100 percent for business, you need to keep a log of your business use, including dates, mileage, and the purpose of your business travels.

For more information, see www.irs.gov/taxtopics/tc510 about the business use of cars.

>> **Make the most of hiring employees.** If you need an employee, consider hiring a family member. A child in a lower tax bracket enables you to keep income in the family. Depending on how much the child earns, no tax at all may be owed on his or her earnings.

>> **Reduce your taxes with a retirement plan.** Putting money into a retirement fund reduces your Adjusted Gross Income, which is what you use to calculate other deductions, such as a casualty loss, medical, and miscellaneous itemized deductions. The self-employed are able to invest more money using plans such as SEPs and SIMPLE Plans than with an IRA. To find out more about retirement plans for the self-employed, obtain IRS Publication 560 (www.irs.gov/pub/irs-pdf/p560.pdf).

>> **Make the most of a bad year.** Consult a tax professional to determine whether you would be better off getting an immediate tax refund or carrying your loss into your next business year. Keep in mind that the tax law on handling losses changes frequently.

Of course, it's against the law to evade paying your taxes, but it's your duty to avoid paying more taxes than you're legally obligated to. The IRS isn't going to give you any gold stars or special privi-leges for paying more taxes than you have to — you're throwing away your money if you do. And that's the last thing any home-based businessperson should ever do.

#32
Ensuring the Survival of Your Home-Based Business in Tough Times

Good planning for your home-based business can help you see far enough out on the horizon to anticipate the most serious financial shortfalls — and then take steps to avoid them — but it's impossible to anticipate each and every bump in the road and miss them when they arrive.

Use these tips to help you weather the unpredictable storms and emerge stronger than ever:

>> **Save for a rainy day.** One of the best things you can do is put aside money when times are good. Although it's tempting (and fun!) to run out and purchase the latest computer, the most recent software update, or a new furniture setup when the money's rolling in, first be sure that you set aside cash in your business savings account or money-market fund to help you through a rough patch of business.

Build a cash reserve sufficient to run your business for a minimum of three months, preferably six to twelve months. After you have your cash reserve established and funded, you can go out and buy all that fun stuff you've had your eyes on.

>> Manage your cash flow. Cash flow — more specifically, maintaining a *positive* cash flow — is by far the number-one financial issue facing every small business owner. And if you rely 100 percent on the proceeds of your home-based business to support you and your family or significant other and to pay for healthcare and other essential benefits, without the kind of steady income that a regular job brings, a shortfall in cash can quickly bring financial disaster.

The solution is to manage your cash flow, which means making a habit of doing the following:

- Keep an eye on your net cash flow.

- Be proactive in bringing cash into your business as quickly as possible.

- Pay your bills only when they're due, but do so in time to avoid interest and penalties.

>> Keep in touch with your customers. When times get tough, your first priority should be to ensure that your current customer relationships are *solid*. Drop in for a visit, schedule a lunch, send an email message, send some flowers, do whatever you can to keep your relationship on the front burner. And while you're busy keeping your relationship active, let your customers know that you're actively seeking more work. This gentle reminder that you're out there often leads customers to send more work your way — exactly what you need when times are tough!

>> Push your clients to pay their bills. How do you know when payments due to your business are running behind? You can find out by monitoring *receivables* — the money owed to your company by your clients and customers. Business accounting programs have built-in receivables *aging reports* that make the task easy by showing you who owes you money, how much they owe, when it's due to be paid, and how late the payment is if you haven't yet received it. And when you discover that one of your client's payments is overdue, act immediately — especially when the amount owed is substantial.

Here are some tried-and-true ways for collecting your money:

- Call or visit your customer, and ask for payment.
- Offer to help.
- As a last resort — and only if you aren't concerned about getting any future business from your client — turn the matter over to a collections agency.

REMEMBER

Whatever you do, when a payment is late, act immediately — don't wait for days or weeks (or months!), hoping it'll come in. Keeping the money coming in on time should be one of your key concerns, and this task needs your immediate attention.

>> **Minimize expenses.** When times are tough, you essentially have two ways to hunker down: increase the amount of money that comes into your business or decrease the amount of money that goes out (or both). Minimizing expenses is one of the quickest ways to help weather the storm, and you need to act immediately when you go into survival mode.

Before you buy anything, ask yourself whether you can survive without it for a while. Can the expense be deferred for a few days, a few weeks, or even a few months? Can you borrow or rent equipment instead of purchasing it? Can you barter your services or products in exchange for the products and services of other businesses?

WARNING

Be careful, however, about exactly what expenses you cut. Do *not* cut expenses that will bring significantly more money into your business; instead, you may actually need to increase them.

>> **Offer a special promotion.** To quickly generate more business, offer your customers a special offer on your products or services — perhaps 10 percent off all orders during July or a two-for-the-price-of-one offer. The exact form of your promotion varies, depending on the nature of your business, but you should be clear to your customers that they need to act quickly to take advantage of the special offer.

Alternatively, offer your clients and customers a premium — a value-added product or service — for placing an order during a specific period of time. For example, every customer who places an order of at least $100 during February receives a gift certificate for $10 worth of merchandise or a free video. You can also offer a special price to customers who are willing to commit to a contract. Be creative!

» **Subcontract for others.** To help offset extreme business swings, develop a network of business contacts — perhaps other home-based businesses — to subcontract your work *to* in times of feast and to subcontract work *from* in times of famine. Sure, it may sound a bit strange to turn work over to a competitor, but it actually makes good business sense. The key is for you to remain the primary contact with the client and to ensure that the work from the contractor is of the same high quality that you would insist on if you did it yourself.

» **Refuse to give up.** When times are tough, you may be tempted to throw in the towel and give up. But what's much more challenging — and ultimately much more rewarding — is to fight for your business and refuse to give up, *no matter what.* When interviewed and surveyed, successful entrepreneurs most consistently attribute their good fortune to *persistence.*

You can fail only if you allow yourself to do so. By not considering giving up an option, you force yourself to focus on doing the things that help pull you through your tough times — things like the other items in this list.

#33

Boosting Your Household Income with a Side Hustle

When you can't make ends meet with expense cuts alone, start looking at the other end of the cash flow equation: income. You may consider starting a side hustle to bring in more income. A *side hustle* is an activity in which you're *materially invested* (basically, what you've started isn't some passing whim, but rather something you're really, really interested in doing) but it's not your full-time, salaried, career-oriented job. Basically, a side hustle is an activity that is on the side of your primary, full-time job and that requires more than a minimal amount of time and energy (at least as you get established).

So how do you get started? You can do an online search for "best side hustles" or "side hustle ideas" or a similar term, and you'll wind up with hundreds of results, many containing dozens of ideas. How do you make sense out of this information overload? How do you find the needle in the haystack: the side hustle that's a great fit for you?

TIP

Fortunately, you can follow a methodical, step-by-step process that can help you narrow down thousands of different side hustle ideas into a small subset that matches your interests, abilities, and goals. Specifically, you need to consider and evaluate the following:

>> Various topical areas available to you to focus on for your side hustle

>> Ways to flesh out and add substance to your initial topical area

>> Various venues or formats through which you can enter the side hustle game

>> How your side hustle should relate to your full-time job or career or possibly other side hustles that you already have underway

>> Financial considerations on both the moneymaking and money-spending side of your side hustle

>> Time considerations, including the highly valued — and often misunderstood — concept of *passive income*

>> Whether you need special skills, training, or licensing for your side hustle

You can then mash the results of each of these areas together, and — presto — that overwhelming list of hundreds or thousands of side hustle ideas is now magically narrowed down for you to make your final side hustle decisions.

3

Putting Your Personal Finances on Firm Footing

Be proactive about protecting the things you've planned for your future: your retirement, your own or your kids' college education, and so on.

Stay in control of your financial goals and simultaneously find savings opportunities for insurance, education, mortgages, and more.

#34

Categorizing Your Financial Records

Getting organized takes time, but you'll be very glad if you invest the time. Imagine no more late payments and fees resulting from misplacing a credit card bill. Imagine organizing your tax records in minutes rather than hours and having critical information or documents ready at a moment's notice.

Organization truly isn't that hard, so if you're ready to put an end to the chaos, the following steps can walk you down the path of organization:

1. **Gather all your financial documents, paperwork, bills, and unopened mail.**

2. **Set up a filing system.**

   See Tip #35 for details on the structure to use.

3. **Separate your paperwork into four stacks: Bills to Be Paid; To Do/Read; File; and Shred.**

4. **Place the Bills to Be Paid stack in your new Bills Due file; place the To Do/Read stack in your new To Do or Read file; file all items in your File stack in their appropriate files; and shred any paper that contains personal or private information before recycling.**

   If in doubt, shred it.

REMEMBER

Every time you retrieve the mail or obtain additional paperwork from work, from the bank, and so on, immediately follow Steps 3 and 4.

#35
Setting Up a Filing System for Your Financial Records

You can use the following list as a guide to organize your personal financial files (either paper or digital). For most of the primary subjects listed here, you need only one file. You may find that fewer or more files are necessary depending on your personal situation, preferences, or the number of documents you have for a particular file.

The following list also outlines how long you should retain these documents for your records.

> » **Wills, trusts, and estate planning:** File all current, executed estate-planning documents, as well as a list of your chosen beneficiaries (heirs) for your insurance policies and your savings, investment, and retirement accounts.

> » **Advisors:** Keep a list of names and contact information for the important people in your financial life, such as your banker, physician, and attorney (among others).

>> **Auto:** Be sure to include the following for each vehicle:

- **Title:** Keep as long as you own the vehicle.

- **Maintenance records:** Keep as long as you own the vehicle.

>> **Bank accounts:** This file includes your checking, savings, and money market accounts. For each account, be sure to include the following:

- **Current monthly statement:** Keep until you receive the next statement.

- **Historic monthly statements:** Keep until the account is reconciled. If you ever need a historic statement for some reason, your bank can provide a copy.

>> **Bills due:** Upon opening your mail, file bills due in this file. After you pay the bills, the file will be empty again.

>> **Contracts:** Keep the following contracts as long as they're in force:

- All legal agreements that aren't listed elsewhere here

- Employment contracts

>> **Credit cards:** Use one file folder for each account and include the following:

- **Current monthly statement:** Keep until you receive and reconcile the next statement.

- **Historic monthly statements:** Keep until the account is reconciled, at a minimum. However, if you purchased an item that's under warranty through your credit card company or if you purchased something that may be a tax-deductible expense, keep the record indefinitely. If in doubt, keep.

>> **Credit history:**

- **Credit report:** Obtain a copy of your credit report for both you and your spouse at least annually. Retain the report until you receive a new report and then compare the two reports.

- **Debt management action plan:** You use this scorecard to track your debt repayment progress.

>> **Education:**

- Enrollment records

- Diplomas and certificates

- Grade cards or transcripts
- Progress reports

>> **Employment:**

- Employee handbook (current)
- Employee benefits handbook (current)
- Paycheck stub (most current only, if cumulative)
- Employee evaluations (all)
- Resume (current)
- Continuing education units (CEU; all required documentation of CEU requirements, if applicable)
- Proof of current licensure, if licenses are required

>> **Healthcare (for informational purposes only):**

- Medical records
- Vaccination information
- Receipts (may be needed for tax return)

>> **Home repairs and maintenance:** Retain records, invoices, estimates, business cards, and so on for any home services or repairs — plumbing, electric, lawn maintenance — as well as any receipts for equipment you've purchased for as long as you own the item.

>> **Insurance:** Retain current copies of personally owned insurance policies, such as auto, home, boat, life, disability, long-term care, or any other type of insurance you may have. In addition to your policies, also keep a copy of your most current annual statement.

>> **Investments:**

- **Bank investment account statements**
- **Brokerage accounts:** Although you aren't required by law to keep your account application, consider putting it in this file. Hopefully, you'll never need it. You should also keep any notes or correspondence from the broker (for as long as you own the asset) and prospectuses (the one issued when the investment was originally made and the most current for each investment position held), as well as annual reports (keep the most current for each investment position held) and monthly or quarterly or annual (if cumulative) account statements (retain

indefinitely). Also file and retain any purchase or sale confirmation statements for at least three years after the investment is completely liquidated.

- **Mutual fund statements:** The documents you need to file include the following: account applications; notes or correspondence from your advisor; prospectuses (initial and most current); annual report (most recent only); monthly account statement (if cumulative, retain the current monthly or quarterly statements as well as each year-end cumulative statement); and purchase and sale confirmation statements (for at least three years after the investment is completely liquidated).

- **Employer-sponsored retirement plans:** Be sure to retain your Summary Plan Description, investment options, current account statement (keep until the next one comes), and annual account summary statement (leave it in the file indefinitely).

- **IRAs:** You need to save your current account statement, any annual account summary statements (retain indefinitely), and any records of contributions, both from traditional (deductible and nondeductible) and Roth accounts.

- **Other investments:** This category includes rental property, limited partnerships, dividend reinvestment plans, and annuities. Anything that doesn't fit into other investment files goes here.

» **Loans:** You need to keep all documents for each loan — whether a mortgage, home equity line of credit, signature loan, auto loan, or school loan — for as long as the loan is outstanding. This documentation includes proof of payments and amortization schedules. After the loan is paid off, keep your paid-in-full verification indefinitely.

» **Read:** Use this folder as a parking place for important financial reading material that you'll get to at a more convenient time, such as an investment account newsletter that came in the mail. (Retain until completed, dropped, or moved to a more appropriate file, which frequently is the recycle bin.)

>> **Tax records:** Hang on to all receipts, 1099s, paycheck stubs, charitable contributions, and other items pertaining to the current year. In most cases, you need to keep tax returns and supporting records — the proof behind the numbers on your tax return that you signed and filed — for three years; however, you may keep them indefinitely.

>> **To do (pending projects):** This category includes to-do items, such as an estimate for work you may have done on your home or an investment prospectus that you haven't read yet. (Retain until completed or dropped.)

>> **Utilities:** Retain current monthly statements for the following: water, gas, electric, phone (both landline and mobile), and streaming, cable, and/or satellite TV.

TIP

As you file these papers, consider recording on a single piece of paper your monthly costs for each service. Take a moment to look at usage trends and you'll likely become more energy-efficient and save money.

>> **Warranties:** Retain the documentation until the item is no longer under warranty. This includes any whole house, appliance, or electronics warranties.

#36
Finding an Insurance Agent

Automobile, home, boat, umbrella, and other personal policies, as they're sold off the shelf, rarely, if ever, cover all your major property and liability risks. But they will cover most, if not all, of those major risks if they're customized to your needs with proper coverage limits and appropriate coverage endorsements. Customizing a policy requires a great deal of coverage expertise and care. And that's why, for most people, locating and hiring the best possible advisor has to be the very highest priority when it comes to buying insurance.

Build a checklist of what you want in your agent. Ask yourself the following questions:

>> **Do I want my life, health, disability, long-term-care, and other coverages with the same agent?** You'll have the best-designed program if you can find one agent with the expertise to oversee your whole program — expertise in every kind of personal policy. At the very least, it's wise not to have more than two agents that you work with.

» **Is a regular, yearly review important to me?** If so, add this to your shopping list. Regular reviews are recommended. A well-designed insurance plan starts to rust with coverage gaps if it's not polished up every year or two.

» **Do I have a home business?** If so, you must find someone with small-business insurance expertise. Add that to your list.

» **Are top claim skills important to me?** Do you want the best possible claims coaching, to maximize your claim when you file it? Do you want an agent skilled enough to fight, successfully, for your rights if your claim is unjustly denied or underpaid?

Then use the answers to these questions to screen potential candidates. You're looking for an agent to probe your needs, identify coverage gaps, solve problems, help you resolve claim disputes, do annual reviews, and, in short, provide greater expertise.

Here are some possible sources for candidates. Try to get at least two to three prospects.

» **Word of mouth:** Word of mouth is always one of the best sources when seeking a professional of any kind. But be careful not to fall into the price trap. Because so many people buy their insurance solely on price, when you ask for a referral for a good agent, you might get: "Call Bob. He's a good guy. He saved me $200 a year. And he always remembers my birthday." So you call Bob, get his quote, save your $200 or more, and end up with a good price for the wrong coverage (and an annual birthday card). And you've done nothing about your uninsured coverage gaps.

TIP

To avoid the price trap, be specific when asking for a referral. You don't necessarily want the best salesperson or the one you'd most like to go to a ballgame with. You want the person who will give you the best professional advice.

» **Professional societies:** An insurance agent can earn a number of advanced insurance designations by completing a series of courses and passing the exams. Here are just a few:

- Chartered Property Casualty Underwriter (CPCU)
- Certified Insurance Counselor (CIC)

- Certified Life Underwriter (CLU)

- Accredited Advisor in Insurance (AAI)

If you want some good leads to an agent prospect with expertise in personal property and liability policies — auto, home, umbrella, and so on — contact

- CPCU Society (www.cpcusociety.org)

- The National Alliance for Insurance Education and Research (www.scic.com)

Whatever names you get from these two societies will be good prospects for your agent search.

>> **Insurance companies:** If you already know you want to be insured with a particular company, go directly to that company for agent referrals. You can also go to the insurance company for agent leads if you've shopped ahead for a certain type of insurance and found one or two insurers that are the lowest priced. (All you know at this point is that they're the lowest priced for the coverage you shopped but not necessarily the coverage you need.)

What you need to find out from the insurer is who the company's best, most knowledgeable agents are. The insurance company knows who these agents are, but the company is unlikely, for legal and other reasons, to give you their names. So try this: Call the local company office and ask them to email you a list of all their agents in your state who have a CPCU or CIC designation. They may not have a list at their fingertips, but they can get it for you. Whichever method you use, it should yield a small supply of quality prospects.

At this point, you've narrowed down your choice to one or two candidates for your "job opening" for an agent/advisor. You're probably thinking, "How do I, with limited knowledge, make this choice? I don't even know what to ask."

Start by requesting a face-to-face meeting for the purpose of doing an insurance review for every policy that you have including your group coverage at work. You'll be able to tell by your gut feel whether this is the person for you.

If you've narrowed your field to two candidates, have both of them do an insurance review for you. The agent with the greater expertise and greater care for your well-being will stand out.

#37
Having a Balanced Insurance Program

A great insurance program has two key components:

» Your program is in balance in all major risk areas:
- Major damage to or destruction of your residence
- Major lawsuits
- Premature death
- Long-term disability
- Major medical bills

» Each policy that you buy is well-designed with high limits for major loss coverages and with all the right endorsements that customize your policy to cover the risks in your life that would not otherwise be covered.

You'll have a better chance of accomplishing both goals if you take time to locate a highly skilled insurance agent who's an expert on every type of personal insurance that you need. (See Tip #36, "Finding an Insurance Agent," for more information.)

Yes, the cost of insurance is important. You want your costs to be competitive and manageable. But the true cost of your insurance program is not only what you pay upfront in premiums but more importantly what you have to pay out-of-pocket at claim time. Most people who shop for insurance put all the emphasis on the front-end costs — the premiums — and then may end up having to pay thousands or hundreds of thousands of dollars in uncovered claims later.

REMEMBER

When it comes to insurance costs, it's far better to pay a little too much in premiums than to pay for an uncovered major claim later.

You face several major risks regularly throughout your lifetime that, if they occur, can cause your financial ruin: major medical bills, major damage to or destruction of your residence, major lawsuits and the cost of defending them, long-term disability, premature death, and — especially for those older than age 40 — the risk of extended long-term care. Your insurance program is in balance if each of these major risk areas are equally well covered and you're not spending too much on one area and too little on another.

Many people have major-loss coverage that's out of balance. They may have a good medical plan with high limits, but no coverage for long-term disabilities. They may have $1 million of life insurance on the breadwinner, but none on the homemaker. Their home may be fully insured, but they have only $100,000 of coverage for lawsuits and no umbrella liability policy.

REMEMBER

A highly skilled agent can help you identify imbalances in your insurance program and suggest the corrective action needed, which is why taking the time to find the right agent is so important. Most people who buy insurance don't take the time to find the right agent for them. They let whoever answered the phone and gave them the quote be their agent, without any knowledge of that person's skill level. And in the end, they get a less-skilled agent than they could have had for the same price.

#38
Deciding between Permanent and Term Life Insurance

TIP

There are really only two types of life insurance — permanent and term — although the two types come in many shapes, sizes, and colors. The biggest difference between them is how long the coverage lasts:

>> Permanent life insurance covers you for your entire life. Your death is certain. And when you die, it pays the death benefit (the amount of money payable at the time of death).

>> Term life insurance covers only a part of your lifetime. When that part, or term, ends, so does the coverage. It only pays a death benefit if you die within the designated term.

Permanent Life Insurance

Permanent life insurance is ideally suited to permanent needs. For example, you may buy permanent life insurance when you're looking to supplement retirement dollars for your surviving spouse, covering estate taxes due upon your death, or paying final expenses — burial, legal costs, and so on.

Every life insurance policy has two core parts to its price:

>> **Mortality cost:** This is determined by your odds of dying at that moment. The mortality charge increases each year as you age and your risk of dying increases.

>> **Policy expense cost:** This is your share of insurance company expenses (rent, staff, and agent commissions). The expense charge stays relatively constant.

Most permanent life insurance policies have level premiums for life. How is that possible if the mortality charge increases each year? The insurance company averages the increasing mortality changes over your remaining expected life. In short, you overpay in the early years so that you can underpay in the later years. That overpayment in the early years is set aside in a reserve for you, called *cash value*. If you cancel a permanent policy, by law you're entitled to get back much of those overpayments — that cash value. The cash value is minimal in the first couple of years because of heavy first-year costs — underwriting, medical exams, and agent commissions.

Permanent life insurance is considerably more expensive than term life insurance for the first several years, for the same death benefit, because permanent insurance has a cash value element.

Term Life Insurance

Term life insurance is ideally suited for covering life insurance needs that aren't permanent. For example, you may buy term life insurance when you want to cover college costs for children or family income needs while the kids are growing up.

Term life insurance costs, unlike permanent life insurance costs, increase regularly as you age. Sometimes the increase is annual, and sometimes it's every five or ten years or more. Term insurance costs can be averaged over 10, 20, or 30 years, so the price is level for the entire term. But term insurance doesn't have a cash value element — if you drop a term insurance policy in its early years, you get no refund of any overpayment.

Because term insurance has no cash value element, premiums in the first several years are considerably lower than permanent insurance premiums for the same death benefit.

#39
Choosing a Permanent Life Insurance Policy

With permanent life insurance, the cost is substantially higher in the first several years of your coverage. However, the cost can't go up. The initial premium rate is as bad as it'll ever get, and the insurance company can't deny benefits as long as you pay your premiums on time. So if you need life insurance coverage indefinitely — for example, if you need cash available for your heirs to pay estate or inheritance taxes upon your death — you're a good candidate for permanent life insurance.

Permanent insurance comes in two primary flavors:

> **Universal:** You may need a lot of life insurance now and well into your retirement years. If that's the case, universal life insurance is likely the type of insurance for at least a portion of your life insurance need. This type of life insurance has an investment as well as an insurance component. Your initial premiums are applied to purchase life insurance. Then, additional premiums either accumulate in a fixed account (universal life) or are invested (variable universal life) to provide more growth (and volatility) opportunities, much like stock and bond mutual funds.

>> **Whole:** If you need coverage for your entire life, no matter how long you live, whole life insurance may be the right option for that portion of your life insurance need.

WARNING

Insurance agents make a lot more money selling universal life, variable universal life, and whole life insurance than they do selling term insurance. This inherent conflict of interest is something that you need to always keep in mind when considering the recommendations of an insurance agent or financial advisor who sells life insurance.

#40
Selecting a Term Life Insurance Policy

Like home or auto insurance, *term insurance* is pure insurance in that it pays off only if you make a claim. The cost of the insurance can go up every year *(annual renewable term)* or remain *level* for a specific number of years (for example, 5, 10, 20, or 30 years). You can lose your insurance coverage if you fail to pay the premiums when they're due, if the term expires and the policy isn't guaranteed renewable, or if you elect not to renew if you have that option. However, term insurance is by far the cheapest form of life insurance.

Here are a few suggestions:

>> Twenty-year level term coverage is generally an excellent option for families with young children, whether or not they need a lot or a little insurance, because the insurance will be there to support the surviving family, at least until the kids are grown.

>> Consider level premium term life insurance coverage. For one thing, the level premium guarantees that you know exactly how much your insurance will cost for a set number of years. And level premium term life insurance can be extremely cost-effective. Consider using level premium term

insurance with a guaranteed level premium for the number of years that you anticipate needing the coverage and also consider adding the guaranteed renewable rider.

WARNING

>> A guaranteed renewable rider is a very attractive feature available with many term insurance policies. It assures that you'll be able to retain a term policy at the end of its initial term — if you still need the insurance — simply by paying the premiums in effect at that time. You don't have to reapply or provide evidence of insurability. This provision provides great flexibility when you're not exactly sure when you'll no longer need coverage.

>> If you need coverage for only five to ten years at most, you may want to consider annual renewable term (ART) life insurance because it tends to be less expensive for the first five or six years of the policy when compared to a 10- or 20-year level term policy. But every year, the premiums continue to increase, and the policy that was once very attractive becomes more expensive than a level term policy. The break-even point is so early in the life of the annual renewable term policy that buying this coverage makes no sense unless you won't need it very long. In every other situation where term insurance would be appropriate, go with the level premium term insurance.

>> Many people need at least $200,000 worth of life insurance, or several times that amount, to provide for their surviving family in the event of premature death, but they can't afford to spend thousands of dollars per year on life insurance premiums. They need life insurance, but they only need the coverage for a limited period of time, so in this case, term insurance is the best fit.

#41
Avoiding Life Insurance Mistakes

People make all kinds of mistakes when they buy life insurance. This list fills you in on the most common ones so that you can avoid falling into any traps:

>> **Trading cash value for death protection needs:** Being underinsured with permanent life insurance may be the biggest single mistake that people make in buying life insurance. They get swayed by the lure of the investment portion or cash value of the policy but can't afford to pay for all the death protection they need plus the investment, so they buy a cash value policy with less death protection than they need in order to have some investment. However, when they do die, their family doesn't have enough money to live on, creating a serious problem.

REMEMBER

The most important thing about life insurance is the protection it offers. So first things first. Determine how much life insurance you need by using a credible method. Then buy as much of that protection as you can afford, using term insurance, even lower-cost reentry products if necessary. If your budget has something left over, only then is it okay to look at permanent life products for part of your coverage. Never trade critical protection for less-important investment opportunities.

>> **Buying your life insurance in pieces:** Buying your life insurance in pieces is a lot more expensive than covering all your needs in one policy. Plus, buying in pieces leaves you vulnerable to a gap in your coverage. Examples of piecemeal buying are having mortgage insurance through your lending institution, credit card insurance through your credit card company, credit life insurance with your car loan, and so on. With some of these insurances, you don't have to qualify medically; therefore, if you're in poor health or near death, buy all you can. Otherwise, they're often several times the price of what you would pay if you're in good health.

TIP

When buying life insurance, figure out how much insurance you need to do the whole job and buy one policy. It's smarter — and cheaper! Only one policy fee instead of several. Plus you have the advantage of a trusted professional agent to help with determining how much coverage you need, the type of policy, and so on.

>> **Buying accidental death/travel accident coverage:** Both accidental death and travel accident policies are varieties of Las Vegas insurance, transferring only the accidental portion of your risk. In other words, you have no coverage for death from natural causes. Buying these policies is an especially bad move if you buy them in lieu of the full life insurance you really need. Anyone who buys travel accident coverage at the airport or from a travel agent is really saying, "I'm not comfortable with the amount of life insurance I have."

REMEMBER

When buying life insurance, buy only coverage that pays for any death — natural or accidental.

>> **Covering the children in lieu of the parents:** When your child is born, you're deluged with a lot of solicitations about life insurance because of the birth announcement. You have hopes and dreams for your children, so you buy a nice cash value policy on your baby. It's understandable — you're so proud. But the economic effect on the family of a child's death is minimal compared to the major impact that one of the baby's parents dying would have.

REMEMBER

When a child is born, reevaluate and raise the amount of life insurance coverage that you and your spouse have.

» **Being unrealistic about how much you can afford to pay for life insurance:** A number of young people commit more money than they can afford to a large cash value life insurance policy and then later have to drop it and take a large financial loss — and perhaps even be exposed to the risk of a death without insurance.

REMEMBER

Term insurance for young families provides the most coverage for the money spent. If you want a permanent policy later with more bells and whistles, you can always convert your term policy.

#42
Saving Money on Your Homeowner's Policy

nsurance companies often offer discounts on your homeowner's insurance if you qualify in certain categories, or you may be able to adjust your deductible to make ends meet.

REMEMBER

If you're considering lowering your *deductible* (the part you pay before your insurance policy kicks in), keep in mind that insurance is intended to cover risks that you can't afford to bear on your own. The higher the deductible, the lower the premium.

Ask yourself these questions, which may save you money:

>> Are your home, auto, and liability insurance policies with the same company?

>> Do you have any safety devices (smoke detectors, fire extinguishers, alarm systems, and so on) in your home?

>> How long have you maintained coverage with the same insurance company?

>> Have you made any upgrades to your home?

>> Could you afford to pay your deductible if you raised it?

If you answered yes to any of these questions, contact your insurance company to see whether you can save money while obtaining top-quality and adequate insurance coverage.

#43
Looking into Umbrella Policies

f you don't have nearly enough insurance protection, what can you do? Here's some really good news: You can buy a second layer of liability coverage, called a *personal umbrella policy*, that sits on top of your other personal liability coverages for your car, home, and so on. It defends you and pays legal judgments against you when a covered lawsuit exceeds your primary liability insurance limits.

Best of all, an umbrella policy is amazingly inexpensive — usually about $150 to $300 per year for $1 million of coverage. And about $75 to $100 per year for each additional $1 million of coverage. This is not a typo. These costs are truly per *year* — not per month!

Buying an umbrella policy is flat-out the best value in the insurance business. It includes some of the broadest coverage in the insurance business at an incredibly low price. Buying an umbrella policy also satisfies two guiding principles of insurance: not risking more than you can afford to lose and not risking a lot for a little.

TIP

Affording an umbrella is easy. You don't even have to increase your insurance bill — just shift dollars away from less important coverages. For example, you can save a few hundred dollars by raising the deductible on your car insurance and homeowner's insurance by $500, or by dropping collision coverage on an older car. Use that savings to more than pay for an umbrella policy.

#44

Buying an Umbrella Policy Wisely

WARNING

H ere are the three most common mistakes people make when buying a personal umbrella policy:

» **They buy their auto and home policies first and then buy the umbrella from the same insurance company.** In short, the mistake is settling for whatever umbrella comes with the auto and home policies, no matter how poor it may be. ***Note:*** Buying your policies from the same agent is usually a good idea, but automatically buying them from the same company is a bad idea if you want the best umbrella policy.

» **They buy their umbrella policy from a different agent than the one who sold them auto and home insurance.** The damage occurs because the two agents don't communicate, leaving you very vulnerable to gaps between your primary and umbrella coverages.

» They buy their umbrella on price and ignore coverage. This usually happens because they think all umbrellas are the same and because they don't realize the importance of gap coverage. They're unaware that they even have gaps.

The three antidotes to these mistakes are building your insurance program starting with the umbrella policy first, keeping your primary and umbrella coverages with the same agent, and considering price last rather than first.

#45

Reducing Risk and the Expense of Car Insurance

The more you know about auto insurance and how the industry works, the better off you'll be, and the more money you can save. The following are key factors that car insurers use to determine the price of your auto insurance and some ways you can keep your premiums as low as possible:

>> **Age:** If you're very young or quite elderly, your risk of being in an auto accident is statistically much higher than it is for middle-aged folks. You can't do anything about your age. However, some insurers may penalize you less than others with regard to your cost of insurance.

>> **Auto insurance claims history:** Safe drivers are rewarded with lower auto insurance premiums. Your history of making claims against your auto policy directly affects the cost of your insurance. The more you use insurance, the more your insurance will cost.

» **Credit history:** Insurance companies have determined that a direct correlation exists between your credit history and your risk as a driver. They figure that if you're careless with your credit, then you may be careless in your driving — just one more reason why maintaining good credit is essential to your financial health.

» **Driving record:** If you've received a traffic ticket for speeding or another form of reckless driving, you'll pay for that carelessness in higher insurance premiums.

» **Place of residence:** Your zip code can affect your cost of insurance. Certain zip codes have a history of more auto theft, vandalism, and so on, and insurance companies are still allowed to penalize you for living in these zip codes.

» **Type of car you drive:** A sensible midsize sedan versus a large pickup truck? Owners of the latter will pay substantially higher auto insurance premiums because it will cause or potentially receive much more damage in the same accident as the minivan, and they cost a lot more to repair or replace than the older, less expensive vehicle.

#46

Getting the Right Car Insurance Coverage

I f you drive, you need to have auto insurance coverage (period). But exactly which type of coverages should you have, and which ones are you required to have? The following are the key features of auto insurance (depending on your unique circumstances, you may or may not need all these features):

>> **Bodily injury and property damage liability coverage:** With this coverage, the insurer agrees to pay damages if you injure someone or someone's property in an auto accident.

>> **Collision:** If you're in an automobile accident, regardless of who's at fault, collision insurance provides protection to replace or repair your vehicle, subject to a deductible.

>> **Comprehensive:** In the event of hail damage or a tree limb falling on your car (risks not involving an auto collision), this coverage insures you. Comprehensive coverage pays to repair your vehicle, subject to a separate deductible.

>> **Medical payments:** This feature provides a limited amount of coverage for you and your passengers' medical expenses as a result of an accident. The coverage pays regardless of who's at fault.

>> **Personal injury protection:** This type of coverage is for medical and other expenses resulting from an auto accident for the people specified in the policy, regardless of fault.

>> **Uninsured and underinsured motorists liability coverage:** If you're in an accident with another driver who doesn't carry any or enough liability coverage, this coverage allows you to collect damages that you personally experience.

REMEMBER

Because states differ in regulations and because you may have unique circumstances, you may need more or less coverage than what's in the preceding list. For state-by-state regulations on required coverages, visit www.insure.com/car-insurance/minimum-coverage-levels.html.

Also consider the following:

>> The additional liability coverage raises your premium; however, increasing your deductible helps offset those additional costs. In fact, increasing your deductible from $250 to $1,000 can reduce your collision and comprehensive coverage premium by 40 percent.

REMEMBER

You buy insurance to cover big financial risks. If you're involved in a major accident and cars are totaled, people are injured or killed, and property is damaged, the total financial impact could be hundreds of thousands, if not millions, of dollars. The liability benefits on your automobile policy help to protect you from this financial devastation. You can't afford to skimp on liability coverage.

>> If you have a much older vehicle or drive your vehicles until they drop, a time will come when maintaining collision and comprehensive insurance coverage isn't financially worthwhile. A general guideline is to drop collision and comprehensive coverage on vehicles worth less than ten times the cost for that portion of your auto policy.

WARNING

Don't drop your liability coverage under any circumstance; your old clunker can still wreak havoc in an accident. Besides, your state law probably requires that you maintain it. And like the money-savvy person that you are, you wouldn't want to put yourself and your family in financial jeopardy.

#47
Cutting the Cost of Your Car Insurance

Here are some tips to help you save money on your auto insurance:

>> **Don't file small claims.** The more you use your insurance, the higher your premiums will be. Submitting claims that exceed your deductible by just a few hundred dollars doesn't make financial sense. You won't come out ahead if you file small or frequent claims; paying for small losses yourself saves you money over the long term.

REMEMBER

The insurance company is in business to make money. Use your insurance to protect yourself only from devastating financial losses.

>> **Don't let other people drive your vehicle.** Multiple drivers create multiple risks. More risk, higher insurance cost.

>> **Wear your seat belt.** Studies prove that more people survive accidents and receive less severe injuries because they wear their seat belts. Less injury, fewer insurance claims, lower cost of insurance.

» **Don't exceed the speed limit.** Speeders cause accidents. Accidents result in claims. Claims jack up your insurance cost.

» **Take a driver safety course.** Many companies provide a discount to drivers who've taken a safe driving course.

» **Practice defensive-driving techniques.** Fewer accidents. Fewer claims. Cheaper insurance rates.

» **Pay your auto insurance premium annually.** Most companies charge a service fee if you pay your premiums monthly, quarterly, and sometimes semiannually.

#48
Continuing Health Coverage When You Leave Your Job

I f you leave your job for any reason, you can lose your group health insurance. But almost all employers are required by law to allow terminated employees to continue group insurance coverage through COBRA (the Consolidated Omnibus Budget Reconciliation Act). Even though you must pay 100 percent of the cost of the insurance, this may be your best option. If COBRA isn't an option for you, or if you're close to exhausting it (generally after 18 months), don't go without health insurance.

Consider these options:

>> **Individual health insurance:** If you're relatively healthy, consider an individual health insurance policy. To use the Health Insurance Marketplace established by the Affordable Care Act, visit www.healthcare.gov/. To find a health insurance broker in your area, visit the National Association of Health Underwriters (www.nahu.org/consumer/findagent.cfm).

>> **HIPAA:** The Health Insurance Portability and Accountability Act requires states to provide minimal coverage after you exhaust COBRA benefits, as long as you haven't had an extended break in coverage, which varies by state. Each state has its own HIPAA rules; to find out the rules in your state, contact your state insurance department.

>> **Medicaid:** Medicaid is a federal program that provides healthcare services to the poor. Medicaid's eligibility requirements and benefits vary by state. Go to the Centers for Medicare and Medicaid Services (www.cms.gov/) for more info.

>> **Local assistance programs:** If you're in a financial crisis, look into assistance programs that provide medical care at no or nominal cost. A small monthly fee pays for medical care at designated facilities for all family members.

>> **State Children's Health Insurance Program:** SCHIP provides healthcare coverage to children whose families make too much money to qualify for Medicaid. Find out more at www.healthcare.gov/medicaid-chip/childrens-health-insurance-program/.

>> **Federally funded community health centers:** These centers provide healthcare assistance to the needy. Go to www.findahealthcenter.hrsa.gov/ for more info.

#49
Capping Out-of-Pocket Health Expenses

Most health insurance plans require some kind of copayment on your part. (A *copayment* is the dollar amount your policy requires you to pay toward your bills.) You may have a copay per visit (such as $25 for each office visit or $75 if you go to the emergency room). Perhaps you have a deductible of $500 a year before your coverage kicks in (meaning that you pay the first $500 of your medical expenses each year). Or maybe your policy pays 80 percent of all covered medical bills, with you responsible for the other 20 percent.

Paying the per-visit copays or the deductible usually isn't a hardship. But paying 20 percent of all your major medical bills in one year, without any limit on the possible amount of your contribution, *can* be. If you have a baby who's born three months premature and who needs pediatric intensive care for a long time, your bill could run $400,000 — and your 20 percent copay would be $80,000! If your baby needs surgeries, your bill could jump to $750,000, and your 20 percent copay would be $150,000! That's too big a risk for almost anyone to assume.

REMEMBER

When buying health insurance that contains a percentage copayment, make sure the policy includes an annual maximum that's reasonable for your out-of-pocket expenses.

#50
Saving on Individual Health Coverage

You can cut costs on individual plans in three ways:

>> You can reduce your coverage and the insurance company will give you a direct premium credit.

>> You can put money into a health savings account (HSA) combined with an approved high-deductible health plan (HDHP). A HDHP is a high-deductible major medical policy that meets the requirements of the IRS for use in conjunction with an HSA. See Tip #51, "Using Health Savings Accounts," for details.

>> You can opt for a higher deductible when your health and self-care are exceptional but when the insurance company has no way of lowering your premiums.

#51
Using Health Savings Accounts

A health savings account (HSA) operates like an individual retirement account (IRA) coordinated with an IRS-approved high-deductible major medical health insurance plan (HDHP). The big advantage of an HSA is that it allows you to pay for your major medical deductible as well as elective medical and dental expenses with pretax dollars. For most people, that's equal to a 25 percent to 30 percent savings on their medical and dental bills!

Here's how an HSA works:

>> As with an IRA, contributions are income tax deductible.

>> Earnings on the account are tax sheltered.

>> The maximum contribution per year is set annually by the government. For each person 55 and older, an additional "catch-up" contribution is allowed.

TIP

To find out what the current allowable amounts are, as well as anything else you want to know about health savings accounts, check out IRS Publication 969, "Health Savings Accounts and Other Tax-Favored Health Plans," at www.irs. gov/pub/irs-pdf/p969.pdf.

>> In order for the HSA contributions to be tax-deductible, you must also have an IRS-approved high-deductible health plan (HDHP). The HDHP must include options for a minimum deductible and a maximum deductible set by the government each year. There usually is a cumulative family deductible amount for policies insuring two or more people in the family. There is no coverage under the policy until the entire family reaches the family deductible in a calendar year. (Be careful when choosing your family deductible!)

>> From the HSA, you can pay your deductibles and most other medical and dental expenses that your health plan doesn't cover (such as laser eye surgery, glasses, contact lenses, hearing aids, and dental work). Because the HSA money has never been taxed, you're paying those bills with pretax dollars — a huge advantage.

TIP

You can make your life a lot easier when using an HSA to pay deductible expenses and other expenses by following these simple suggestions:

>> Don't pay any medical bill or pharmacy charge until your insurance company has reduced the cost to its negotiated discount pricing.

>> Fund the account early in the year so you have plenty of cash available if medical bills are sizable in the first quarter of the year.

>> Keep all your receipts for all services you've paid through your HSA (medical bills, pharmaceutical bills, dental bills, and so forth) in a medical folder in case you ever get audited. For a complete and current list of IRS-approved medical and dental expenses, see IRS Publication 502, "Medical and Dental Expenses (Including the Health Coverage Tax Credit")" at www.irs.gov/pub/irs-pdf/p502.pdf.

#52
Tapping into Short-Term Health Insurance

Many states allow health insurance companies to offer the public temporary health coverage to meet short-term needs (such as covering a person who's between jobs or waiting for open enrollment to begin at www.healthcare.gov). Coverage is usually available for up to 364 days.

WARNING

Short-term coverage has several disadvantages, including these:

>> Preexisting conditions aren't covered.

>> Short-term plans cover fewer instances and less in expenses than long-term plans and Affordable Care Act plans.

>> You have no guarantee that you'll be accepted.

TIP

For general information on short-term insurance, visit www.investopedia.com/best-short-term-health-insurance-4844942 and www.healthinsurance.org/short-term-health-insurance/.

#53
Examining Health Insurance Options for the Self-Employed

W hen seeking health insurance as a self-employed per-son, you have a number of options available to you. For example:

>> If you start up your business while you're still working your regular job, you can simply keep your current healthcare plan as it is.

>> If your spouse has health insurance at work, you can decide to use their plan to meet your healthcare needs as you establish your own business. This option, too, can be a relatively inexpensive one for you and your business.

>> If you decide to leave your regular job to start your own business and you live in the United States, COBRA — the Consolidated Omnibus Budget Reconciliation Act — requires your employer to extend healthcare benefits to you for a minimum of 18 months (and in some cases, even longer) at the same rate offered to all other company employees (a piece of which most companies pay as an employee benefit)

for comparable coverage. After the 18-month period elapses, you can generally convert to an individual plan with little muss or fuss, but usually at a significantly higher cost.

» If you want to find your own coverage as you begin your business, you can conduct your own search for health coverage. You can find a plan via the Health Insurance Marketplace at www.healthcare.gov, established by the Affordable Care Act. Other sites, such as www.eHealth-Insurance.com, are dedicated to helping small business owners select and apply for health insurance. Alternatively, a good insurance agent or broker can find the best coverage for you while saving you precious time in the process.

#54
Considering Long-Term Care Insurance

Knowing whether you'll need long-term care is difficult to predict, but can you afford the risk? Can you afford to pay for this type of care out of your retirement nest egg? If so, you can self-insure. If not, you have two primary options:

>> **Take your chances.** Maybe you'll be one of the fortunate ones who doesn't require long-term care assistance, or possibly your extended family will provide the care you need.

>> **Buy long-term care insurance.** Long-term care insurance is insurance you purchase to help offset the cost of long-term healthcare.

You should *consider* buying long-term care insurance if

>> You have substantial assets and income, and you want to protect the majority of your assets for your loved ones.

>> You don't want to depend on or become a burden to others to provide for your care or support.

#55
Seeing the Tax Benefits of a 401(k) Plan

A 401(k) plan lets you put some of your income away now to use later, presumably when you're retired and not earning a paycheck. When you sign up for a 401(k) plan, you agree to let your employer deposit some of the money you earn into the plan as a pre-tax contribution, Roth after-tax contribution, or a combination of the two, instead of paying it to you. (You always pay tax on contributions before they go into a Roth account.) Your employer may even throw some money, known as a *matching contribution*, into your 401(k). You don't pay federal income tax on any of this money except the Roth contribution until you withdraw it.

WARNING

Of course, there's a catch. Some 401(k) plans don't allow you to withdraw money while you're still working. Even if your plan does allow withdrawals, if you're under 59½ years old, those withdrawals can be difficult and costly.

A 401(k) lets you pay less income tax in two ways:

REMEMBER

>> **Lower taxable income:** You don't have to pay federal income tax on the money you contribute with pre-tax contributions to your 401(k) plan until you withdraw it from the plan.

If you're making contributions to a Roth 401(k), you must pay tax now on the amount you put into the plan.

>> **Tax deferral:** You don't pay tax on your 401(k) investment earnings each year. You pay tax on your pre-tax contributions, any employer contributions, and your investment gains on these contributions only when you make withdrawals.

The investment gains on your Roth contributions are never taxed if you follow the rules.

#56
Knowing the Limits on 401(k) Contributions

The federal dollar limit for pre-tax salary deferrals is probably the best-known 401(k) limit. It's the cap on how much income you can have your employer put into the 401(k) rather than into your paycheck. In 2022 the limit is $20,500, plus an additional $6,500 catch-up contribution if you're age 50 or older. The limits rise in $500 increments due to inflation and occur as often as inflation warrants.

REMEMBER

Another federal limit to be aware of is the *percentage-of-pay limit*. This limit applies to all contributions made to your 401(k) by you and your employer, as well as to all contributions to other defined contribution plans, such as profit-sharing plans or 403(b) plans. These contributions can't total more than 100 percent of your pay, or $61,000 for 2022, whichever is less. The $61,000 limit is expected to rise periodically with inflation.

The 100-percent-of-pay limit includes catch-up contributions, but the $61,000 dollar limit doesn't.

#57
Reducing the Amount You Invest in a 401(k)

Why start planning now (and deprive yourself of cash every month) for a retirement that's 30 or 40 years away? The answer is *compounding*. Small amounts of money saved regularly over time can grow to large sums, especially in an account like a 401(k) or IRA-based plan that lets you save without paying taxes on your investment gain each year. Invest $1,000 a year from age 20 until age 65, with a 9 percent average return, and you'll end up with $525,000. Start saving five years later, at age 25, and you'll only have about $338,000. See how much better off you are if you start early?

You don't have to start big, either. Just $20 a week adds up to about $1,000 a year. As you move up in your career and your salary increases, you can increase your contributions.

TIP

If you don't like your 401(k) plan because you think that the fees are too high or the investment selection is inadequate, don't simply throw in the towel and not participate. One strategy you can try is to contribute only enough to get the full company match.

#58
Timing Investment Allocations to Match Employer Contributions

How you time your 401(k) contributions is important. Some people like to contribute more to their 401(k) early in the year to ensure that they reach the maximum before, say, having to think about buying holiday gifts at the end of the year. This is sometimes referred to as *front-loading* the 401(k).

WARNING

The potential problem with this strategy is that it can cause you to lose some of your employer matching contributions. Before you decide to go with this strategy, ask your employer about its timing for depositing matching contributions. Many employers only make these deposits during the pay periods when you contribute to the plan because it's easier for them. If this is how your plan works, you'll lose out by front-loading.

The following example uses 2021 limits for 401(k) contributions. Say your employer matches 50 cents on the dollar, up to 6 percent of your salary. If you earn $150,000 and you contribute at least $9,000 (6 percent of your salary), you should receive an employer match of $4,500. Now, say you want to contribute the full $19,500 permitted in 2021, and you want to do it early in the year. You fill out your form indicating that you want to contribute 20 percent of your pay every pay period. You're not allowed to contribute $30,000 to a 401(k), so you'll be forced to stop contributing partway through the year when you reach the $19,500 limit, unless you are at least age 55 and eligible to make a catch-up contribution. (You'll get there after you've earned $97,500, because 20 percent of $97,500 is $19,500.)

Say your employer stops making matching contributions then, because you're no longer making contributions at that time. You will have received only 3 percent of $97,500 in matching contributions, or $2,925, which is lower than the $4,500 you would've received if you had spread out your contributions evenly over the year. By using this strategy, you lose $1,575 of employer contributions.

In this case, it makes more sense to reduce your contribution rate so that you contribute for the entire year and still hit the $19,500 limit. In this instance, 13 percent would be the percentage to use (13 percent of $150,000 equals $19,500).

#59

Protecting Your Retirement Goals with a 401(k)

nvesting money always involves some risks, but money in a 401(k) plan is protected in some ways that money in an ordinary savings account, brokerage account, or IRA isn't. The following sections explain the safeguards.

Meet Minimum Standards

A federal law called ERISA, the Employee Retirement Income Security Act, governs 401(k) plans. Passed in 1974, ERISA sets minimum standards for retirement plans offered by private-sector companies. Some nonprofits also follow ERISA rules, but local, state, and federal government retirement plans, as well as church plans, don't have to.

ERISA requirements include

>> Providing information to you about plan features on a regular basis, including a *summary plan description* outlining the plan's main rules, when you enroll in the plan and periodically thereafter.

>> Defining how long you may be required to work before being able to sign up for the plan or before employer contributions to the plan are yours to keep if you leave your job.

>> Detailing requirements for the *plan fiduciary*, essentially including anyone at your company or the plan provider who has control over the investment choices in the plan. (A fiduciary who breaks the rules may be sued by participants.)

REMEMBER

This last point, *fiduciary responsibility*, is important to understand. Essentially, it means that anyone who has a decision-making role in your 401(k) plan's investments is legally bound to make those decisions in the best interests of the plan participants (you and your co-workers), and not in the best interest of the company, the plan provider, or the fiduciary's cousin Joe. For example, the committee in charge of choosing a 401(k) provider shouldn't choose Bank XYZ just because the company president's cousin runs the bank.

Avoid Losses in Bankruptcy

Many people wonder whether their 401(k) money is at risk if their employer goes out of business. The answer is usually no, with a few caveats:

>> If the money is in investments that are tied to your employer, such as company stock, and the employer goes bankrupt, you may lose your money. (This is a compelling argument for you to limit the amount of your 401(k) that you invest in a single stock.)

>> In the case of fraud or wrongdoing by your employer or the trustee of the 401(k) account, your money may be at risk. (The trustee would be personally liable to return your money, but that's no help if they have disappeared.)

These situations are rare; what's more, your employer is required to buy a type of insurance — a *fidelity bond* — when it sets up the plan that may enable you to recoup at least some of your money in the event of dishonesty. (Fidelity bonds generally cover 10 percent of the amount in the entire plan, or $500,000, whichever amount is smaller.)

>> Part of your money may be lost if your employer goes out of business or declares bankruptcy before depositing your contributions into the trust fund that receives the 401(k) money that is deducted from your paycheck.

REMEMBER

Federal law says that if you declare personal bankruptcy, your creditors generally can't touch your 401(k). They may be able to get at your other savings, but your 401(k) should be protected. Exceptions include if you owe money to the IRS or if a court has ordered you to give the money to your ex-spouse as part of a divorce settlement. In both of those cases, your 401(k) money is vulnerable.

#60
Withdrawing Money from Your 401(k) with the Fewest Penalties

t can be difficult, if not downright impossible, to make a withdrawal from your 401(k) while you're working for the company that sponsors the plan.

The tax breaks you get with a 401(k) plan come with a price. It can be very costly to take your money out of the plan before you retire — if you can even do it at all. Many employers permit you to borrow money from your 401(k), but not necessarily for any old reason. Most plans permit *hardship withdrawals,* which are withdrawals from your account to pay expenses when you're in financial difficulty. Your employer may permit withdrawals only for reasons approved by the IRS.

People often think that they're automatically allowed to withdraw money from a 401(k) for higher education expenses or for buying a home, and that they won't owe an early withdrawal penalty on the amount. This is false. Your plan *may* allow you to make a withdrawal for these reasons, but it doesn't *have* to.

When you leave your employer, either to retire or to change jobs, you generally have a window of opportunity to get your money. In most cases, you can receive payment of your account or transfer the money into an IRA or another employer's retirement plan. Transferring the money to another plan or IRA, or leaving the money in the plan to avoid a high tax bill, is highly recommended.

TIP

Don't wait for an emergency to check on the rules for accessing your money. You may find that you can't make a withdrawal or that you'll lose about half the value in taxes and penalties if you do make a withdrawal.

Federal law allows three ways to get money out of your 401(k) while you're working for the employer sponsoring the plan. But keep in mind that your employer isn't *required* to allow these features, so they may not be available in your plan. The three ways to obtain money from your 401(k) are as follows:

>> **Unrestricted access to plan assets after you reach age 59½:** The amount withdrawn becomes part of your taxable income for that year.

>> **Withdrawals for financial hardships as defined by law and IRS regulations:** *Hardship withdrawals,* as they're known, are fully taxable and are usually also subject to an additional 10 percent federal early withdrawal penalty (and possibly additional state and local taxes as well).

>> **Plan loans:** These are subject to numerous restrictions. You may get a plan loan to pay for excessive medical expenses, but you won't get one to buy a yacht.

The first two options listed are known as *in-service withdrawals* because you make them while you're "in the service of" your employer.

Strangely enough, federal law makes it theoretically easier to withdraw your employer's contributions than your own pre-tax deferrals while you're working. Your employer may allow you to take the employer contributions out for any reason. But most employers place restrictions on withdrawals of their contributions because they want you to use the money for retirement, so you won't be able to use those to buy your yacht.

#61

Borrowing from Your 401(k)

Most 401(k) plans allow loans, but your plan may limit your ability to borrow from your 401(k). Your employer may not want you to squander your retirement money on something that's not really a necessity. The following sections lay out general rules for loans. Keep in mind that the rules for your specific plan may differ.

Figure Out How Much You Can Borrow

You can take out a loan only if your 401(k) plan document allows you to borrow for the specific reason that you have in mind. Some plans permit borrowing for any reason, but another common approach is to permit loans only for hardship withdrawals (see Tip #62, "Taking a Hardship Withdrawal"). You can get specific details about account loans from your summary plan description or from your benefits office or 401(k) plan provider.

The government sets the limits on how much you can borrow. Generally, you're allowed to borrow no more than 50 percent of your account value up to $50,000 maximum. The other half stays in the account as collateral. However (there always seems to be a "however"), government rules permit borrowing 100 percent of an account up to $10,000. For example, if your account value is $15,000, you may be able to borrow $10,000, even though 50 percent of $15,000 is only $7,500. Some plans don't allow this, though — they limit all loans to 50 percent of the account value for the sake of simplicity. Some plans also impose a minimum loan amount because it's not worth the hassle for them to administer a loan for only a few bucks.

Determine How Much Interest You Pay

The interest that you pay on your 401(k) loan is determined by your employer and must be at a level that meets IRS requirements. It's usually the *prime rate* (the interest rate that banks charge the most creditworthy companies) plus 1 or 2 percentage points. In most plans, the interest that you pay goes back into your account, so you're in the interesting position of being both the borrower and the lender.

Know Repayment Rules

You normally have to repay the loan within five years, but you can repay it faster if your plan permits. Also, your employer may permit a longer repayment period if the money is used for a home purchase.

Employers usually require you to repay a loan through deductions from your paycheck. The loan repayments are taken out of your paycheck after taxes, not pre-tax like your original contributions. Then, when you eventually withdraw this money in retirement, you pay tax on it again. This bears repeating: *You pay tax twice on money used to repay a 401(k) loan.*

The fact that most employers require you to pay back the loan with payroll deductions means that if you're laid off or you quit your job, it becomes impossible to keep repaying the loan. What happens then? You have two choices: Either repay the entire outstanding loan balance right away or take the amount as a taxable *distribution* (payment from the account).

If you don't have the money to repay the loan, you must declare the entire unpaid loan balance as income on your tax return. Adding insult to injury, if you're younger than 55 when you leave your job, you'll probably have to pay an early withdrawal penalty of 10 percent.

If you take a loan, you should be pretty sure that you're going to stay with your employer long enough to repay it. At the very least, try to have a Plan B in the works to help you scrape together enough money to repay it in full if you're laid off.

#62
Taking a Hardship Withdrawal

Most 401(k) plans allow hardship withdrawals, but not all of them do. The following sections assume that your 401(k) plan offers a hardship withdrawal possibility.

Know the Definition of a Hardship

REMEMBER

Hardship withdrawals are limited to specific situations and are permitted only if you have an *immediate and heavy financial need* that can't be satisfied from other resources. Certain expenses are deemed to be immediate and heavy, including

>> Costs related to the purchase of your primary residence

>> Tuition and related educational expenses for the next 12 months for you, your spouse, a dependent, or a nondependent beneficiary

>> Medical expenses for you, your spouse, dependents, or a primary beneficiary not covered by insurance

>> Payments necessary to prevent either eviction from your principal residence or foreclosure on the mortgage for your residence

>> Burial and funeral expenses for you, your spouse, dependents, or a primary beneficiary

>> Certain expenses for the repair of damage to your primary residence such as fire, flood, hurricane, or earthquake that qualify for the casualty deduction under IRC Section 165

WARNING

A distribution isn't considered necessary to satisfy an immediate and heavy financial need if you have other resources available to meet the need, including your spouse's and minor children's assets. You must also have obtained all other currently available distributions from the 401(k) plan and all other employer plans maintained by your employer.

You can also withdraw Roth contributions to a 401(k). Any investment gains withdrawn are taxable, and the 10 percent penalty tax applies if you haven't made contributions for at least five years, and you haven't reached 59½. The penalty tax doesn't apply for distributions due to death or total and permanent disability. Any Roth contribution withdrawal must include a pro-rata portion of any investment gains.

All withdrawals of non-Roth contributions prior to age 59½ are taxable including the 10 percent early distribution penalty except in the following circumstances:

>> You're a highly compensated employee required to take a distribution to make the plan comply with a nondiscrimination test.

>> Your death.

>> To pay a qualified domestic relations order (QDRO), issued as part of a divorce decree.

>> To pay an IRS levy of your account.

>> A series of substantially equal periodic payments (SEPP).

>> To pay medical expenses in excess of 10 percent of your adjusted gross income.

» You withdraw money within 30 to 90 days of your first automatic enrollment contribution deduction. You forfeit any matching employer contributions if you do this.

» To add a child to the family. The Secure Act passed by Congress in December 2019 permits each parent who has an IRA or 401(k) account to withdraw $5,000 for the birth or adoption of a child.

» To make certain payments to a reservist called to active duty.

» You are totally and permanently disabled.

The IRS definition of total and permanent disability requires you to be "unable to perform substantial gainful activity" because of an identifiable physical or mental impairment that is expected to be of "long-continued and indefinite duration." Your doctor needs to confirm that you're unable to work due to a physical or mental disability and that you'll continue to be unable to work permanently or at least for a very long period of time. You must submit IRS Form 5329 when you submit your tax return to claim the exemption. Enter Code 03 for disability where it asks for the code for the exemption. Also look at Box 7 of the 1099-R you received for the distribution to be sure that the distribution code used is 03. If not, contact your former employer or service provider to get a corrected form.

REMEMBER

Participants who are unhappy with their 401(k) investments frequently ask whether they can take their money out of the plan as a hardship withdrawal, while they're working, and roll it into an IRA. The answer is no.

WARNING

If you withdraw your money using a hardship withdrawal before you turn 59½, you'll be heavily taxed. Not only will you owe federal and perhaps state and local income tax on the amount withdrawn, but you'll also owe a 10 percent federal early withdrawal penalty on the entire amount unless the withdrawal is for one of the reasons that qualify for an exemption. If you take a hardship distribution, the money you withdraw is no longer eligible for a rollover.

Taking out a loan lets you avoid these penalties; however, other costs are involved. See Tip #61, "Borrowing from Your 401(k)."

Determine the Amount

You can withdraw only the amount you need to meet your hardship expense. Because you have to pay tax on a hardship withdrawal, you can include the taxes you'll owe.

The money you're allowed to withdraw for a hardship may be limited to the money you've contributed (excluding investment gains), or it may include vested employer contributions and money you've rolled into the plan from an IRA or another retirement plan. Your employer decides the rules. Many employers don't permit their contributions to be withdrawn for a hardship because they want this money to stay in the plan and be used to provide retirement benefits.

TIP

If your plan lets you borrow money from your 401(k), you may be required to take a loan before taking a hardship withdrawal. It depends on your plan's rules.

#63

Rolling Over Your 401(k) to Avoid Taxes

When you leave your job, one of the many forms that you'll likely have to fill out is a 401(k) *distribution election form. Distribution* is employee-benefit-speak for the payment to you of your vested 401(k) money.

The most sensible thing to do with your 401(k) from a tax-management point of view is a *direct rollover* (also known as a *trustee-to-trustee transfer*) of the money. With this type of rollover, your old service provider writes a check directly to the financial institution where your new account is. The money goes directly from your 401(k) plan into another tax-deferred account:

>> An IRA.

>> Your new employer's 401(k) plan.

>> A 403(b) plan: 403(b) plans are offered by many nonprofit organizations.

>> A 457(b) plan: 457(b) plans are offered by state and local governments.

By doing a direct rollover, you don't have to pay any tax on the money when it comes out of your old employer's 401(k). The money also continues to grow tax-deferred in the new account.

Instead of transferring the money directly to the new plan or IRA, the service provider may write you a check for the 401(k) balance, which complicates things for you. If the check is payable to you, the service provider is required to withhold 20 percent of the account value as federal withholding tax. So, if you have $10,000 vested in your account, you'll receive a check for only $8,000.

In order to avoid paying income tax and an early withdrawal penalty, you have to deposit the $8,000 check plus $2,000 of your own money into an IRA or your new employer's plan within 60 days of receiving the distribution. (The IRS will return the $2,000 to you when you file your tax return if you do the rollover correctly.) The amount that you don't deposit in the new account will be considered a cash distribution on which you'll owe applicable tax and penalties. The IRS is firm on this 60-day limit. The only leeway is in the case of a national disaster when the IRS can decide to extend the 60-day period.

Your employer may also require your spouse to sign if you're married because you have the right to name a beneficiary other than your spouse if the money is transferred to an IRA. If so, the spouse's written consent is usually required on the election form, and it must be notarized or approved by a plan representative.

If your account balance is less than $5,000, you may be forced to take the money out of your employer's 401(k) plan when you leave. If it's more than $1,000 (and less than $5,000) and you don't tell your employer what you want to do with the money, your employer can automatically roll the money into an IRA on your behalf. If the balance is $1,000 or less, your employer can simply issue a check to you for the entire amount without giving you any alternatives, but you'll owe tax and penalties on the money.

Let your employer know right away that you want to do a rollover if your balance is less than $1,000 to prevent paying taxes and penalties.

If your vested 401(k) balance is $5,000 or more, and you're younger than the normal retirement age specified in the plan document (usually 65), your employer is required to let you leave your money in the 401(k) if you want to. Leaving your money in the plan can be a useful strategy, at least as a temporary measure. See the next tip.

#64
Leaving Money in Your Old Employer's Plan

Leaving your money in your old 401(k) plan may be a good temporary solution while you figure out your next step, but it's probably not the best long-term solution.

Leaving the money in the 401(k) may have advantages for some investors because

» Some people don't want to make new investment decisions. If you're satisfied with your 401(k) investments, this strategy is fine. However, be aware that an employer can change the investments offered by the plan at any time. If your money is in your former employer's 401(k), you have to go along with the change. During the switchover period, which can take several weeks or months, you won't be able to access your account.

» Money in a 401(k) generally has more protection from creditors than that in an IRA should you declare personal bankruptcy.

WARNING

Consider some of the drawbacks to leaving your money in your former employer's 401(k):

>> After you leave a company, you'll be low in the pecking order for service if you request a distribution from the 401(k) plan or if you have questions or complaints. Companies can change a lot over time, including being acquired, restructured, or even going out of business. The level of support you receive as an ex-employee usually drops dramatically if this happens.

>> While the money is in a former employer's 401(k) plan, you can't take a loan. (You have to pay back such a loan through payroll deductions.)

>> You can no longer contribute to the old 401(k) plan, but you can rebalance the investments.

#65
Avoiding Lump-Sum Withdrawals

This option isn't advisable, but just so you know all your choices, when you leave your employer, you can withdraw all the money in your 401(k) account in what's called a *lump-sum withdrawal.*

WARNING

Unless you have a serious financial need, cashing out the money and spending it is something you should avoid. Even if your account balance is small, it's worth leaving the money alone. If you take cash, you'll have to pay income tax on it. You'll also owe the 10 percent early withdrawal penalty if you're younger than 59½ when you leave your employer unless you qualify for one of very few exceptions.

REMEMBER

Some people take a cash distribution and spend the money, figuring it's such a small amount that it won't matter. This is a mistake. An amount as small as $5,000 when you're 25 can grow to $157,047 by the time you're 65, assuming a 9 percent rate of return. That additional income can mean puttin' up at the Ritz rather than puttin' up a tent during your retirement travels.

What's more, you wouldn't even get the full $5,000. You'd get just $4,000 because your employer must withhold 20 percent for taxes.

While you're still with your employer, the magic age for withdrawing money from the plan without a 10 percent early withdrawal penalty is 59½. That's also the magic age if you have an IRA. However, the IRS lets you avoid the penalty if you're at least 55 when you leave your job (the job with the employer who sponsors your 401(k) plan). The reasoning is that if you lose your job at age 55 or older, it can be particularly hard to find a new one, so you may need the money. Imagine that — for once, the IRS gives you a break.

#66
Taking Your 401(k) Plan with You to Your New Job

You may be able to roll the money from your old 401(k) over into your new employer's plan. You may decide to do this for a number of reasons, including the following:

>> Your new employer has a terrific plan with great funds and low expenses.

>> You want to consolidate all your retirement savings in one place for ease of management.

WARNING

Before you decide to roll over your 401(k), get a copy of the new plan's summary plan description to find out all the rules your money will be subject to. After the money is in the plan, you may not be able to withdraw it and move it into an IRA unless you leave your job.

TIP

You also need to find out whether your new employer's plan accepts rollovers. In theory, you're allowed to roll a 401(k) plan into another 401(k) plan or into a 403(b) plan or 457(b) plan. In practice, not all employer plans accept rollovers. If yours doesn't, you can leave your money in your old 401(k) or roll it into an IRA to preserve the tax advantage. (See Tip #64, "Leaving Money in Your Old Employer's Plan.")

Your new plan may require you to wait until you're eligible to participate before accepting a rollover from your old 401(k). Although many employers allow you to roll money into the plan before becoming eligible to contribute, some employers restrict the availability of rollovers until you actually become eligible for the plan. For example, if your new employer has a waiting period of one year before you can contribute to the 401(k), you have to wait one year to roll the money into the 401(k). In that case, you can either leave your money in your former employer's plan or move it to a rollover IRA, ready to be transferred into the new 401(k) when the time comes.

#67
Investigating Tax-Deferred Ways to Save for College

Saving money is a good thing, or so the federal government would have you believe. Uncle Sam is prepared to back up that philosophy with a variety of savings programs for college that contain built-in tax incentives. These sections discuss them.

Section 529 Plans

One incentive savings plan is the Qualified Tuition Program, or Section 529 plan, which is designed solely for the purpose of saving for college or any other type of qualified postsecondary education, either tax exempt or tax deferred, depending on a number of factors. Like almost everything else the government cooks up, though, Section 529 plans aren't as simple to navigate as everyone selling these plans would have you think.

WARNING

Section 529 of the Internal Revenue Code is long, complex, and not for the faint of heart. Still, savings accounts that fall under its regulations can be a fantastic way to save for future educational expenses. To make it work, though, you have to understand its requirements. Your account will either qualify under the regulations for tax deferrals or exemptions, or it won't. And if it doesn't, the consequences may be costly.

In order for a Section 529 plan to qualify under the IRS's rules, it must meet the following criteria:

>> Contributions may be made only in cash, including checks, money orders, or payroll deductions, but not in stocks, bonds, or real estate.

>> After a contribution is made into a specific plan, you may not direct the investments. You may, however, change plans once each year.

>> You may not pledge the value of the account as security against any sort of loan.

>> The plan or program in which you invest must provide each designated beneficiary a separate accounting.

>> You can't contribute more into an account, or group of accounts, for the benefit of a single designated beneficiary than the beneficiary will use in the payment of qualified higher education expenses. You have to try to estimate this amount.

When you make a contribution to a Section 529 plan, you're not allowed any federal income tax deduction for the amount of your contribution (unlike many sorts of retirement plans, which defer income tax not only on the accrued earnings in the account but also on your contributions). Depending on what state you live in (and if you use its plan), you may get a current state income tax deduction for part or all of your contribution each year.

After your money is safely tied up in a Section 529 plan, interest that you earn on it isn't taxed until *distributions* (amounts of money you take out of the plan to pay your student's expenses) are made to your designated beneficiary. And, if you use distributions from these plans to pay the qualified education expenses of a student at an eligible educational institution, accrued earnings generally aren't taxed at all.

REMEMBER

In other words, a Section 529 plan allows you to save for college, and it exempts or defers income tax on the accrued earnings until the designated beneficiary begins taking distributions from the plan.

Coverdell Accounts

If the world of tax-deferred/tax-exempt savings accounts were an ice cream parlor, Coverdell Education Savings Accounts (ESAs) would be a new and improved flavor, still not everyone's favorite, but just what you may want on a particular day. And, not surprisingly, many people, when shopping for a place and a way to save money for college, prefer Coverdell accounts, whether for their wider range of investment options, the account owner's increased level of control over the account, or the fact that certain expenses qualify for tax exemption under Coverdell rules that aren't under Section 529 requirements. Whatever your reasons, Coverdell ESAs may be just the flavor of account you want today.

Coverdell ESAs are savings plans described in Section 530 of the Internal Revenue Code (IRC). They're accounts that Congress created to allow you to save now for future educational expenses, whether primary, secondary, or postsecondary, of a designated beneficiary.

You can invest money in Coverdell accounts in a variety of ways: stocks, bonds, money market accounts, certificates of deposit, and so on, although you may not invest in life insurance policies. Under the Coverdell rules (and unlike Section 529 rules), if you designate yourself the one responsible for all decisions on this particular account (also known as the *responsible adult*, who must be the parent or legal guardian of the minor child), you keep control of the money and make all the investment decisions for your child's account. Over the years, the investments will hopefully earn significant income through interest, dividends, and capital gains, until the time that the account is closed.

You pay no income tax on the income when it's earned, and as distributions are made from these accounts to your designated beneficiary for qualified educational expenses, the income portion of the distribution isn't taxed, either to you or to your student.

REMEMBER

A Coverdell ESA must be opened as such, in writing, and you need to designate a beneficiary when you create it; you aren't allowed to take an already existing account and decide that it's now the Coverdell account for your student. Money that you contribute into the account is held by a trustee or a custodian, which must be a bank, mutual fund company, or any other entity that's approved by the IRS.

#68
Considering Costs of Different Colleges

N
o matter where your student decides to attend college, you have to pay the tuition and the books and supplies, and then you have to come up with some solution to the housing question. But because you may need a crystal ball to figure out where your child plans on attending college, the next piece of the puzzle isn't quite as straightforward — estimating the tuition and fees you need to save for.

However, after you have an idea of what type of school your student plans on attending, or, if your up-and-coming student is either not yet born or just recently populating the planet, you have decided on what type of school you *hope* your student attends, you can begin some significant planning for the future.

Career and Vocational Training Schools

Smaller, more specialized schools, such as career and vocational training schools, train students in very specific areas for specific careers, such as funeral services, dental hygiene, piano tuning, or even bartending. The cost of these programs (which may exist entirely independently of or be attached to community colleges or even four-year colleges) tend to be much smaller than your typical college.

Community College and Continuing Education Classes

Almost every city of any size has at least one community college, an institution of higher education that gives college level learning without the college-level price. In addition, many large universities have a division of continuing education that provides much the same function as a community college, including the low cost.

TIP

Don't assume that because you can't afford an Ivy League college through the normal channels that you also can't afford to take courses in the continuing education division.

TIP

Funds from all of your college savings plans can be used to pay either community college or continuing education tuitions, provided the school you attend is an eligible institution. However, in order to pay for housing using savings from these plans, you need to be at least a half-time student. Be aware of this and be vigilant; a mistake here will cost you not only income tax on the distribution but also a penalty.

A Four-Year Public Education

Each state has its own public university/college system. Because the universities are larger than the colleges and offer much more programming, they tend to be considerably more expensive than the colleges. If your student has a very clear idea of where they're going in life, it's going to be most cost effective if you can find that program at a state college rather than a state university, especially for in-state students.

Unlike public elementary and secondary schools, public universities and colleges aren't funded totally by tax dollars (and may actually be funded very little by tax dollars). However, state-run colleges and universities are one of the best bargains around, especially for in-state students. Any state subsidy, no matter how small, is better than no state subsidy for keeping costs down, and this is reflected in the size of tuition bills.

A Private Education

Public education may be the cornerstone on which the United States is built. However, a vast network of private schools is available at every level, for those who can afford to pay. And because no college education is free (unless you look at the U.S. military academies, where the payment is in kind or you get a full-ride scholarship), all schools that don't rely on public subsidies are referred to as *private*.

Private universities can refer to various types of institutions, from the Ivy League schools to hundreds of private four-year institutions throughout the country. Each of these colleges and universities offers a unique educational opportunity, as well as a unique price tag.

Overall, prices are high, climbing higher every year, and no relief is in sight. Tuition and room and board fees are set by the college, and there is no public oversight. Furthermore, college presidents and trustees retain their jobs on the basis of how well their institutions are doing financially — if it takes tuition hikes to keep it that way, that's just too bad.

TIP

If your savings are a bit lacking when the time comes to start forking over tuition payments, the smartest way to look for a private school may be to shop by *endowment* (the amount of money that the school has invested, with the income available for building projects, professors' salaries, and tuition grants), rather than tuition ticket price. Schools with large endowments usually devote a large percentage of the earnings from the fund to outright grants, awarded on the basis of need.

#69
Working Part-Time and Summer Jobs

You can't send your elementary student to work at the factory after school. As they enter middle and high school, however, their potential to make money to help defray college costs increases significantly. So start encouraging your college hopeful to get off the couch and get a job. Young teens can begin earning their own money with timeless neighborhood jobs such as babysitting, working as a mother's helper, lawn mowing, and snow shoveling.

But your child can tap into even greater college money potential by working for an employer who

> **»** **Provides a tuition-reimbursement program:** One of the most prized fringe benefits today is the tuition reimbursement plan, meaning that your employer essentially pays for some or all of the employee's tuition. Generally, larger employers (including many large retailers and fast-food restaurants) offer these plans, and usually the plans cover only education expenses that apply to the employee's current job or that improve the employee's general job skills.

Other restrictions may also apply, such as limiting participation to full-time employees or to employees who have completed a certain period of service. However, if your child works for such an employer and meets all the requirements, they may be able to have their employer pay for at least a portion of tuition at a local college or university. Although the number of students who qualify for tuition reimbursement plans is small, if you (or your child) fall into this category, you could offset a significant portion of the eventual cost in this way.

>> **Offers discounts:** Working for discount or retail stores may not sound glamorous, let alone lucrative, but most places offer discounts of some kind. Just think about all of the stuff that college kids need — school supplies, dorm room gear, and so on. When you add up how much you can blow on the small stuff, remember that the money has to come from somewhere. And no matter who's paying the bill, you can reduce it significantly by getting it all on discount.

>> **Teaches a marketable skill:** Beyond the fast-food restaurants and discount and convenience stores, teens can find summer or part-time jobs that provide them with a marketable skill or with experience in a field they may otherwise not have considered. Even working at jobs like lifeguarding can give teens skills and an experience that lasts much longer than a summer — your teens may have an easier time finding a job at school because of their experience or skill. In addition, if they can keep working while in school, they can further defray incidental and everyday costs that otherwise you or their college savings plans would have to fund.

TIP

Yes, nepotism is a dirty word — strictly defined, *nepotism* is when a relative is shown favoritism in getting a desirable position. However, most people don't consider typing up commercials at Uncle Dave's AM radio station a desirable position. So when it comes to getting your kids started earning money, it's a who-you-know-not-what-you-know kind of world, and asking your family and friends about any possible openings is a great way for your kids to find work.

TIP

After your child begins working, take that time to emphasize what portion of college expenses you expect your child to contribute — whether it be the cost of books, incidentals, or a computer. Be clear about your expectations. Just like most people, your child is more likely to reach a tangible goal than one that has no boundaries.

#70
Applying for Financial Federal Aid

n the world of financial aid, equitable allocation of available resources is the name of the game. This allocation can be made only when comparing apples to apples, assets to assets, and income to income. The financial aid powers that be make this comparison by using financial aid applications. You and your student have to apply for financial aid every year.

Depending on where your child intends to attend school, you may have to complete more than one financial aid application. Although individual schools and many states have their own forms that they require you to complete, here are the two most common and the information you must provide:

>> **Free Application for Federal Student Aid (FAFSA):** As long and as seemingly complicated as the FAFSA is, everyone needs to fill one of these out each academic year if you need or want aid from any of the federal grant or loan programs. These applications are free (as the name suggests). You use income figures and current asset information for both you and your student. You can take most of the required information directly from your, and your student's, income tax returns; the rest comes from current bank and

investment account statements and your business's balance sheet (if you own part or all of a business). The amount of debt that you have, including mortgages, car loans, and credit card debt, isn't included on the FAFSA.

TIP

You can get detailed info on the FAFSA and complete the online form of the application by visiting https://studentaid.gov/h/apply-for-aid/fafsa.

>> **CSS PROFILE:** Administered by the College Scholarship Service, this form is required by many private colleges and universities in place of or, in most cases, in addition to the FAFSA. The CSS PROFILE contains much of the same data you put on your FAFSA; however, the information it requests is far more detailed and includes the amount of your *net home equity* (the value of your primary residence less any outstanding mortgage loans). Unlike the FAFSA, this isn't a free service; you pay a nominal application fee, plus an additional fee for every school you request your application be forwarded to.

TIP

For more info, go online to https://cssprofile.collegeboard.org/.

REMEMBER

The purpose of financial aid applications is to help the federal government and your student's school determine your family's need for outside sources of funding and your ability to repay loans. Federal financial aid eligibility is determined by a strict formula known as the Federal Methodology based on FAFSA information. Although CSS PROFILE information is far more specific, it impacts only institutional aid (not federal grants, loans, and work-study). Individual financial aid officers are allowed to exercise great latitude in determining need based not only on the CSS PROFILE but also on any other information you may provide. If you believe your financial circumstances aren't accurately reflected in the information provided on these forms, talk with the financial aid officer at your prospective colleges about your circumstances and the possibility of a "professional judgment," which allows the financial aid officer to make an aid award based on all the factors you present, not just the ones contained on your financial aid applications.

WARNING

Don't lie on a financial aid application or even try to bend the truth a little.

#71

Squeezing Out Every Drop of Available College Money

After you begin to suspect that your savings and amounts available from current earnings will fall short of your child's anticipated educational costs, some planning may well increase the amount of outright grants and very low-cost loans your student may qualify for.

Time the Receipt of Taxable and Tax-Exempt Income

Do your best to schedule large infusions of income and cash two years or more before your child is due to start college; the financial aid folks won't care about what's on your income tax return in any years other than your *base years* (the calendar years used to determine how much financial aid you receive).

So if you need to sell an investment, do it sooner rather than later. If you're going to receive a year-end bonus, try to defer it to a non-base year if possible. You want to avoid large amounts of extra income in your base years.

Pay Down Debt

The folks who process your FAFSA (Free Application for Federal Student Aid; see https://studentaid.gov/h/apply-for-aid/fafsa) are concerned with how much you have in income and assets, not how much you owe, which means you don't even get any credit for your debts. So to minimize the value of assets you show on your aid application, get rid of your debt. Sell some assets, if necessary, to pay off your car loan, make extra mortgage payments, and bring your credit card balances to zero. Complete all these transactions before you fill in your aid applications; the FAFSA folks are concerned only with the value of your assets on the day that you complete the application — not the day before and not the day after. Your good intentions will be worth less than nothing if you raise the cash but fail to pay off your debt before filing your application.

Anticipate Your Expenses

Most people have large expenses they tend to postpone, such as replacing a car or a roof, when facing the first college tuition bill. But while a certain amount of self-deprivation is normal for parents, indulging yourself a little may actually help your student's overall financial aid picture. Replace that old rust bucket that's been held together with duct tape for the last three years (but pay cash — don't finance it unless you absolutely must) and repair the roof. Paying for these items depletes your cash and asset balances, which you must, of course, report accurately on the FAFSA. Because the value of the new car and the house repairs isn't included on your aid application, you can successfully convert reportable assets into nonreportable assets and also take care of some necessary expenses in the process.

Spread Your Available Assets across Multiple Students

You may be surprised to find out that although each of your children has to file their own FAFSA application, your EFC isn't the same for each student. The portion of the EFC that's calculated based on your income is divided by the number of students you currently have in college. The student's portion (based on his income and assets) is then added on each application, arriving at the EFC for each student. The more family members who are attending a postsecondary school at any given time, the greater the potential financial aid award for each student. Although the total that you'll be expected to pay will likely be greater for multiple students than it would be if you just had one in school, the per-student cost should be less (unless your income and/or asset value is very large).

#72
Looking into Federal Assistance Programs

You can choose from a wide variety of financial aid programs, but be aware that they come with a broad expanse of qualifying rules and regulations.

>> **Pell Grant:** These need-based outright grants — given by the federal government — currently are available in amounts up to $6,895 per academic year (adjusted annually as a result of federal appropriations — and not always upward). They're generally only for undergraduate students who haven't yet received a bachelor's or professional degree. These grants aren't subject to any work requirements or loan repayments, and they may be used to pay for any portion of the college's established cost of attendance, including room and board, books, transportation, and so on.

>> **Federal Supplemental Educational Opportunity Grant:** The federal government awards this grant to undergraduate students with exceptional financial need (the need requirements here are even stricter than for Pell Grants). These grants, which presently range from $100 to $4,000, don't need to be paid back, nor is there any work requirement.

#73
Using Federal Loans

As college costs soar and grant amounts remain fairly constant, loans have become the meat-and-potatoes measure that parents and students use to plug funding gaps. Some of these loans come directly from the federal government. Others come from private sources but carry federal guarantees so that, if the borrower doesn't pay the amount due, the lender isn't left holding the bag. Still others come from private sources and carry no guarantees (for which you'll pay a higher rate of interest) but may provide you with some added flexibility.

According to the U.S. Department of Education, several types of federal student loans are available:

» **Direct Subsidized Loans:** They're made to eligible undergraduate students who demonstrate financial need to help cover the costs of higher education at a college or career school.

» **Direct Unsubsidized Loans:** They're made to eligible undergraduate, graduate, and professional students, but eligibility isn't based on financial need.

>> **Direct PLUS Loans:** They're made to graduate or professional students and parents of dependent undergraduate students to help pay for education expenses not covered by other financial aid. Eligibility isn't based on financial need; however, a credit check is required. Borrowers who have an adverse credit history must meet additional requirements to qualify.

>> **Direct Consolidation Loans:** They allow you to combine all of your eligible federal student loans into a single loan with a single loan servicer.

TIP

For the full scoop on federal student loans, visit `https://studentaid.gov/understand-aid/types/loans`.

#74
Deferring or Discharging Student Loan Debt

Under special circumstances, you can receive a deferment on the repayment of your federal student loans. In some circumstances, you may also be able to have your entire debt forgiven (or to use the technical term, *discharged*).

REMEMBER

Deferment lets you temporarily stop making payments on your student loan. See https://studentaid.gov/manage-loans/lower-payments/get-temporary-relief/deferment for ways you can defer your federal student loan.

According to the U.S. Department of Education, the terms *forgiveness, cancellation*, and *discharge* are used in the following ways:

>> If you're no longer required to make payments on your loans due to your job, this is generally called forgiveness or cancellation.

>> If you're no longer required to make payments on your loans due to other circumstances, such as a total and permanent disability or the closure of the school where you received your loans, this is generally called discharge.

TIP

Visit https://studentaid.gov/manage-loans/forgiveness-cancellation for full details.

#75
Consolidating Your College Loans

Direct Consolidation Loan helps students and parents simplify the college federal loan repayment process. As you may guess from its name, a Direct Consolidation Loan combines or *consolidates* various federal student loans that are active under your account.

TIP

You can get more information about loan consolidation options at `https://studentaid.gov/manage-loans/consolidation`.

#76
Getting Tuition Discounts and Waivers

Confusion may arise when people discuss the forms of financial aid known as *tuition discounts* and *waivers*. Some consider these to be strictly the financial aid offered based on eligibility. Others define tuition discounts as including anything offered by the college that reduces the amount a student is required to pay for tuition.

When you're offered a tuition discount, the college quotes you its full sticker price and then offers to reduce the amount for you. The reduction may be a specific dollar amount of money or a percentage of the total. You never get to see or hold the money when you receive a tuition discount. Your college bill is simply *reduced* by the discount amount so that you only have to pay the net amount.

WARNING

Tuition discounts, by definition, only cover tuition. Some colleges may extend the discount to other required fees, such as lab fees, but that's rare and must be confirmed in advance.

TIP

The money the college offers you may be called a tuition discount, an entrance award, or a specific college-based grant, but the effect is the same: The amount you have to pay is less than the quoted sticker price.

Eligibility-Based Discounts

Colleges often offer to reduce tuition as part of a benefits package or as part of their general policy. For this sort of tuition discount, you can't negotiate for a better deal, and eligibility tends to be strictly defined. You either qualify or you don't. Here are a few examples:

>> **College employees often get tuition discounts.** If you're the spouse, child, or (rarely) grandchild of a faculty or staff member, you're often entitled to a tuition discount or a tuition exemption.

>> **Some colleges also offer discounts to alumni and their dependents.** Colleges often do this as a way of keeping a tradition alive or rewarding return business. A university, for example, may offers a 20 percent tuition discount to alumni returning for continuing education courses.

>> **Eligibility may be based on age.** Some colleges offer discounts to seniors. For example, a university may offer a 50 percent discount for students aged 60 years and older.

>> **Discounts may be offered to students with siblings attending the college.** For example, a university may offer a 10 percent discount to students whose brother or sister attends the university.

>> **Tuition discounts are often tied to employment.** A university may operate a liaison program with various corporations, offering a tuition reimbursement to employees who complete a course of study with them. The reimbursement amount is capped at a set figure.

>> **Some employee tuition discount programs also apply to the rest of the family.** Programs for state employees and their dependents exist in most states, so definitely investigate this possibility if your parent, or even your grandparent, works for (or used to work for) the state. While you're at it, don't forget to check on discounts available if your parent works for the city in which a college is located.

>> **Some programs are tied to religious institutions or organizations.** Several religious institutions offer discounts to groups.

>> **Some tuition discount programs may not be for college tuition.** Instead, discounts for a private school, a daycare, or other similar institution may be offered to the children of those attending or working at a particular college.

>> **Some discounts are offered for non-peak school times.** A school, for example, may have an early-start program, offering students a 25 percent tuition discount on specific courses if they take them in the summer term, which typically has lower enrollment than the rest of the year.

Incentive-Based Discounts

Some colleges use incentive-based incentives to meet their enrollment objectives of increasing the quality or diversity of students, or to ensure that they acquire a sufficient number of students for the year. The effect for you, the student, is that the college offers you a discount to register with it. In effect, the college waives all or a portion of your fee because it believes that you'll make a significant contribution to the college environment.

The college itself funds this amount through internal budgets, endowment funds, and income. Generally, a certain amount is set aside in the college admissions budget for these incentives. You can try to negotiate for a better financial aid package or ask for the financial aid officer to work with you to obtain extra financing through other sources.

WARNING

To make the terminology even more confusing, sometimes this discount is also known as an *entrance scholarship.* If you receive one, take special note of whether or not the award is recurring or renewable. Many entrance scholarships only apply to your first year. Then, after you're a registered student, happy at the college with friends and enjoying an established relationship with your professors, the amount you must pay in subsequent years effectively rises dramatically.

#77
Finding College-Based Scholarships

TIP

Begin your scholarship search at your child's college, both in the admissions and the financial aid offices. Every college has a list of scholarships that are available if a student applies for them. Some of them are well known and very prestigious; others, though, are buried in obscurity, and you just have to be proactive enough to look for them and apply. Although the size and seeming abundance of the athletic scholarships have become the stuff of legend, your child may also qualify for academic scholarships.

Both athletic and academic scholarships are generally awarded before your student even begins their college career, and they need to be renewed for each subsequent year. Substandard performance may lead to a reduction in, or even total loss of, the scholarship.

Don't forget, though, that there are often smaller scholarships awarded to students who have already proven themselves at the college level. The annual history award may not carry much cachet outside the history department, but that's real money they're handing out with it.

#78
Accessing State and Local Scholarships

Most states and some cities and towns provide some scholarship aid to some of their neediest students. Even if you're not sure that your child will qualify, there's no harm in accessing the information and making sure.

TIP

If you're not sure how to begin searching for these taxpayer-funded scholarships, the Internet is always a good place to begin. You can plug in your state's (or town's) name and *scholarship* into any search engine and come up with a fairly extensive list of what's available to you from local sources. You should also check with your student's guidance counselor for any smaller grants. And, last but not least, check with your state and local departments of education to see whether they have any pertinent information for you.

Generally, when you do receive assistance from the state, some strings are attached — for one, your student must attend a public institution in that state, whether it's a community college or a four-year college.

#79
Looking into Charitable Foundations for College Funds

The United States has thousands of charitable foundations. Many of them, according to the terms of their establishing documents, can't give scholarship money directly to students. Instead, they must set up scholarships through another organization, such as a college or university. Check with your student's financial aid office to obtain a list of these charities.

TIP

Some charitable organizations, however, do provide scholarship and fellowship money directly to students to help defray the cost of education. Unfortunately, finding these organizations may be difficult (because many keep a very low profile). Still, you can locate them. Here are some tips:

>> **Check with your state's attorney general.** The AG's office in each state usually keeps a list of all organized charities operating within the state. They're obligated to provide annual reports, and this information is available to the public.

» **Check with regional associations of grant makers.** Their lists may not be as complete as the one you get from the attorney general because charitable foundations don't have to register with them, but this may be the easiest way to access information from charitable foundations around the nation. Keep in mind that if you can find a local foundation that's giving away money for schooling, your chances of snagging a scholarship from them may be greater than from a national charity because you're competing against a smaller pool of applicants.

» **Search the Internet.** You can often find the major charitable foundations that do provide scholarship assistance on the big scholarship search websites, such as www.scholarships.com and www.fastweb.com.

#80
Tapping Organizations for Scholarships

Undoubtedly, you have an inkling that some organizations offer scholarships, but you may not know *which* organizations to approach. Following is some help:

>> **Service and social clubs:** The Elks Club, Lions Club, Rotary Club, 4-H Club, Boy Scouts and Girl Scouts, and Greek organizations (college fraternities and sororities) are just a few examples of service and social clubs.

>> **Foundations formed by corporations, groups, or individuals:** These foundations include large organizations with multiple awards, midsized organizations, and small organizations offering as few as one scholarship a year.

>> **Employment or trade groups:** Professional organizations, trade unions, and military service organizations fall under this category.

#81
Accepting Work-Study Opportunities

I f your student is able to juggle their schoolwork with employment and has demonstrated financial need, the federal Work-Study Program may be the answer to your prayers. This program provides part-time employment for eligible undergraduate and graduate students through their university or in public service work in the community. These jobs generally pay at least minimum wage, and earnings are subject to federal and state income taxes; however, Social Security and Medicare taxes (FICA) aren't withheld.

Although the federal government provides the funds for this program, they're allocated directly by the individual schools based on the need of a particular student and the number of students who can demonstrate need.

TIP

Check out https://studentaid.gov/understand-aid/types/work-study for more details.

#82
Receiving College Funding in Exchange for Service

In all the examples in this section, either the federal or state government pays for all or a part of your education, while you give a period of service as a payback. Clearly, from the government's position, this is a winning strategy — it gives higher education to people who otherwise might do without and gets services in exchange. But for many people who enroll in these programs, it also helps to solve what otherwise might be an unsolvable problem: how to pay for the education they need in order to begin the career they want.

You and your child should ponder a few points before embarking on this road:

REMEMBER

>> **Your student may have very little control over what type of service he does and where he does it.** While the military, the Public Health Service, and AmeriCorps try very hard to put people where they want to be, not everyone can play in the Marine Corps Band, fly fighter jets, or be in the Army Corps of Engineers.

» **After your student actually begins to receive money, their window to back out of the deal closes quickly.** Although the various branches of the service allow a freshman ROTC scholarship student to cancel their scholarship, for example, after that first year, your child has pretty much committed to fulfilling the military service obligation.

» **The amount of money your student receives may not be enough to pay for the education they want.** Even if you can get benefits to help pay for an education at a public college or university, you'll come up short if your child's greatest desire is to attend a private four-year college. Even with additional benefits available, you still won't have enough, and you'll have to make up the difference, either through savings, current earnings, or loans.

#83
Searching Out Merit-Based Financial Aid

O nly people with the top grades across the country win merit scholarships, right? Wrong. It's surprising, considering that merit-based awards are, by definition, supposed to award the most meritorious students. But the concept of "merit" means more than just high grades.

Besides, even those awards that grant prizes to the students with the top grades *in the applicant pool* don't necessarily have the country's top students *in* the pool. Most awards start off whittling down their applicant pool through eligibility requirements.

When looking for merit-based financial aid, follow this path.

REMEMBER   1. **Start with the financial aid office.**

Collect applications for federal, state, and college based financial aid.

Ask for information about any college-based scholarships.

Ask for information about any scholarship offices that may exist, resources, guides, and other advice about tracking down private scholarships.

Ask for contact information regarding departmental scholarships for all the departments relating to anything you may wish to study.

2. **Move on to the scholarship office if one exists.**

   Work with one of the helpful people who work at the campus scholarship office to figure out what scholarships are best for *you*.

   Search online, in guidebooks, and use all other resources available.

   Come back periodically to find out whether anything new is being offered.

3. **Continue to the individual departments.**

   Ask about any and all scholarships, grants, fellowships, bursaries, and other forms of free money that may be available to students.

   Find out about eligibility, application requirements, the frequency the awards are given, who chooses the winners, and exactly how the winners are chosen.

   Don't limit your questions to information about first-year student awards. You need to consider your *entire* college career, so make a financial plan that will address all four (or more) years.

   For fine arts scholarships and grants, find out how the audition process works and where you'll be playing (or singing or dancing). Visit the actual room, if possible, to familiarize yourself with its equipment, size, acoustics, lighting, and other factors.

4. **Repeat the process at all your prospective colleges.**

   If you find one with an excellent scholarship office, use it for all its worth.

   Always thank people for their help and let them know if they helped you get any money.

#84
Negotiating Better Financial Aid

So you've been accepted, you filled out your financial aid forms, and your colleges have offered you their packages. What can you do to get more? First of all, think about it from their perspective. The financial aid office has a set amount of need-based and merit-based funding that they can disperse, and they want to know that they're getting the best possible students for the money.

Need-Based Money

Getting more need-based money is generally your best option. This strategy isn't as much negotiating as it is *appealing*. To put it in a slightly better light, you're reinterpreting your financial information or introducing new financial information to explain why you have a greater need than the amount you received.

You may qualify for more need-based funding for all sorts of reasons, including the following:

>> **Your circumstances have changed.** The FAFSA and most college financial aid applications base their assessments on

your financial situation months before you enter college. In that time, a supporting parent may have lost their job, someone in your family may have required an expensive and non-insured medical procedure, your parents' retirement fund may have been devastated by the stock market, or any number of other events may have occurred that renders you more needy.

>> **The financial effects of certain parts of your information may not be properly understood.** For example, it may not be clear that your grandparents who live in another country are dependent upon your parents. Or the extent of a medical impairment and its future financial implications may not have been fully explained previously.

>> **Your assessment may not take into consideration other factors.** A good example relates to retirement funds. Colleges may assess a student's expected family contribution (EFC) differently from the federal government. A university, for example, may *include* the value of the family home but may not include retirement savings that are kept in a retirement savings plan. If your parents are approaching retirement age and have no retirement savings plan but expect to live off the equity in their home, the college assessment doesn't recognize the home as retirement savings. However, if you explain this situation to your financial aid counselor, you're likely to have your financial aid situation reassessed in your favor. In this situation, your family's home equity may be reassessed to zero, which would significantly *increase* your demonstrated need.

When appealing your financial aid package based on need, make sure that you bring along as much documentation as possible to prove the points you're making. Not all changes in your financial position will warrant a revised need assessment. The fact that you blew your savings on a trip to Europe won't induce the financial aid officer to give you any more aid.

Merit-Based Money

In a strictly need–based school, showing off your science prizes and honors and SAT scores in hopes that the college will suddenly change its policy just to entice you won't do any good. Most financial aid officers, however, are very willing to help guide you toward *external* merit-based scholarships. After all, it's in a college's best interest that you find extra money.

Negotiating for more merit-based money is a challenge because most financial aid officers pledge almost all their money when they send out admissions offers. Still, convincing a financial aid officer that you truly should've been offered a greater entrance scholarship based on your vastly improved final marks or SAT/ACT scores is possible, depending on the school. If the officer has any discretionary budget left, your position may be reassessed. If not, the officer can certainly help you apply for other sources of funding.

The sources of merit-based money are

>> **College entrance scholarships:** These scholarships are usually fixed by a predetermined college formula. What you're offered is what you get.

>> **Departmental scholarships:** These awards may or may not be included in the financial aid packages, and you must apply for them separately.

>> **External scholarships:** Many financial aid officers are knowledgeable about them, and some colleges have separate offices specifically set up to help students apply for these types of scholarships.

Of course, any money you bring along in the form of scholarships will be included in your need assessment. Yes, this may reduce the amount of need-based funding you receive. However, because the purpose of the funding is to get you to 100 percent of what you need to attend college, factoring in scholarship money makes sense. After you hit the full amount, you have no further need. If you were given more, you'd be *making* money, and that's not the purpose of need-based financial aid.

You can, however, request that the scholarship money you receive be directed toward the *loan* portion of your financial aid package. If you don't ask, you won't get.

#85
Carefully Considering Retirement Accounts for College Expenses

As you begin the run-up to college, you may be patting yourself on the back, sure in the knowledge that you've saved every penny you're likely to need to pay for your child's college education. If so, fantastic! You've overcome a huge obstacle, and now all your child needs to do is be accepted to the college of his or her choice.

If, on the other hand, you've left saving for college until late in the day and are now sweating because you don't have enough funds in your Section 529 plan or Coverdell Education Savings Account, all isn't lost. If you're like many people, especially those who had children later but who started saving for retirement early on in their careers, you may actually have adequate money saved to not only fund your retirement but also to make up the difference between college costs and college savings.

WARNING

Although using some or all the money in your traditional IRA may make perfect sense when you're still relatively young and retirement seems distant and unreal, you need to remember that, while you can borrow for college, you can't borrow for retirement.

Use retirement funds of any variety for college expenses only if you're certain that you'll have enough for retirement without that money. If you're far from retirement age, you still have the opportunity to increase your contributions into retirement plans. If, however, you're paying for college expenses only shortly before you'll be needing these funds yourself, be certain that you're not condemning yourself to a lifetime of limited opportunities and beans-on-toast dinners. Retirement now lasts longer, on average, than it ever has, and raiding your retirement savings now could sentence you to 20 to 30 years of subsistence living without adequate funds.

As you look at all the assets you have available to pay for college expenses (including your retirement accounts), keep the following in mind:

>> **Tax deferrals:** Should you take a distribution to pay for college expenses, you'll be picking up that income on your current year's tax returns. Many people are in their highest earning years when their children are in college, so you may find that you pay tax on these distributions at an even higher rate than you would have if you'd never put the money into the account.

>> **Reduction in available retirement income:** You have no idea how long you'll live or how much money you'll need to see you through the end of your life. Using retirement funds to pay for college expenses may compromise your future standard of living.

>> **Great flexibility in uncertain family situations:** Face it: You don't know for certain whether your children will attend college, or where, or exactly how much it will cost. If you don't want to put too much into specific college savings accounts because of your uncertainties, adding a cushion to your retirement accounts may provide you with whatever extra you may need to meet all contingencies.

#86
Knowing When to Refinance Your Mortgage

REMEMBER

When you're considering refinancing a loan, inspect many of the same issues that you initially looked at, including the following:

>> How long do you plan to stay in the home?

>> What's your current interest rate?

>> What interest rate can you obtain on a new mortgage?

>> How much will refinancing cost?

>> Will you be refinancing your mortgage and pulling out additional cash to use for other purposes such as paying off credit card debt?

Refinancing isn't the only option for tapping into home equity. A home equity line of credit is another possibility.

WARNING

Don't use any cash that you obtain through refinancing as a quick fix for a systemic problem. If you put your home at risk to pay off your credit cards, don't let it happen again. With the refinancing, you need to keep in mind that closing costs are levied against you. Check with potential lenders and compare closing costs as well as interest rates.

#87
Calculating the Cost of Refinancing

Loan origination fees, points, processing fees, notary fees, attorney fees, wire transfer fees, and so on should always be included on the good faith estimate that the lender provides you prior to closing. The cost of refinancing also includes the increased amount of interest you end up paying over the life of the loan.

If you have enough equity in your home, these costs can be paid for out of the proceeds from the refinance. However, you should be aware of the costs, so you can make a well-informed decision as to whether refinancing is worth it (see Tip #86 for more information).

Tabulate Loan Fees (Including Those Notorious Hidden Fees)

If you're refinancing through a traditional lender, you're probably getting your loan through a mortgage broker or a loan officer who works for a mortgage broker. This person usually earns money in two ways: receiving a commission from the bank that ultimately lends the money and charging you a loan origination fee. In addition, other services related to the processing of the loan are going to charge fees.

You don't have to worry about the commission because you don't pay that, but you do need to be aware of all the fees. Here's a short list of fees that were pulled from a good faith estimate on the refinance of a $100,000 mortgage:

Loan origination fee	$750
Loan discount (points)	$1,000
Appraisal	$325
Processing fee	$375
Underwriting fee	$175
Administration fee	$375
Flood certification	$21.50
Closing or escrow fee	$215
Document preparation fee	$50
Notary fees	$60
Title insurance	$280
Title search	$175
Recording fees	$60
State tax/stamps	$8
Total	**$3,869.50**

The total is an example of what you can expect to pay at closing, either out of pocket or from the proceeds of the refinance (the equity you cash out).

TIP

When shopping for mortgages, be sure to obtain a good faith estimate, in writing, from each lender. This estimate can be very valuable when comparing the cost of loans. What the lenders won't tell you is that many of these fees are negotiable, and the cost of processing a loan isn't as steep as some lenders make it out to be.

Calculate Interest Over the Life of the Loan

A 30-year, $200,000 mortgage at 7 percent interest is going to cost you over $479,000 when all is said and done, assuming you live in the home for 30 years. How much interest are you scheduled to pay on your current mortgage? How much interest can you expect to pay on your new mortgage?

The formula for calculating this is pretty straightforward:

Interest = (Monthly Payment × Term × 12) – Loan Amount

For a 30-year, $200,000 mortgage at 7 percent interest, the monthly payment is $1,330.60, so the formula looks like this:

($1,330.60 × 30 × 12) – $200,000 = $279,016 in interest

TIP

These numbers are only for comparison purposes. Very few people end up staying in their homes for 30 years. Most people sell by the fifth year. The actual life of the loan is however long you own the home and pay on the mortgage. Unfortunately, because of the way banks calculate mortgage payments, you end up paying way more in interest during those early years compared to what you pay in interest during the last five years.

Calculate the Total Cost of the Loan

After you know the total fees that the lender charges for the loan and the amount of interest you can expect to pay over the life of the loan, calculating the total cost of the loan is fairly easy:

Fees + Interest = Total Cost of Loan

Using this formula, calculate the cost of your current mortgage and your new mortgage. Depending on the interest rates and fees, you may actually save money by refinancing. If, however, the new loan is going to cost significantly more over the life of the loan, you may want to reconsider.

Two schools of thought may influence your decision of whether refinancing is worth it:

>> Some people focus solely on the monthly payment. If they can refinance and consolidate their debt so they have one affordable monthly payment that's less than the total payments they're now making on their home, car, and credit cards, they consider refinancing a great option.

>> Other people look at the total cost of the loan over the life of the loan, and if refinancing is going to cost them significantly more over the course of 30 years, they want no part of it.

The choice is up to you.

4

Living a Recession-Busting Life

Be smart about where your money goes, especially in tough economic times, and cut back in ways that don't feel like deprivation.

Keep your household humming along quite nicely with a little planning and a few changes here and there.

Reduce typical household expenses and still enjoy quite a few of life's luxuries.

#88
Developing Good Shopping Habits

Shopping can often feel like a black hole on your finances. Money goes in and disappears into a vacuum. Every time you step into a grocery store or discount department store, you may feel like you're out of control and you come out flat broke. In order not to allow your shopping trips to turn into guilt trips, take time to think about how you can spend more thoughtfully.

TIP

When considering a purchase, always keep the following in mind: Reduce, reuse, and recycle. Ask yourself these questions: Do you really need it? Do you already own or have access to something that you can use instead?

For example, don't buy processed, prepackaged foods. The more packaging and processing involved, the more the food costs you. By reducing your purchase of packaged and processed items, you save money and resources. Prepackaged groceries generally cost at least twice as much as whole foods, often multiple times more.

Also try to buy whole foods in their natural state whenever possible: fresh fruit, vegetables, meat, and dairy products. Yes, cooking is required, but cooking doesn't have to be drudgery. Sharing a home-cooked meal brings people together, saves money, and can be much healthier than the alternatives.

You can reduce trash and save money by minimizing your use of paper towels, disposable plates, and cups. Instead, reuse cloth towels and napkins and use durable dishes because you can wash and reuse these again and again. Go for permanent or reusable over disposable every time possible.

TIP

Take your shopping bags with you to the grocery store. Many stores credit you 5 cents per bag for bringing your own or charge you if you don't. You're not only saving money but also saving landfills. Over the course of a year, simply reusing shopping bags, napkins, plates, and cups can save you $40 to $60. Just think of how many other items you can apply this concept to. If you can cut costs without cutting your lifestyle, why not? Use your money in other ways that give you more enjoyment and satisfaction.

The following are some other ways to keep your shopping expenses at a minimum:

>> **Use a shopping list and purchase only the items on your list.** Organize your list based on the layout of your store and stick to the outer walls where all the healthy options are. By following this guideline, you can begin to better plan your expenditures. And if you stick to your list and a routine, you can eliminate those nasty impulse purchases.

>> **Don't go grocery shopping when you're hungry.** People typically spend more and buy more processed — and, therefore, more expensive — food when they're hungry.

>> **Buy merchandise when it's going out of season.** Buy next year's winter coat or swimsuit when the prices are dirt cheap instead of at the beginning of the season, when the item's not on sale. And when you're shopping for clothes, buy wash-and-wear clothes rather than dry-clean only.

>> **Buy second-hand.** eBay and Craigslist have changed the landscape of shopping for pre-owned items. Before you buy something, check online first to see whether a pre-owned version is available. You can also find treasures at thrift stores and garage sales.

>> **Shop at discount stores.** Deep-discount grocery stores, such as Aldi's, can save you a lot of money.

#89
Buying Store Brands and in Bulk

Many stores carry *store brands*, items with the store's name on the label. Or they may carry *generic products*, those items labeled without a brand name of any sort. If you're willing to be a bit adventurous, keeping your eye out for inexpensive store brands and generic products can shave a substantial amount from your grocery budget. People often say that they don't care for the taste or quality of store brands or generic items, but you may be surprised to discover that many products carrying generic or store brand labels are actually top quality, name brand items packaged under a different label.

You may have the best luck with generic versions of

» Tomato sauce and paste

» Canned and frozen vegetables

» Canned soups

» Cookies and crackers

» Dairy products (milk, butter, and cheese)

» Coffee and tea

» Bread, rolls, and buns

Do you think you don't have room for bulk purchases because you don't have a pantry? Well, look at the back of your linen closet shelves behind the folded towels. If you're like many people, you may have some empty space just waiting to be filled with a stack of cans, boxes, or packages. What about that empty corner in the garage? Or look underneath your beds, and what do you see? Empty space and dust bunnies? Any of these places can be potential storage spots for a case or two of extra stewed tomatoes or refried beans. You can also split bulk orders with a friend or relative if you really don't have the room but want to experience the savings to be found in bulk purchases.

#90
Seeing through the Gimmicks Grocery Stores Use

G rocery stores spend money to learn how to fool you into spending more in their store. Whether they're enticing you into the store in the first place with sale items or convincing you to buy more expensive items, be aware of some of these tactics:

>> **The aisle switcheroo:** If you shop at a particular store regularly, you know where everything you buy is located in each aisle. Without realizing it, you've developed a form of tunnel vision and don't really see anything except what you need. When the store rearranges the aisles or moves items from one position on a shelf to another, you have to look around and actually focus on each aisle and every shelf. By losing your tunnel vision for a time, the possibility of something new catching your eye increases dramatically, and consequently your impulse purchases increase, too.

>> **The store's layout:** Most grocery stores have the same general floor plan — they keep produce, bread, dairy, and meat products along the edges of the store or up against the walls. By putting commonly purchased items against the farthest wall or way off in a back corner, customers have to walk past numerous displays and shelves full of goodies.

TIP

Shop the edges of the store to save considerably on your grocery bill. Added benefit: The perimeter carries the healthiest items in the store. Your waistline — and your budget — will be healthier.

>> **Shelf arrangements:** If you want to find the best values on the grocery store shelves, look high on the top shelves or bend down and look at the bottom shelf. The brand-name and higher-priced products (as well as products designed to entice children) are located at eye level, while the generic, store brand, and lower-priced items are in the more awkward places to see.

#91
Using Coupons and Rebates

People either love coupons and rebates or find them to be more work than they're worth. Coupons and rebates are a valuable addition to a well-rounded approach to saving money.

To make the most of your coupon savings, follow these suggestions:

» Look for double-coupon and triple-coupon deals.

» Look for coupons for items that are already on sale or that are deeply discounted.

» Don't assume you get the best deal with the coupon; store brands can still be cheaper.

» When shopping online, look for online coupon codes to save on the purchase price or on shipping and handling charges; just type the name of the site you're shopping at and **coupons** into your favorite search engine to see what you find. You can also try websites like Rakuten (www.rakuten.com/), Honey (www.joinhoney.com/explore), and RetailMeNot (www.retailmenot.com/).

>> To receive a rebate, you must fill out a rebate form and mail it along with proof-of-purchase materials — usually your original cash register receipt and the Universal Product Code (UPC) or barcode — to the manufacturer. Occasionally, a store will offer rebates in the form of store credit rather than money back from the manufacturer. If you shop in a store regularly, credit for shopping there again can be helpful to the budget. But be careful you don't use the store credit as an excuse to buy things you normally wouldn't purchase. The store isn't really trying to save you money — they're trying to entice you into spending more money.

#92
Targeting Seasonal Grocery Sales

Throughout the year, food items are seasonally offered at discounts. The lower prices usually reflect what's currently growing at local farms. Fruits and vegetables that aren't in season can still be found in the produce department, but the price is higher because the stores need to pay higher shipping costs for importing the food from other regions.

TIP

The following list includes food items you can find on sale or at the lowest prices each month of the year:

- ❯❯ **January:** Turkey, apples, grapefruit, oranges, and pears
- ❯❯ **February:** Post–Valentine's Day candy and chocolates
- ❯❯ **March:** Frozen vegetables, meats, breakfast items, and TV dinners
- ❯❯ **April:** Eggs, broccoli, and cauliflower
- ❯❯ **May:** Soda, hot dogs, hamburgers, buns, asparagus, and pineapple
- ❯❯ **June:** Dairy products and tomatoes

» **July:** Strawberries, raspberries, blueberries, corn, cherries, squash, watermelons, cantaloupes, tomatoes, plums, peaches, and nectarines

» **August:** Squash, green peppers, salad fixings, berries, apples, melons, peaches, apricots, and fresh fish

» **September:** Apples, broccoli, cauliflower, and canned goods

» **October:** Pumpkins, cranberries, grapes, oranges, sweet potatoes, and yams

» **November:** Turkey, sweet potatoes, yams, and post-Halloween bags of candy

» **December:** Oranges, apples, and grapefruit

#93
Planning Your Meals Economically

Whether you're feeding yourself or a family, mealtimes present a challenge when you want to save money without sacrificing your favorites. You want healthy, tasty menus that everyone will enjoy and that won't send your budget into cardiac arrest.

Find a Breakfast You and Your Wallet Will Love

TIP

With $5 boxes of cereal that are gone in a day, breakfast bars not much cheaper, and egg prices going up and up, breakfast can be one of the most expensive meals of the day. Here are ways to save:

>> **Make homemade versions of frequently purchased breakfast items, such as frozen waffles or instant oatmeal.** For example, make instant oatmeal at home by briefly whirling oats in the blender or food processor. Then just stir in boiling water as you normally would for instant oats.

» **Keep a list of favorite breakfast ideas.** Examples of quick, healthy, and inexpensive options include

- **Breakfast shakes or smoothies:** Blend a few ice cubes with your choice of fresh or generic canned fruits and juice.

- **Fresh or canned fruit:** Whole, sliced, or stewed.

- **Rice, oats, or other cooked grains:** Serve hot with milk, sweetener, raisins or finely diced apples, and a dash of cinnamon or nutmeg. Many grains can be purchased inexpensively in bulk and stored in air-tight containers in your kitchen cupboard for several months without getting stale.

- **Omelets:** Use leftover pieces of meat, vegetables, and cheese to keep omelets inexpensive.

- **Bagels:** Serve toasted and spread with butter or spread with generic cream cheese. Sliced strawberries, when they're in season, and generic cream cheese on bagels is an almost decadent breakfast treat. Look for sales on bagels and stock up. They keep for weeks in the freezer.

- **Use leftovers:** Cold pizza makes a nice breakfast. So does a cheese enchilada and vegetarian lasagna.

Brown-Bag It in Style

Bringing homemade lunch items with you to work or school is a sure-fire way to save money every day during the week. Sandwiches don't always need to come served between two pieces of white bread . . . or even whole wheat bread. For a change of pace, make sandwiches with bagels, English muffins, raisin bread, or pita pockets. Look for sales on day-old bread items and stock up your freezer with a variety of sandwich fixings.

Some simple, frugal, and always family-friendly sandwich filling ideas to consider are

» Tuna or egg salad

» Peanut butter and jelly (yes, kids still love the old standby)

- Cream cheese with sliced cucumber, avocado, or alfalfa sprouts
- Assorted leftover meats and cheeses
- Leftover salads or rice stuffed into pocket bread
- Bean spreads with assorted sliced veggies

Here are some other frugal lunch ideas to get you started:

- **Cheese cubes:** Purchase large blocks of cheese on sale. Cut into small cubes and put in small zip-top bags to add to lunches for an easy finger food.

- **Cut-up veggies:** Cut up fresh celery, carrots, radishes, broccoli, cauliflower, or other vegetables your family likes to eat raw. Store in a large bowl filled with water in the refrigerator (to keep crunchy veggies from wilting), and then just grab a small handful to put in a reusable zip-top bag for a healthy addition to the lunch box.

- **Cake or brownies:** Buy several boxes of cake mix or brownies on sale or if you have a good coupon. Prepare and slice the cake into individual servings, wrap in plastic, and store in the freezer. When packing a lunch, just toss a frozen square directly into the lunchbox. The frozen dessert keeps the other lunch items cold and thaws easily by lunchtime.

- **Pudding or gelatin:** Stir a batch of pudding or gelatin and store covered in the refrigerator. When you or your kids crave pudding for lunch — or want a change from slices of cake — just spoon big dollops into small plastic containers and go.

- **Mini-muffins:** Make brownies, muffins, cupcakes, or quick breads in mini-muffin pans. Place several into sandwich bags for easy, freezable desserts.

Save on Scrumptious Dinners

Living well involves setting priorities; if yours include being healthy and omitting needless spending, you know that dinner-time makes it difficult to stay on track. The following list offers a few ideas to help you save time and money and still end up with a great dinner:

>> **Serve breakfast for dinner.** Bacon and eggs may be a fairly expensive breakfast to serve the family, but it's a very cheap meal compared to most dinner menus. Making an occasional breakfast for dinner can be a real treat.

>> **Focus on the sides.** If you're not a vegetarian, think of meat as a side dish rather than the main course. A small serving of chicken with a large tossed salad and a generous serving of steamed vegetables or rice is better for you and can save tremendously compared to having the meat be the largest item on your dinner plate.

>> **Serve salad.** A chef salad, for example, includes a little meat and a lot of vegetables, and it's even better and less expensive if the vegetables are in season.

#94
Stretching One Meal into Two (Or More)

TIP

Tossing a glob of warmed-up old noodles onto a plate doesn't entice many appetites. But if you use a little creativity, leftovers can be fun, tasty, inexpensive meal starters. By camouflaging the leftovers from meal to meal, even your pickiest eaters will have trouble recognizing the roasted chicken from dinner two nights ago in today's pasta salad lunch.

Here are some ideas:

>> **Make a leftover buffet.** Plan one meal each week that uses the assorted leftovers accumulating on the refrigerator shelves. It's like getting a free meal every week.

After accumulating about half a dozen containers of leftovers, reheat them in the microwave and portion out a little bit of everything onto each person's plate. Generally, nobody ends up with more than a spoonful or two of any one item, but the variety of items gives it the look of a full plate after you've gone through a buffet line at a party: a dab of lasagna, a slice of roasted chicken, half a black bean enchilada, a forkful of several types of salad. Toss some crackers, sliced cheese, and fresh cut-up veggies into the mix, and you have an easy dinner that the whole family enjoys.

» **Sandwich your leftovers into savings.** A favorite use for leftovers is to make sandwiches for lunch or dinner. Whether it's leftover roast beef made into French dips, sliced meatloaf with mayo and ketchup, or an open-faced turkey sandwich smothered in gravy, your family will love the results. Rolling leftover meats and veggies into a cold flour tortilla with a bit of cream cheese and a pickle is also a delicious way to add some variety to the typical sandwich presentation.

#95
Finding Alternatives to Store-Bought Food

S tore-bought isn't always a necessity, and homemade ideas are often healthier and better tasting than their more expensive store-bought counterparts. Whether you're looking for alternatives to store-bought mixes, or you just want to add a little fresh produce to your backyard garden, you can find several money-saving ideas worth considering in this section.

Grow Your Own Produce

Whether you have a large or small yard (or no yard at all), you can grow a garden that drastically cuts down your produce bill five months out of the year. Here's how:

>> **Pick a prime location.** The garden should get 6 to 8 hours of sun a day and be in close proximity to both your house and the water supply.

If you don't have a big sunny spot in your yard for a full garden, just scatter vegetable plants throughout the yard. Or try container gardening, which works wonders on small decks and patios.

>> **Decide what veggies to grow.** Start with about four or five easy-to-grow varieties of vegetables (such as tomatoes, bush beans, lettuce, cucumbers, and zucchini) — whatever your family eats regularly and works well with your soil and climate conditions. For specifics about regional growing recommendations for your area, consult a local home and garden center or ask your friendly gardening neighbors what they suggest.

>> **Weed and enjoy!**

Make Your Own Mixes and Convenience Items

For the sake of convenience — and sometimes just out of sheer laziness — you probably buy expensive premade and prepackaged products (such as salad dressing, taco seasoning, and cookie and cake mixes) to ease your time spent in the kitchen. But when money's tight, all the convenience in the world doesn't make up for spending too much on groceries and going over your budget. And it goes without saying that homemade isn't only cheaper, but it's also considerably healthier. You can choose which ingredients to use, and you know that no flavorings, colorings, or preservatives are added.

TIP

You can find recipes for convenience items by looking at the ingredient lists on the package and getting a good idea of what to use, browsing through all-purpose cookbooks and cooking-related books at the library, and logging on to different cooking websites. When you find a good recipe for something you use regularly, like taco seasoning, prepare the mix ahead of time to store in the refrigerator or on the pantry shelf. Pre-measure the mixes into individual plastic zip-top bags, and then place the individual bags into larger zip-top bags. When you need some taco seasoning, you can just reach in and grab out a small bag. You're ready to cook without worrying about running to the store for last-minute ingredients.

#96
Saving on Baby Food

Frugal hardly seems like a word to use in the same sentence as "baby food," which can really take a bite out of the ol' budget. But buying the expensive prepackaged baby foods isn't the only way to feed baby. You have less expensive (and more healthful) options:

» **Process your own baby food.** Serve your baby tiny servings — well-processed in the blender or food processor first — of most anything the family is already eating: potatoes, carrots, peas, or even homemade chicken soup. Take care to leave out spices and any additives in baby's portion.

Prepare a large batch of baby food at one time so you don't need to do it at every meal. For example, cook and puree a big bunch of carrots, freeze the puree in ice cube trays, pop out the frozen food cubes, and place in labeled zip-top freezer bags. When your baby is ready to eat, just take out a frozen carrot cube, thaw it, warm slightly, and dinner is served.

WARNING

Be careful not to heat the food too hot. Microwaves can be efficient but often heat the center of the food to temperatures inappropriately hot for a baby. Be sure to stir the food thoroughly and double-check the temperature before feeding your child.

» **If you buy premade baby food, buy the largest jars available.** The little bitty jars may be meal-sized for baby's tiny appetite, but they're expensive too. When you open a large jar, spoon out a small portion onto a plate or bowl, and then cover the jar and refrigerate it. The large jar of food lasts for about two meals this way, rather than just one.

#97
Cooking Up Money Savings

E ating out often can zap your budget, but busy schedules make it difficult to find the time to fix healthy, tasty, and economical home-cooked meals. The suggestions here can help.

Cook in Bulk

The idea of cooking in bulk and freezing the premade meals puts off many people. They hear terms referring to *monthly* cooking or *30-day* cooking, and they roll their eyes. But think of it more as a concept. If you don't have the freezer space, the energy, or organizational where-withal for a full month of cooking in one pop, try twice-a-month, or even once-a-week. Or just double and triple recipes as you prepare them.

Here's how bulk cooking works: When you make chili, make enough for three meals. Eat one tonight, and then package the extra in labeled freezer bags. You now have two meals ready to go in just minutes for those nights when you're in a hurry. Just pop the freezer bag in the microwave or pour the thawed chili into a pan on the stovetop, toss together a green salad, and dinner is served.

For additional savings, plan your bulk-cooking sessions around the supermarket's sales. Suppose, for example, that your grocery store has whole fryers on sale. You buy the maximum number of fryers the store allows (four in this example) and do a chicken mini session: You cut up the fryers, and then prepare and freeze the following meals:

>> **Two or three meals' worth of marinated thighs and drumsticks in plastic freezer bags:** The chicken marinates while it's frozen and also while it thaws. You can use homemade Italian-style salad dressing for a marinade or generic or store-brand dressing. To serve, thaw completely, pour off the marinade, and then cook the chicken pieces on the barbecue or under the oven broiler.

>> **Two meals of chicken cacciatore:** A tasty freeze-ahead version consists of sliced chicken breast, a jar of spaghetti sauce, stewed tomatoes, and some sautéed onions and green pepper strips. Thaw the cacciatore and serve it over pasta or rice.

>> **Several meals' worth of cooked chicken:** Cut the chicken into medium-sized chunks to use in skillet meals or casseroles. Having freezer bags with precooked and frozen chicken pieces makes later meal preparation a snap.

>> **A large pot of homemade chicken noodle soup:** Soup is usually good for at least two meals, maybe more, depending on how hungry the troops are when they're ready to eat.

REMEMBER

Be sure to vary your menus to keep your family happy. Even when foods are dressed differently, few people like the same thing night after night. Just because you've prepared all these chicken-based meals doesn't mean you have to serve them one day after another.

Use a Slow Cooker

A slow cooker is both convenient and a money saver. When you come home at dinnertime, dinner's nearly done, eliminating the temptation to run out for something quick (and usually less healthy and definitely more expensive). But slow cookers can save you money in other ways:

>> You can cook larger meals, providing leftovers and possibly a second meal from one cooking time.

>> You can buy tougher (and less expensive) cuts of meat because the slow cooker acts as a tenderizer.

>> Meat shrinks less when cooked in the slow cooker and doesn't dry out. Also, flavors have time to develop while your meal cooks all day.

>> A slow cooker doesn't use as much electricity as an oven, nor does it heat up the kitchen nearly as much as the stovetop or oven, so it's a perfect hot-weather cooking appliance.

>> A slow cooker frees up oven and stovetop space during a large cooking session for the freezer.

Use an Instant Pot

Also referred to as a pressure cooker, an Instant Pot has many benefits similar to the slow cooker and is also much faster. If you don't have all day for your meal to simmer on the counter, the Instant Pot is a great option.

Did you know that pressure cooking can help save money on your electricity bill? The Instant Pot is one of the greenest kitchen appliances you can have in your arsenal. Compared to other kitchen appliances (like your oven or stove), the Instant Pot uses 70 percent less electricity. Plus, the Instant Pot cooks food much quicker than other appliances, meaning less energy is used during the entire recipe process. The Instant Pot cooks most food in 70 percent less time!

Another important feature built into the Instant Pot is the sealing mechanism, which requires significantly less water for cooking (resulting in less steam produced as well). This is actually a double whammy because not only will you save from less energy being used for cooking, but it'll also help keep your house cooler versus using an oven and hopefully preventing have to turn on the air-conditioning!

Finally, peak energy usage hours are typically from 4 to 9 p.m., typically prime dinner hours. Enlisting the help of your Instant Pot, you can keep your costs down while still putting a home-made, delicious meal on the table in a matter of minutes.

#98
Canning and Preserving Your Food

C anning and preserving are ways to protect food from spoil-age so you can use it at a later time. Some methods, like dehydrating (also referred to as drying), date back to ancient times; others, like canning, are a little more recent. There's no doubt that being able to offer fresh-tasting, home-canned or home-preserved foods to your family and friends throughout the year is definitely satisfying.

Whatever food-preservation method you choose, your efforts will give you the following:

>> **A pantry full of freshly preserved, homegrown foods:**
Having a stocked pantry offers a cushion against the
fluctuating cost and availability of healthy foods. If you enjoy
specialty foods from gourmet stores but dislike the high
prices, home-canning is a safe and economical way to
preserve large or small quantities of high-quality food.

>> **Convenience:** You can build a pantry of convenience foods
that fit into your busy lifestyle and that your family will enjoy.

>> **Confidence in the ingredients that go into your food:** If you love fresh ingredients and like to know what goes into your food, doing your own canning and preserving is the answer.

>> **Protection against rising food costs and temporary shortages:** The whole idea of canning and preserving is to take advantage of fresh food when it's abundant. And abundant food generally means lower costs. If there is a temporary shortage of food, you'll have what you need in your pantry.

>> **A sense of relaxation and accomplishment:** For many people, working in the kitchen and handling food provides a sense of relaxation, and watching family and friends enjoy the products of your efforts gives you a great sense of accomplishment. Taking the time to select your recipe, choosing and preparing your food, and packaging and processing it for safety is fulfilling and a source of pride for you, the home-canner.

>> **A good time:** Producing canned and preserved food in your kitchen is fun and easy — and can be a great family activity.

REMEMBER

The price of food has skyrocketed in the last few years. Food safety and availability have become a concern for everyone. Canning is the answer to both the price dilemma and the desire to offer nutritious foods throughout the year. Home-canning and home-preserving instantly reward your efforts when you follow the proper steps for handling and processing your food.

REMEMBER

In both water-bath canning and pressure canning, you heat your filled jars of food to a high temperature in order to destroy microorganisms and produce an airtight vacuum seal. The only way to reliably produce a safe canned product is to use the correct method for your type of food, follow your recipe instructions to the letter, and complete each processing step.

Canning and preserving methods are simple and safe, and they produce food that's nutritious, delicious, and just plain satisfying to your taste buds. Becoming a successful food preserver takes time, effort, and knowledge of the rules. Follow these tips for achieving success as a home canner and preserver:

>> **Start with the freshest, best products available.** Preserving doesn't improve food quality. If you put garbage in, you get garbage out.

>> **Know the rules and techniques for your canning or preserving method before you start your work.** Don't try to learn a technique after you've started your processing.

>> **Work in short sessions to prevent fatigue and potential mistakes.** Process no more than two items in one day, and work with only one canning method at a time.

>> **Stay up-to-date on new or revised guidelines for your preserving method.** The latest edition of *Canning and Preserving For Dummies* by Amelia Jeanroy (John Wiley & Sons, Inc.) is a great start. You can also go to websites like www. freshpreserving.com, created by the makers of Ball canning supplies. Here you can find tips and directions for canning just about anything.

>> **Use the correct processing method and processing time to destroy microorganisms.** The recipe will tell you what method to use, but it helps if you understand the difference between high- and low-acid foods and how the canning methods for each differ.

>> **Know the elevation you're working at.** Adjust your processing time or pressure when you're at an altitude over 1,000 feet above sea level.

>> **Put together a plan before you start your preserving session.** Read your recipe (more than once). Have the proper equipment and correct ingredients on hand to prevent last-minute shortages and inconvenient breaks (make a list of what you need and check off items as you gather them).

>> **Test your equipment.** If you're using a pressure canner or an electric dehydrator, test out the equipment to ensure everything's working properly. And always check the seals on your jars.

>> **Do a trial run.** Before canning for the first time (or the 40th), it's a good idea to do a trial run. Canning jars of water is a great way to be certain that you have all the equipment you will need, and that you are using the techniques properly. Do your jars seal? It's also a good way to experience the sounds that both a water-bath and pressure canner make.

#99
Freezing Fruits and Vegetables

Freezing foods is the art of preparing and packaging foods at their peak of freshness and plopping them into the freezer to preserve all that seasonal goodness. Freezing is a great way to preserve foods that can't withstand the high temperatures and long cooking times of conventional canning methods.

The keys to freezing food are to make sure it's absolutely fresh, that you freeze it as quickly as possible, and that you keep it at a proper frozen temperature (0 degrees).

REMEMBER

The quality won't get better just because you throw it in the freezer. Properly packaging food in freezer paper or freezer containers prevents any deterioration in its quality. Damage occurs when your food comes in contact with the dry air of a freezer. Although freezer-damaged food won't hurt you, this does make the food taste bad. Here are three things to help you avoid freezer burn:

>> **Reduce exposure to air.** Wrap food tightly.

>> **Avoid fluctuating temperatures.** Keep the freezer closed as much as possible. Know what you want to remove before opening the door.

>> **Don't overfill your freezer.** An overly full freezer reduces air circulation and speeds up freezer damage.

Freezing fruits and vegetables is the second-best preserving method after canning. Preparing and processing fresh fruits and vegetables for the freezer takes about a third of the time of water-bath or pressure canning.

Fruits

When freezing fruit, follow these general steps:

1. Select quality, ripe fruit.

2. Work with small, manageable quantities, about 8 to 12 cups of fruit, which yields about 2 to 3 quarts frozen.

   Note: Many recipes use about 2 cups of fruit, which yields 1 pint. You can easily do multiple batches at a time to get the yield you want.

3. Wash your fruit.

4. Pack your fruit for freezing based on your final use.

5. If called for in your recipe, add an *antioxidant* (or anti-darkening agent).

6. Fill your container, allowing the proper headspace.

7. Label the package and let your freezer do the rest!

Veggies

Follow these simple steps for freezing vegetables:

1. Choose quality, ripe vegetables.

2. Work with small, manageable quantities, about 2 pounds at a time.

3. Wash and drain your vegetables and prepare them according to your recipe (which usually specifies blanching the vegetables).

Be sure to allow the vegetables to dry thoroughly before freezing to prevent them from sticking together when frozen.

4. **Chill your vegetables before packing them for freezing.**

5. **Fill your container, allowing the proper headspace if you're using rigid containers, or removing all of the excess air from the freezer bags.**

6. **Label your package and add it to your freezer.**

#100
Trying Other Ways to Save in the Kitchen

Every tip helps when you're trying to save money in the kitchen, so here's a list of easy ideas to help cut the cost of family meals.

>> **Keep lettuce fresh longer by rinsing and drying it thoroughly.** (Use a salad spinner, if available.) Then cut the lettuce into salad-size pieces (use a lettuce knife to reduce the risk of bruising), place in a zip-top bag, try to get all the excess air out of the bag, and then store the bag of lettuce in the refrigerator. Each time you use some of the lettuce, press the air out again.

>> **Don't rinse produce until you're going to use it.** Otherwise, it can mold and get slimy faster.

>> **Cook a large pot of your favorite dry beans (kidney, white, red).** Look in a general cookbook for instructions. Scoop the cooked beans into zip-top freezer bags, two cups to a bag. When you're making soup, casseroles, chili, skillet meals, or burritos and need some cooked beans, thaw a frozen bag and throw it in the pot.

» **Use half the amount of meat called for in the recipe when making a casserole or skillet meal.** Add inexpensive vegetables or pasta to fill in for the missing meat.

» **Buy blocks of cheese when they're on sale, grate, and place in a large zip-top freezer bag.** Use it as needed. If the cheese clumps together in the freezer, bang the bag against the kitchen counter to loosen.

» **Buy eggs when they're on sale and freeze for later use in baking, omelets, and scrambled eggs.** Don't freeze the eggs whole; crack each egg into a section of a clean plastic ice cube tray. When frozen, remove the egg cubes from the tray and package in a large zip-top freezer bag. Use as needed. The thawed-out eggs should be used quickly — they're very perishable.

#101
Getting Toiletries on a Budget

Making your own toiletries saves money. For example, brushing your teeth with baking soda works great and is cheaper than buying brand-name pastes. Baking soda not only cleans your teeth, but it also freshens your breath! Think about that open box of baking soda on the back shelf of your fridge. What's it there for? Absorbing odors! So if it works for your fridge with all the atrocious odors brewing there, baking soda is bound to work wonders on a little dose of morning breath. (If you don't think it tastes all that great, make a paste by mixing peppermint oil and baking soda.)

TIP

Here are few more simple and frugal home alternatives for expensive toiletry items:

» **Wipe on rubbing alcohol with a cotton ball as a substitute for deodorant.** You can also try using witch hazel in the same way (allow to dry thoroughly before dressing) or baking soda (dusted on underarm with a powder puff or cotton ball).

» **Use a mild solution of salt and water for mouthwash (about four parts water to one part salt).** The saltwater rinse and gargle keeps your mouth clean after eating and kills some of the bacteria that lead to bad breath.

» **Substitute cheap, bought-in-bulk hair conditioner for shaving cream.** A large container of conditioner is considerably less expensive than even the most inexpensive cans of shaving cream. Plus you only need to add one item to your shopping list instead of two.

If you want to try your hand at making your own frugal body cleansers, you can find recipes on the Internet for bubble bath, facial masks, lotions — you name it. If you're not interested in making homemade body cleansing products, at least watch carefully for sales and coupon specials at your local stores. Buy several tubes of toothpaste or a couple bottles of your favorite shampoo when it goes on sale. And give generic products a try.

#102
Saving on Salon Expenses

When you're trying to be a conscientious consumer, salon visits pose a dilemma. On the one hand, visiting a stylist once every six weeks is a luxury you can surely do without. On the other hand, looking and feeling good is darn near priceless. The key is to find a balance that lets you have your cake and eat it to. Here are some ideas:

- >> Negotiate services with your stylist.
- >> Extend time between visits.
- >> Go to a discount salon or a beauty college between visits with your regular stylist.
- >> Trim your own bangs to extend the life of your style between salon visits.

WARNING

Trimming your own hair under ideal conditions is a good thing. But impulsively cutting your hair in elevators, at stoplights, or seconds before dashing out on a date is a bad idea. Even minor trims take planning and a sensible work area so you can concentrate on what you're doing!

- >> Cut your kids' hair yourself rather than taking them to the salon. They don't need the extra pampering just yet. (See Tip #103 for more details.)

#103
Cutting Your Kids' Hair

Most children are far less enthusiastic about getting their hair cut than you are about transforming their locks into neat little works of art. Five minutes seems like a long time to a young child — and 20 minutes like an eternity. Coaxing them to happily stay put for an entire haircut means using every trick in the book. In a sentence, you need to provide an experience that's fast, fun, tasty, and filled with kid–size activities.

REMEMBER

Before you plunge headlong into cutting kids' hair, make sure you have these tools, supplies, and equipment at the ready:

>> Chair (preferably a styling chair or barstool with a back and low arms)

>> Child-size beanbag pillow (to place on the chair)

>> Child-size cutting cape

>> Thin, small towels or dish towels (to put under the cape to catch stray bits of hair)

>> Large, fluffy face brush

>> Cornstarch (to apply to the face brush; tap it to remove the excess, and brush away any remaining snippets to stop the "itchy-hair syndrome" dead in its tracks)

>> Spray bottle filled with warm water

>> Hair conditioner (mix a small amount — no more than a capful — into the warm water in the spray bottle) to painlessly remove any tangles as you go

>> Quality combs and soft brushes

>> Haircutting scissors

>> Small toys

>> Entertainment

>> Healthy snacks (toys, entertainment, and snacks can buy you a few minutes during a kid's cut!)

>> Rewards for good behavior

#104
Expanding Your Wardrobe

Dressing well doesn't have to equal dressing expensively. A great place to find clothing is at thrift stores and garage sales. Even if your family's wardrobe consists of almost nothing but secondhand clothing, you can all still look great. The following list suggests other ways to expand your family's wardrobe without decimating your budget.

>> **Make the most of hand-me-downs.** Using hand-me-downs for your kids is a wonderful way to save money and recycle still serviceable clothing items. If you have friends and family with kids slightly older than yours, ask them to save their children's outgrown clothing for you. Most parents are happy to save clothes for a friend but may not know who's interested in their hand-me-downs.

>> **Exchange clothing.** Start a regular group clothing exchange throughout the year. Here's how it works: Everyone brings their family's outgrown or discarded clothing to someone's home, displays it on a table, and then sorts through everyone else's castoffs to find clothing for their own family. At the end of the exchange, the leftovers are boxed up and donated to a thrift store.

» **Shop seasonally and plan ahead.** At the end of each season, you can find huge savings on seasonal clothing items. The best *selection* of clothes is usually at the beginning of the season, but the best *bargains* are at the end. Watch for seasonal sales at local stores, where you can stock up on items you'll use throughout the year.

TIP

If you're buying for your kids and you see an excellent price, stock up on larger sizes. Your kids can grow into them as time passes.

» **Save on school clothes.** Wait until the school year begins to buy the bulk of your kids' school clothing, so they can see what's in style and what's out of fashion. Waiting until after school starts allows you to take advantage of clearance sale prices at department stores, thrift stores, and secondhand shops.

#105
Getting Stains Out of Kids' Clothing

Small, stubborn stains can ruin an otherwise perfect piece of clothing. Finding simple ways to take care of grass stains and spilled juice can prolong the wearability of a garment. Here are some ideas to try for some common stubborn stains:

» **Blood:** Rinse immediately with cool water. Hot water sets the stain and makes it harder to remove. Dab hydrogen peroxide on white fabrics. If the stain persists, soak overnight in a solution of non-chlorine bleach and warm water.

» **Chocolate:** Rinse immediately with cold water. If the stain persists, soak overnight in a solution of non-chlorine bleach and warm water.

» **Grass:** Apply a stick stain remover immediately. Let sit overnight. Wash as usual. Or pretreat overnight in non-chlorine bleach mixed with water.

» **Ink:** Apply a stick stain remover as soon as possible. Gently work stain remover into the fabric. Let it sit for several hours before washing. Launder in cold water.

» **Juice:** Pretreat with liquid dishwashing detergent or stick stain remover. Wash as usual in hot water. Repeat pretreatment and laundering if necessary.

» **Ketchup:** Rinse the stain in cold water immediately. Soak the garment in cold water for several hours. Launder in cold water. If the stain remains, use stick stain remover, let sit overnight, and launder again.

#106
Reconstructing Your Clothes

Reconstructing clothing is the practice of creating new clothes from existing garments. Some examples of this include

» Adding a simple hood to a jacket

» Cutting the sleeves off a T-shirt

» Cropping a sweater

When it comes to saving cash, reusing and reconstructing clothes just can't be beat. People with all levels of sewing skill can reconstruct clothes. Creative types who don't like to use patterns excel at this, and it's a fun way to make old or out-of-style clothing new again.

Sometimes clothing is just fine in its present form, but it needs a little something. Maybe you want to add a little pizzazz and individuality to your garment, or maybe you want to fix a poor fit, hide stains, or spruce up a worn 'n' torn favorite.

Lots of clothing is well-made and practical. But it can also be boring and can look exactly like every other piece that was mass-produced from the same factory! Some less intense reconstruction techniques serve to elevate your ho-hum hoodie to a truly unique piece of self-expression:

>> Sewing a hem with contrasting color thread

>> Taking in a seam with the seam placed externally

>> Decorative patching on wear 'n' tear

>> Decorative stitching on patches and hems

>> Decorative painting over stains

These techniques are exciting for all levels of skill and creativity. And they're perfect for those pieces that you're on the fence about banishing from your closet! Plus you have lots of no-sew options with this method.

#107
Shopping for Secondhand Clothes

Shopping for secondhand items at garage sales, thrift stores, and consignment stores can be fun, rewarding, and incredibly inexpensive. By checking for hidden flaws and avoiding some problem items altogether, your adventures in the world of bargain hunting can yield more big game than big duds.

TIP

Double-check each item of clothing before heading to the checkout counter. Refer to the following list as you decide on any clothing purchases:

>> Check tags for brand name, size (especially when the outfit has multiple pieces), and fabric content.

>> Read any special laundry instructions. You aren't saving money if you buy a $2 blouse that needs dry cleaning.

>> Look carefully at seams (under arms, across shoulders, legs, crotch, and back end).

>> Make sure pockets aren't ripping out or coming undone. Check for holes inside the pockets.

>> Check the buttons. Are they all there? Do they match? Have they been replaced?

>> Make sure zippers work properly and aren't broken or previously replaced.

>> Carefully check the entire garment for stains, rips, holes, snags, runs, bleach marks, loose hems, or defects.

>> Try the clothing on. Don't trust the sizes on the labels. The previous owner may have laundered the sweater inappropriately and changed its size, or the item may have been altered after someone lost weight.

TIP

If you know how to sew, or someone who knows a good one, you can alter some clothing slightly (for example, shorten a skirt or pant length).

#108
Utilizing Community Resources

Before you plunk down your hard-earned money to join a gym or for various types of entertainment and activities, consider what your community has to offer — usually at little or no cost!

>> Community colleges and universities

>> Community swimming pools

>> Gymnasium or exercise classes

>> Community centers

>> Local parks or jogging trails

>> County libraries

>> Museums and galleries

>> Concerts

>> Festivals

#109
Having Fun in Your Own Backyard and Beyond

The family activities highlighted here are not only fun and cost next to nothing, but they also help build family relationships because you spend time together pursuing enjoyable pastimes.

Take a Family Field Trip

A meaningful family field trip can be simple, like taking a leisurely walk down a local nature trail and watching a pair of red squirrels do aerial acrobatics. Or extend the field trip and follow the path of Lewis and Clark across the United States for a long — but relatively inexpensive — educational family vacation. Even camping in your own backyard can be an adventure of sorts. Here are the rules:

>> **Choose an event the entire family enjoys.** The weekly "What's Happening?" section of the newspaper and monthly issues of regional parenting magazines — often available for free in libraries and bookstores — provide a never-ending variety of activities that appeal to the entire family, from

preschoolers to adults. Also, your local library may offer classes, readings, and live performances for kids. Check your library's bulletin board for notices about family-friendly activities and attractions. And don't forget to check online for free local activities.

>> **Do a little pretrip planning.** A little advance planning can make for a more enjoyable — and less expensive — trip. Before you leave home, pack some inexpensive snack supplies and drink bottles, confirm driving directions, check on admission prices, and check your destination's website for any "online only" coupons (this would also be a good time to check for unanticipated park closures or hour changes).

Discover the Games People Play

Family games can be enjoyed whenever you want some inexpensive entertainment and time together. Institute a family game night.

TIP

If you don't have a closet full of board games, you can acquire them inexpensively at garage sales and thrift stores. If someone asks what to get you or your family for a gift at the holidays, suggest a board game.

Board games aren't the only family-friendly games to play on a family game night. Do you remember Charades? How about Spoons? Twenty Questions? Hide the Thimble? Spotlight Tag? Rummy? Crazy Eights? Delve into the recesses of your mind and try to remember the games you played as a kid. The games may be old to you, but they're *new* to your kids!

Plan a Movie Night

Going out to a movie can be real treat — and, given the price of tickets nowadays, even matinees can break the bank. But even if heading to the cineplex is no longer within your budget, you don't have to forego the enjoyment of watching films. Rent a video (or choose a movie available for free on a streaming service), pop some corn, and invite the kids to a movie night.

#110
Saving for a Family Vacation

Finding money in the family's budget for a trip — large or small — can be challenging but not impossible. If you cut back on smaller activities during the year, you can pocket the money you save and put it into your vacation fund. Here are some ideas for saving a little here and a little there to fund a family getaway:

» Eat at home — skip the drive-thru.

» Save all your loose change in a jar.

» Have a yard sale.

» Sell some clothing at a consignment store.

» Babysit or work a part-time job during the school year.

» Cut back on "extras" like cable television and dry cleaning to jump-start your vacation savings.

» Wash your car yourself rather than take it through the automated car wash.

» Tally up the money you save by using coupons at the grocery store each week and put that amount in a vacation fund.

#111
Traveling on a Few Dollars a Day

Al travel seems to have the same basic expenses: food, accommodations, and fun activities. What you spend on these things can amount to a lot or a little. The difference depends on where you go, how you get there, and what you do when you get there.

Choose Less-Expensive Travel Times

If possible, take your vacation during off times. The months of May and September (in the Northern Hemisphere) are especially good times to travel because they're not as hot as July or August, they're not prime tourist season, and the weather is usually nice. Many resorts offer a schedule of rates, showing their peak and off-seasons. To maximize your money and enjoyment of available perks, make your reservation for the week just before the peak time starts or right after it ends.

REMEMBER

Be aware that "off times" in your area may not be "off times" at your destination. Holidays and regular breaks from school (winter and spring break, summer vacation from school) are also usually expensive times for travel.

Also, when picking a destination and time of year to visit, you may want to make sure the dates you choose aren't during local festivals or events, which usually run up hotel rates and make sightseeing a nightmare (unless you actually want to participate in the festival or event, of course).

Book Affordable Accommodations

Accommodations are often one of the most expensive parts of any vacation. But less-expensive alternatives exist:

>> **Camping:** If you have a tent or a trailer, you can often pull into a campground almost anywhere and find a spot to sleep for about $40 per night for the whole family.

>> **Hotels:** If you plan to stay at a hotel, be sure to find out about special prices or seasonal deals when you make a reservation. Depending on when you're traveling, check Sunday nights, which are often slow and hotels offer cheaper rates to encourage customers to stay.

>> **Vacation home rentals:** Check out Airbnb (www.airbnb.com/) and Vrbo (www.vrbo.com/) for homes you can rent in your destination.

TIP

Traveling in a group can cut accommodation costs. Take a vacation with some other families or your in-laws. Rent a big house at the ocean or stay in a mountain lodge and have everyone split the cost.

Eat Well for Less

Don't eat all your meals in restaurants. Here are some ideas for restaurant alternatives:

>> If your hotel or motel offers a free breakfast, take full advantage of it.

>> Eat a huge breakfast, and then have a light lunch of fruit and cheese or an energy bar.

- » Visit a local supermarket and pick up the ingredients for a picnic. Make your own sandwiches, grab a bag of chips, and buy whatever drinks are on sale.

- » Stay hydrated. Thirst can be mistaken for hunger, and getting something to drink is usually a lot cheaper (think water fountain) than getting something to eat.

- » Carry snacks with you so you're not tempted to buy pricey snacks to satisfy your hunger pangs.

TIP

You'll likely want to eat in restaurants at least part of the time — you're on vacation, after all. Plan your main meal around lunchtime. Restaurants' lunch menus are similar to dinner menus, but the cost is greatly reduced.

#112
Finding Transportation Bargains

Transportation has progressed a long way from the horse and buggy, which is a good thing . . . most of the time. But when a car payment can be higher than a mortgage and the cost of gasoline can outpace your commuting budgets, you may want to think twice about the sanctity of the family car. Do you have other options? More frugal alternatives? Ways to afford more car for less money? Yep. Read on!

Find a Deal on a Set of Wheels

Unless you live in the city on an excellent bus line, you're going to need a vehicle at some point in your life. But paying $400 (or more) each month on car payments isn't necessary if you follow some of the simple ideas in this section.

Most people today choose to take out a loan for a car, but you can save on your car loan by purchasing a vehicle with fewer extras. You can carve as much as $100 a month off your monthly car payment by doing so.

An obvious alternative to buying a new car is to buy a used car. Doing so can save you quite a bit of money. The moment you drive a brand spanking new vehicle off the car lot, it becomes a used car and begins to depreciate rapidly and drastically. Why not pay thousands of dollars *less* for a used car rather than pay top dollar for a soon-to-be-used car? Either way, you're driving around in a used car the moment you leave the car dealership.

Also, carefully consider the type of car you're buying. You can buy a wide range of car models for the same price, but the insurance rates for those cars can vary significantly. Cars with higher safety ratings insure for less. But if you want the snazzy red sports car, be prepared to pay through the nose to insure it!

TIP

If you're thinking of buying a used car, check for the ratings on used cars that interest you by looking at back issues of *Consumer Reports'* annual auto report. You can also search online for used cars in the price range and locality you need. You can get a general feel for what's available in your price range. For a good place to get started, check out www.autotrader.com.

Get the word out to friends, neighbors, and co-workers when you're in need of another car. If you buy a car from an individual or even a dealer, pay the $30 or so to have it checked out by a mechanic before you sign the papers. One person learned this lesson the hard way. They bought a great-looking car a couple of years ago for $2,500 and had an $800 repair bill within two weeks. But the car still wasn't fixed, so they decided to cut their losses and trade it in at a dealership. The car needed a new engine; the dealer gave them $1,200 for it. So a month after purchasing the "great deal," the buyer found themselves recovering from a financial bloodbath that could have been avoided if they'd simply taken it to a mechanic before buying it.

Another good idea when you're considering a used car is to view the car's history report online. (You can do this for a $10–$20 fee at www.carfax.com.) You can tell whether the car has ever been in an accident, how many owners it has had, and whether it has been a rental or fleet car.

TIP

Other excellent resources for used cars include the following:

>> **Rental car companies:** They have to clear out their entire inventory every couple of years, and even though the cars are used, sometimes heavily used, rental cars often get a higher level of continuous maintenance throughout their lives than most cars owned by private individuals. Call and find out when your local rental car businesses are holding sales of their out-of-service fleet of cars.

>> **Auctions:** Be sure to check in various local classified advertisement listings for auctions. Many cars at auctions either have been repossessed, have been confiscated by the police, or are trade-ins from car dealerships.

>> **Dealer repossession sales:** These sales provide reasonably good cars at less-than-market prices.

Use Public Transportation

If you live out in the country somewhere, chances are good that public transportation isn't much help in your situation. But most people in moderate-sized communities and large cities have access to several transportation options other than their own private vehicle.

A monthly bus pass easily pays for itself if you live and work near a local bus route. Buses usually offer low rates, discounts for multiple rides, and convenient locations near business and office centers. Commuting on the bus can be a relaxing way to catch up on reading or to just sit back and watch the scenery go by without worrying about doing the actual driving. Bus passes for teens also provide some much-desired independence for the teens and cut down on the amount of time Mom and Dad spend running a taxi service all over town.

Larger cities like Chicago and New York have additional public transportation options like the subway or commuter train. Both of these alternatives offer the same benefits of bus systems. You've probably heard scary stories about subway systems, but most of them are quite safe if you use common sense.

Bike or Walk

Few people consider foregoing the health club and simply biking or walking to work or school five days a week. You also save on parking fees if you usually park your car at a pay lot near your office.

TIP

If you have things you need to carry into work with you each day, get an inexpensive saddlebag for bicycles that can probably hold anything you need to transport back and forth. If you're walking to work or school, invest in a comfortable backpack. You can also keep a change of shoes in the pack so you don't have wear your dress shoes for the two-mile walk to work.

If your work attire isn't conducive to biking or walking, bring a change of clothes with you and make use of the company washroom to touch up your hair and makeup before work.

#113
Saving on Phone Bills

Cutting back on the monthly phone bill is a welcome relief to many wallets:

>> Check your phone bill and make sure you're not paying for extra services you never use or don't need.

>> Look into Internet phone services that offer free or reduced plans. For example, if you (and the person you want to call) have webcams, you can use Skype (www.skype.com) to make free video calls anywhere in the world.

>> To save money on cellphone bills, look for plans that offer minutes the entire family can share; instead of getting a phone for each child, get a single phone your children can share; examine your monthly bill to see how you're using your minutes; and if you consistently have minutes left over, ask about dropping to a cheaper plan.

>> Investigate package deals. Getting phone, Internet, and TV service from one provider can often save you money.

>> Send an email (it's free) or rediscover the joys of letter writing. Sending cards and letters via the U.S. Postal Service doesn't have to cost much more than the price of a first-class stamp if you watch for specials on stationery while you're shopping.

#114
Staying Cool on the Cheap

Following are some ways to stay cool, even when it's hot outside:

>> **To drop your cooling (and heating) bills dramatically, add insulation to your home.** First insulate your attic floor, and then when time and money allow, add insulation to your basement, exterior walls, floors, and crawl spaces (in that order).

>> **Improve attic ventilation.** Adequate ventilation under the eaves allows cooler air to enter and circulate throughout the attic. If you don't have a permanent exhaust fan, you can set a box fan with the air flow pointed outward to pull the hot air out of the house.

>> **Shade your house from the sun.** If your house isn't shaded by trees, install awnings over any windows that are exposed to direct sun during the day. Many awnings are removable and adjustable.

» **Cover your windows.** Windows are a major source of heat during the summer. Reduce the heat coming in through your windows by closing the drapes during the day, adding reflective window tint to southern windows, and hanging bamboo shades on the outside of heat-producing windows.

» **If you use an air conditioner to cool your house, turn the thermostat up a bit higher than the temperature you usually set.** If you normally set the A/C for 72 degrees Fahrenheit during the summer, switch to 78 degrees. When it's 95 degrees in the shade outside, 78 degrees still feels comfortable and not too warm. Also set the temperature higher for times when you're not there.

» **Use fans to circulate air.** Moving air feels several degrees cooler than still air.

» **Reduce how much heat you create inside your house.** Use your outdoor grill more often to keep from heating up the kitchen. Cook in the microwave, slow cooker, electric skillet, or toaster oven, rather than the stove and oven. Don't use the heat setting on your clothes dryer.

#115
Keeping Warm

S tay cozy and still save money on your heating bills by following these hints.

Turn Down the Thermostat

TIP

The simplest way to save money on heating is to turn down your furnace a couple degrees. If you usually keep your thermostat set at 72 degrees Fahrenheit during the winter, turn it down to 70. If you're used to 70-degree temperatures, set the thermostat at 68. Lower the temperature even further at night when you're sleeping. Toss on an extra blanket if you're still a bit chilled.

Consider these other ways to stay warm without running up your heating bill:

>> Close the vents and doors in rooms that aren't in use for long periods of time.

>> A ceiling fan set to push air down keeps warm air circulating to the lower regions of the house.

>> Higher humidity keeps the air warmer. Here are a few simple ideas to add warm moisture:

- Let steamy air from the bathroom escape into the rest of the house after a shower.

- Boil water on the stovetop.
- Keep a kettle or pan full of water on top of your wood-burning stove or radiator.

Deal with Drafts

A well-insulated house can help you save quite a bit on your heating bills (and cooling bills, too). New houses are often built with energy-efficient features such as thermal-paned windows, well-insulated walls, and energy-efficient water heaters and furnaces. If you don't live in a newer house, consider using some of the following ideas to increase the benefits of your home's current heating system.

>> Add a layer of air between your windows and the great outdoors (the air insulates much better than the window glass alone). Some ideas:

- If you have storm windows, use them.
- Stretch thick sheets of plastic across the inside of your window frames.
- Hang heavy curtains that you can pull closed at night. During the day, open your curtains, especially those on southern windows, for passive solar heating.
- After dark, hang blankets or quilts in front of the windows for added insulation. Install a decorative curtain rod above your existing window treatment, and then simply fold a blanket or quilt over the rod.

>> Use a draft stopper at the bottom of outside doors. You can make one, buy an inexpensive one, or roll up a bathroom towel and place it next to the bottom of the door.

>> Fill areas behind electric switch plates that are on outside walls with plastic foam or purchase plastic insulation that's already cut to size and made for this purpose.

>> Close the flue on your fireplace when you're not using it. Leaving a fireplace flue open is like having a vacuum hose hooked to your house, sucking the warm air right out the chimney.

#116
Making Your Own Cleaning Solutions

Y ou don't need a cabinet full of the latest cleaners from your local supermarket. Rather, a few simple household ingredients can provide all you need to keep your house and appliances sparkling.

REMEMBER

All cleaners, whether commercial or homemade, work best when left to sit for varying periods of time. Generally, the tougher the stain, the longer you let it sit to work.

White Vinegar

Full-strength white vinegar is an excellent cleaning option that kills many germs, bacteria, and molds. Keep a spray bottle of full-strength vinegar around the house, and spray it on countertops, toilet seats, doorknobs, and even cutting boards. Vinegar helps deodorize, and you can use it in your wash and get the same results as store-bought detergent additives.

Here are a few easy ideas for cleaning around the house with vinegar:

>> Use full-or half-strength vinegar for cleaning windows, mirrors, chrome, and tile. (Wash your windows with newspapers to cut down on the lint left behind from cloth or paper towels.)

>> To easily clean the microwave oven, heat ½ cup of white vinegar in a microwave-safe bowl or mug on high for 3 minutes. Let the vinegar sit undisturbed for about 15 minutes, and then remove the vinegar container and wipe down the inside of the microwave with a sponge and clear water.

>> Use full-strength vinegar in the rinse-aid container of your dishwasher.

>> Add ½ cup of white vinegar to the rinse cycle or pour it into the washing machine's fabric softener container to remove any leftover soap residue from the clothes. The clothes will smell clean and fresh.

Baking Soda

You can find bulk containers of baking soda in the baking supplies aisle of the supermarket. Baking soda is fairly inexpensive normally, but when you buy it in bulk, it's really a bargain. Baking soda works well for the following:

>> Mix a 50/50 paste of baking soda and water for scrubbing bathtubs, tile, sinks, chrome, and pots and pans. Rinse thoroughly with water.

>> Add about 1 teaspoon of baking soda to 1 cup of water, stir, and use in a spray bottle with a fine mist setting for an easy air freshener to spray around the room.

>> Add about ¼ cup of baking soda to the washing machine's rinse cycle as a fabric softener and odor remover.

>> Use a paste made from a mix of 50/50 baking soda and water to pretreat spots before putting clothes in the wash.

Bleach

When it comes to killing germs and removing household mildew, you won't find a less expensive disinfectant and cleaning agent than common household bleach. Here are some simple cleaning ideas that use bleach:

>> Use a 50/50 mixture of bleach and water to remove stubborn stains and mildew from tile and grout.

>> Pour a 50/50 bleach-and-water mix into teacups or coffee mugs with difficult stains. Allow them to soak overnight. The next day, pour out the bleach and water and wash the cup as usual.

WARNING

>> Mix 1 cup of bleach with 1 gallon of water for general cleaning and disinfecting, but be careful not to let the bleach mixture touch fabrics or anything that can have color bleached out of it (such as carpets, window treatments, clothing, and so on).

#117

Fixing Squeaky Floors

No matter what kind of finish flooring you may have — carpet, vinyl, tile, or hardwood — unless your home is built on a concrete slab, underneath it's wood. And it's that wood that causes the squeaks — well, sort of. Usually, the squeak is a loose nail rubbing inside the hole it was originally driven into. Lumber used to build homes contains a certain degree of natural moisture, which makes the wood easy to cut and minimizes splitting when it's being nailed together. Unfortunately, as the wood dries, it shrinks — a natural process that can take years. When the wood shrinks enough, once tightly seated nails can loosen and rub when the wood flexes below the pitter-patter of foot traffic, creating the familiar irritating sound: a floor squeak.

TIP

If you have company coming or you're expecting houseguests for a week and you don't have time to make the repair, try this temporary fix: talcum powder. Talcum powder works particularly well in quieting a squeaky hardwood floor or wood stairs. Sprinkle a generous amount of the stuff wherever the floor makes noise. Work the powder into the joints and around any exposed nail heads. Make sure that you completely remove the excess powder because it can make the floor dangerously slippery. The relief lasts for a few weeks or months.

TIP

The first step in repairing a floor squeak is to find the nail that's rubbing up against the wood floor — a task akin to finding a needle in a haystack. Here's a trick to pinpoint a floor squeak so you can make a repair: Use a short length of garden hose as a stethoscope. Hold one end of the hose to your ear and the other end on the floor while someone else walks across the floor to make it squeak. If you can listen to the floor from a basement or subarea, the makeshift stethoscope yields more accurate results.

If the problem is a loose *subfloor* (the wood floor beneath the carpet, vinyl, hardwood, and so on), the repair can get sticky depending upon the type of finish flooring you have. However, if access below is available (that is, you can get to the subfloor through the basement or crawlspace), installing a wood shim shingle between the subfloor and the floor joist is a quick and easy means of preventing the subfloor from flexing, and it quiets the squeak. Just squirt some carpenter's glue on the thin end of the shingle and tap it in with a hammer.

TIP

Another means of quieting a squeaking floor by preventing it from flexing is a nifty gadget called a Squeak-Ender. It consists of a metal plate and threaded-rod assembly that's screwed to the underside of the subfloor and a steel bracket. You slip the bracket beneath the joist and over the threaded rod; then you tighten a nut onto the rod to pull down the floor and close the gap. For more information on the Squeak-Ender, go to www.squeakender.com.

If access below isn't available, after you locate the culprit nail, the next step is to create a better connection. Don't use nails to make the repair — use screws. Just follow these steps:

1. Locate the squeak using the method discussed earlier.

2. Near the existing squeaking nail, drill a small pilot hole through the carpet, pad, and wood subfloor and into the floor joist.

The floor joist is the horizontal floor framing member that the wood subfloor is attached to. Drilling a small pilot hole makes the job easier. You can leave the old nail in place or, if it's loose, remove it using a nail puller or pry bar.

3. **Drive a construction screw into the pilot hole, through the carpet, pad, and so on.**

   When working on a hardwood floor, *countersink* (recess) the screw head so that it can be concealed with hardwood putty. Use a putty knife to install hardwood putty. Touch up the floor finish with 400- to 600-grit wet/dry sandpaper.

Construction screws are easy to drive and grip like crazy. You can purchase ones with a finish head (like a finish nail), which makes them a particularly good choice when working on a hardwood floor. You simply countersink them slightly and putty over them. You can also drive them directly through the carpet, pad, and sub-floor and into a floor joist. A construction screw's course threads and really sharp tip make it the perfect fastener for old, dry wood. The sharp tip gets through harder lumber easier, and the course screw threads go in faster and hold better.

If you do decide to use nails, choose a ring shank nail, which has a barbed shank for superior holding power. (Ask a clerk at the hardware store to help you find these nails if you don't know what they look like.) Like construction screws, ring shank nails can be driven through the carpet and pad; however, due to the size of the nail head, they aren't a good choice for hardwood flooring.

If the squeak persists, it may mean that your foundation has settled, in which case pier post shimming may be required. This process is similar to installing a shim shingle. Instead, the shingle is inserted between the top of the pier post and the bottom of the girder. Coat the end of the shingle with glue and tap it in snuggly using a hammer. And if you're still struggling with a squeaking floor? Major foundation settlement or an out-of-level floor could be the problem.

#118
Extending the Life of Your Roof

Because shingles become more flexible when warm, this task is best saved for a sunny day. Here's all you have to do:

1. Fold back the shingle(s) above the one to be removed.

2. Use a flat pry bar to remove the nails that hold the damaged shingle in place.

3. Slip a new shingle in position to replace the one that was removed.

4. Nail the new shingle in place by using a flat pry bar as a hammer extension.

With this technique you can drive a nail in from beneath an overlapping shingle: First, press the nail into the shingle by hand. After the nail is in place, position the bottom of the flat bar so the straight end rests atop the nail head. As the hammer strikes the flat bar, the offset below drives the nail home.

#119
Fixing Roof Leaks

The first step in repairing a roof leak is finding its point of origin. Although finding a leak on a flat roof can be extremely difficult and should be left to an industry professional, do-it-yourselfers can find a leak on a pitched roof. To water test your roof, you need two people, one on the roof and one in the attic (or living space below if you don't have an attic). You also need a ladder, a garden hose, and a flashlight.

Although water testing a pitched roof isn't a difficult process, it can be time-consuming and tedious, so be patient. Follow these steps:

1. **Station your partner in the attic and tell them to holler at the first sign of water.**

2. **Use the garden hose to run a modest amount of water over the roof at a point below the area where a leak is suspected.**

   Work from the lowest point of the roof (near the eaves or gutters) in an area about 4 to 6 feet wide. Work your way up the roof a couple of feet at a time. Stand on dry roofing above the water to help prevent a slip.

Don't run the hose full blast. Don't use a spray nozzle, and don't force the water between the shingles. Doing so may force water into the home, creating the illusion that you've found a leak when, in fact, you did nothing more than temporarily create one.

3. **The moment your helper sees water, they should let you know.**

   A wailing screech usually does the trick. Or use your cellphones to communicate without yelling. Mark the spot with chalk.

After you find the leak, hire a contractor to repair it.

#120
Prolonging the Life of Your Siding

No siding surface is perfect; no material perfectly withstands the rigors of nature and the force of the elements. But you can do a thing or two to add life and beauty to your home's siding.

Vinyl Siding

Vinyl siding doesn't warp, split, or buckle and, according to what several manufacturers espouse, it doesn't ever have to be painted. Actually, it can't be painted — paint simply will not stick to vinyl in the same way it sticks to wood or aluminum.

Like all types of exterior siding, vinyl does have its shortcomings. Over time, its surface oxidizes. As the surface deteriorates, the pitted result causes the material to become dull and prone to stain. The only way to combat this problem is to regularly clean the siding. Twice a year is good — once in the spring and then again in the fall. Use a pressure washer with laundry detergent to get the surface sparkling clean.

Keeping the surface of the vinyl clean won't prevent it from oxidizing, but it will prevent corrosive chemicals in the air from attacking the surface.

Stucco

Stucco is cool stuff. It doesn't rot, and compared to other types of siding, it's relatively easy to maintain. Stucco is very porous and holds on to paint better than most other kinds of siding. Also, it's one of the easiest surfaces to prepare and paint. So, if you have stucco, count your blessings.

The most challenging stucco maintenance is crack repair. Stucco's tough but brittle surface sometimes can be a drawback. When the house shifts, rigid things crack.

REMEMBER

You can turn your home into an interstate road map of ugly, obvious crack repairs if you aren't careful. When it comes to stucco crack repair, less is more. Don't try to patch every crack. Hairline cracks and those that you can't get your fingernail into should not be patched; in fact, paint usually will fill those cracks. Wider cracks (those up to ¼ inch wide) should be filled with a high-quality, exterior-grade, acrylic latex caulk. Have a damp sponge handy to wipe away excess caulk that escapes.

Just follow these simple steps:

1. **Clean all loose debris from the crack.**

   The V end of an old-fashioned can opener and a vacuum cleaner work wonders here.

2. **Use a paintable silicone caulk — and your finger — to make an invisible repair.**

   Don't use a putty knife because it prevents you from matching the existing texture. And don't use just any caulk; use the 50-year kind, which really does hold better and longer than the other types.

3. **With a damp sponge, wipe off the excess caulking in all directions.**

4. **While the caulk is still wet, place fine texturing sand into the palm of your hand and, holding your hand in front of the caulking, blow across the sand to scatter it onto the surface of the damp caulk.**

   The sand makes the patch less obvious and prevents the road-map effect by helping the caulk blend into the surrounding finish.

You can repair wider cracks and gouges with a stucco patching compound. Follow mixing instructions carefully because the amount of water you use can change the properties of the compound. If the properties of the compound change, it may not hold as well. Follow these steps:

1. **Clean all loose debris from the crack or gouge.**

2. **Use a latex patching product and a putty knife or trowel to fill the area.**

3. **Apply a second coat to match the surface texture.**

   Thin the patching compound to a pancake-batter consistency. Dip the end of a paintbrush into the mixture. Holding your hand between the wall and the paintbrush, slap the handle of the brush against your hand. The patching compound splatters onto the surface, matching the texture of the stucco. If the texture is flat, wait for the splattering to become slightly firm and then wipe it to the desired flatness with a putty knife or a trowel.

Wood Siding

When wood's moisture content reaches 20 percent to 30 percent, fungi deep within its fibers begin to grow and flourish, causing dreaded wood rot. To prevent wood rot, treat your wood siding with an application of oil, stain, or paint. These materials act as a barrier, preventing water from coming into direct contact with the wood.

Which finish you choose is mostly an aesthetic choice, although practicalities like ease of application, how long lasting the finish is, and so on are also factors:

» Oil, a clear finish, is absorbed into the wood and fills all pores and voids, displacing water that would otherwise be absorbed. It's easier to apply than paint, and if the oil is clear (or almost clear), mistakes are nearly impossible to detect. In addition, oil doesn't split, chip, or blister. Unfortunately, oil tends to evaporate and doesn't last as long as paint.

» Oil stain is the same as oil except that a pigment has been mixed into the oil. The added pigment makes application of oil stains slightly more difficult (mistakes show more readily). But the pigment also helps filter out more of the sun's damaging ultraviolet rays. Like oil, oil stains don't split, chip, or blister. The more wood that you can see when the job is complete, the more often you can expect to redo the finish.

» Paint penetrates and protects in the same way that oil does. Additionally, paint coats the surface of the wood with a thin, durable waterproof hide. Paint certainly lasts longer, but it is the most difficult to apply and is more prone to chipping, splitting, and blistering.

REMEMBER

Everything's a trade-off. With oil you won't ever have to sand, scrape, or chisel the surface to prepare it for another application. But be ready to reapply a new coat every several years. With an oil stain, figure about three to five years of lasting quality. A good grade of paint, applied to a properly cleaned surface, lasts seven to ten years or more.

The exterior of your home is no small area, so when it comes to preparation (removing old layers of loose paint, a tattered layer of stain, a discolored layer of wood, or just plain dirt), you can expect to do some major work. Fortunately, tools like sand blasters, soda washers, and pressure washers are available at home centers, paint stores, and rental outlets; these tools help make cleanup and removal an almost fun job. Our personal choice is a pressure washer.

To prepare surfaces for repainting, follow these steps:

1. **Completely remove all old loose paint and sand the spots where a painted surface meets a bare spot.**

   A new coat of paint won't stick any better than the old paint below it; that's why removing all loose paint is so important, and tapering or feathering these transition points makes them less visible and guarantees a nicer looking finished product.

2. **Prime all bare spots with a high-grade oil-based primer.**

Tinting a standard white primer a shade or two lighter than the finish coat can improve coverage. For example, a light-brown finish coat covers a beige primer more effectively than it covers a white primer.

3. **Caulk all joints with a high-grade, 50-year, paintable silicone or polyurethane product.**

Doing so prevents water from getting behind the siding.

Now you're ready to paint.

To prepare an oiled surface for refinishing, clean the wood with a pressure washer, apply a coat of wood bleach, let it stand (following the manufacturer's instructions), and pressure-wash again. At this point, the wood is ready for a fresh coat of oil or oil stain. Your oiled siding will look so good, you won't believe you did it yourself!

#121
Using Less Energy

Saving money on electricity and gas utilities can be as easy as making a few minor adjustments in your day-to-day life. Every penny and dime saved add up to a considerable amount of money day after day. The following tips, when combined together, can help cut your electricity and gas use considerably.

>> Wash clothes in cold water. The majority of electricity used for washing clothes is used to heat the water. Save hot water washes for white towels, socks, and undergarments.

>> Wash only full loads in the washing machine and dishwasher.

>> You use less electricity to heat a cup of water in the microwave than on the stovetop. When you're boiling water on the stove, always keep the pot covered because water boils much faster in an enclosed pot. Or use a teakettle. Don't boil more water than you actually need to use, or you're wasting energy to heat water that's just going to cool off again or end up dumped down the drain.

>> If you're preparing food and the recipe says something like, "Heat to a boil; then simmer for five minutes," don't simmer! Just heat it to a boil, cover the pan tightly, turn off the burner, and let the whole thing sit undisturbed for 5 to 10 minutes. It actually simmers and stays hot long enough to cook your soup, ramen noodles, oatmeal, or instant rice.

» Keep indoor lights off during the daytime. Position your desk near a window for adequate lighting.

» Turn off your computer, printer, scanner, monitor, and any other office equipment at night. Even when they're turned off, a lot of devices (TVs, for example) use electricity. Instead of trying to remember to unplug each device every night, plug them all into power strips that can be flipped off easily.

» Find out whether your local energy provider has off-peak hours when electricity use is less expensive. If they do, do your laundry and run the dishwasher accordingly.

» Many power companies allow users to pay a flat rate every month of the year, so they don't have really high energy bills in the heat of the summer and dead of winter. If the total energy use is higher or lower than the amount paid over the course of the year, the extra amount will be charged or refunded accordingly the next year.

» If you have an outdoor pool or pond, circulate the water for only one hour per day. Set it on a timer so that you don't forget.

» Put a timer on your hot water heater so it runs for only four hours total each day during peak use times (morning showers, evening dishes, and children's bath times).

» Use a programmable thermostat in your house that you can set it for different temperatures at different hours. This costs a bit upfront but can quickly recoup any money spent by not overheating the house all day while the family's at work and school or at night while everyone's sleeping.

#122
Keeping Your Fridge Running Well

Refrigerators are big, and they have many components to keep clean. You've got the exterior, the interior, the freezer, water lines, drain lines, and coils to worry about. Not that the maintenance they require is difficult — you just have to stay on top it to make sure the fridge does a good job of keeping everything cold.

Take Care of the Condenser Coils

The most important thing for any refrigerator is to keep the condenser coils clean. The coils are usually located at the bottom of the refrigerator behind a removable grille; on some older refrigerators, they're located on the back of the refrigerator. Air passing over these coils is what cools the refrigerator, and if they're dirty, the unit has to work harder to do its job.

To clean the coils, first unplug the refrigerator. Remove the grille by grabbing both ends and pulling gently. Use a vacuum cleaner with a brush or crevice attachment to get as far into and under the unit as possible (being careful not to force access, which can bend condenser tubing and the thin metal coil fins). While the grille is off, also remove the refrigerator drain pan and wash it.

Typically located inside your refrigerator is an electric heater power switch. It controls small electric heaters that keep the outside of the cabinet from sweating. Only turn the switch on when it's humid and you see moisture beads. When both the weather and your refrigerator are dry, turn this switch off to save energy costs. The electric heater also helps prevent rust and nasty mold buildup.

Clean the Gasket

The chilled air inside a refrigerator is kept there primarily by a gasket at the perimeter of the door. In good condition, it provides a good airtight seal. It can get tired and worn, or hard, and also is a prime candidate for mold. Here's how to take care of it:

>> **Every six months or so, check the gasket to make sure it's in good condition.** How can you tell if your gasket is in good condition? Place a dollar bill between the gasket and the door jamb. If it's difficult to pull out, the gasket is okay. If it pulls out easily, you need to replace the gasket.

>> **Wipe the gasket every few months with a wet cloth, making sure to get all the surfaces and to go completely around the door.** If the gasket seems a bit hard, apply a light coat of lemon oil, mineral oil, or any type of body lotion with lanolin.

>> **As soon as you notice any mold around the gasket, remove it.** To do so, clean it with a solution of liquid chlorine bleach and water (4 tablespoons of bleach in 1 quart of hot water), and scrub well with an old toothbrush. Afterwards, completely wipe off all residue with warm water and a mild, liquid dish soap.

>> **Always wipe off any food or liquid spills, drips, and runs from around the door and gaskets.** If you don't, they dry and become sticky, possibly ripping away the gasket when you open the door.

>> **If the gasket has pulled away in spots, stick it back down with a little contact cement.** Use a Popsicle stick to neatly smear a small blob of glue into the gap and hold it in place for 10 seconds. Then close the door. Make sure there is nothing sticky where the gasket meets the refrigerator — otherwise, your work will be in vain.

Defrost the Freezer and Drain Line

Defrost your freezer when ice begins to build up on the interior. Aside from decreasing usable freezer space, the ice can prevent the door from sealing properly. Most freezers need to be defrosted at least once and sometimes twice each year. Start by turning off the power to the freezer and removing all the contents. You can allow the ice to melt on its own or you can speed things up by placing a pot of hot water in the freezer and closing the door. Clean the interior of the freezer using the same method described for cleaning the interior.

While you're defrosting the freezer, defrost the freezer drain line leading to the drain pan, too. (This task needs to be done at least once a year.) Mold buildup starts retaining moisture, which, in turn, starts freezing and ultimately completely blocks the line. Here's how to defrost the drain line:

1. Turn off the freezer (so that you can melt the ice in the drain line).

2. Put very hot water into a turkey baster and insert it into the ½-inch drain hole located at the back of the freezer floor.

3. Release the hot water into the line until it runs free.

4. Blast in more hot water to blow out any mold buildup.

5. Put 2 tablespoons of chlorine bleach in 1 cup of hot water and pour it down the drain to kill off any remaining mold spores.

All this liquid should be running into the drain pan at the bottom of the unit. Make sure it doesn't overflow, and empty and clean the drain pan when you're done.

Maintain Inline Water Filtration

Many, if not most, refrigerators offer automatic ice makers and water dispensers. A filter somewhere under the unit ensures clean ice and water. Typically, the only maintenance required is periodically changing the filter. Many units even have a red-light/green-light alert to tell you when the filter needs to be replaced. You can order the filters from the manufacturer, get them at an appliance parts dealer, and may even find them at your home center or the retailer that sold the unit. Consult your owner's manual to get step-by-step filter-replacement instructions.

#123
Insulating to Save Energy Costs

Most home-maintenance projects save you money over time. But only a few of them produce an immediate and measurable return. Maintaining an energy-efficient home is one such project, and one of the best ways to do this is to make sure everything's properly insulated.

Attic Insulation

If you have loose fill insulation, look to see whether the insulation in your attic has shifted. If some areas of your ceiling are bare, solve the problem by using a plastic lawn rake to gently move the insulation from high spots onto the bald areas. (Be sure to use a plastic rake; with electrical wires present in the attic, it wouldn't be wise to use a metal rake.) You can also use a piece of batt insulation to cover a hole. Simply use a razor knife to cut batt insulation to the approximate length required and lay it in place.

If your insulation appears to be in good shape, but you still feel a chill, you may need to add more. Check with your local public utility or a local building inspector for advice on what to do.

WARNING

Keep attic insulation clear of light fixtures. If the light boxes are covered with insulation, they can overheat, and a fire can result. And above all, don't plug attic vents. An attic must be able to breathe; otherwise, trapped hot air can convert even the best insulated home into a sweatbox on a hot summer day. In addition, a buildup of humidity can occur, which over time can result in wood rot, mildew, mold, and fungus growth.

Wall Insulation

Adding insulation to a wall is a bit more difficult than adding it to an attic. In an attic, the insulation is usually exposed. In a wall, the insulation resides between the interior and exterior wall coverings. To insulate a wall, you have to either remove the wall covering or create small penetrations and blow the insulation into the wall cavity. It's simply not cost-effective to remove a wall covering to insulate the wall cavity. Therefore, blown insulation is usually used to insulate the walls of a completed home.

Because wall studs are spaced every 16 inches or so, penetrations to add insulation must be made at the same intervals, thus filling one cavity at a time. In some homes, a horizontal block exists midway between the top and bottom of a wall cavity. In such cases, two penetrations must be made into each cavity: one above the horizontal block and one below it.

Floor Insulation

An insulated floor substantially reduces the loss of heat, helps to eliminate mildew-and rot-causing condensation, and generally helps to keep your toes warm when you go barefoot through the kitchen.

Periodically crawl beneath your home with a flashlight to check the condition of the floor insulation in your basement or sub-area. You want to ensure that it's properly positioned. Sagging is the biggest problem. Floor insulation is normally held in place (between the floor joist) with netting or bailing wire attached from one joist-bottom to another. If the insulation netting sags, reattach or replace it.

Lightning rods (named for their speedy installation) are a handy alternative to netting or bailing wire when maintaining sagging floor insulation. These lightweight, flexible steel rods hold the insulation in place by spring tension. You place one end of the rod against the side of a floor joist and bend it slightly so the other end is forced into place against the face of the opposite joist. Use one hand to hold the insulation up and the other hand to whip the lightning rod into place.

#124
Insulating Pipes

Putting insulation around all accessible water pipes saves energy, prevents freezing during most moderate to medium chills, and reduces condensation when pipes flow through attics and crawlspaces.

Properly maintained pipe insulation can be cheap insurance. A pipe that bursts in the attic can destroy a substantial portion of your home before the leak is stopped.

Be sure the tape that holds the insulation in place is in good shape, and make sure the insulation is still in good condition as well. If either the insulation or the tape crumbles to the touch, the material should be replaced.

Pre-formed, tubular, foam pipe insulation is slit lengthwise for easy installation. All you have to do is open the slit and lay the insulation onto the pipe. Pipe insulation comes in 6-foot lengths and is easy to cut with scissors or a razor knife.

#125
Insulating Heat Ducts

As with other kinds of insulation, the material that surrounds your heat ducts reduces energy costs while improving the effectiveness of your central heating and cooling system. It also helps prevent unwanted condensation in attics and crawlspaces, thereby reducing the chance for mold, mildew, and the foul odors associated with them.

Wrap insulation around and around the duct in a corkscrew fashion. Air currents, rodents, house movement, and vibration in the heating system can cause the insulation to loosen and fall away from the ducting. While you're there, add an extra layer if your budget allows. It can't hurt.

TIP

You can hold insulation together by "stitching" a nail into it. Simply insert the nail the same way a seamstress uses a sewing pin to hold two pieces of fabric together.

#126
Stopping Air Leaks

Air leaks mean excessive energy loss — and cost. Summer or winter, you don't want your house to leak air, especially when you spend your money warming or cooling it.

Air Leaks around Windows

Test a window for leaks by holding a lighted candle near all its joints and connections. If the candle flickers, you have an air leak. Check

>> Where one section of the window meets another

>> Where the windows meet the frame

>> Where the frame meets the wall

To fix air leaks, try these tactics:

>> **Caulk around the window.** Often air leaks at a window result from a breakdown in the connection between the frame of the window and the frame of the house. To prevent leaks, caulk the window where its frame meets the exterior

siding. If the window is surrounded by wood trim, seal all gaps between the trim and the siding (and the trim and the window frame) with a high-grade polyurethane caulk.

» **Replace the weatherstripping.** Leaks occur when weatherstripping wears out. You may have to remove the operable portion of the window to find the weatherstripping. Most home centers sell replacement weatherstripping in peel-and-stick rolls. If you aren't sure about what to do, take the section you removed to the store with you, or snap a picture of the area that needs attention and take it with you.

» **Inject foam sealant between the frame of the window and the frame of the house.** Foam sealant is a major deterrent to air infiltration and also prevents water from leaking into the house.

Air Leaks around Doors

An air leak in a door frame is pretty common. As the moisture content changes in soil, your home shifts. Your doors also shift, creating gaps large enough for a dump truck to pass through.

You can add foam sealant between the frame of the door and the frame of the house by removing the interior door casing. The casing is the wood trim that covers the joint between the door frame and the wall. Use a flat pry bar to slowly remove the trim so you don't damage it.

Other air leaks can occur between the door and the door frame. An easy-to-find and easy-to-install weatherstripping consists of a rubber bead attached lengthwise to a strip of metal. Standing outside the door, with the door in the closed position, gently press the rubber portion of the weatherstripping against the door and frame at the same time. Attach the metal section of the weatherstripping to the door frame with the nails or screws provided. Here, oblong holes allow the weatherstripping to be adjusted later as house movement causes the door to shift.

#127
Identifying and Fixing Plumbing Leaks

Water leaks can be expensive, not only for the damage they cause (think rot and mildew), but also because you're stuck paying for the leaking water, even if, as is the case with some leaks, you don't know you have one.

TIP

If you're on a public water system, you have a water meter somewhere on or near your property. Besides telling you how much water you're using, it can also help you detect leaks. Take a meter reading, and then turn off every plumbing fixture in your house (including the built-in icemaker or other water-consuming appliances) for a couple of hours. After everything is off, take another meter reading. If the reading changes, you have a leak. You can tell how much water you've used in any given timeframe by subtracting the first reading from the second reading. A cubic foot contains 7½ gallons of water.

If you find a leak, you need to identify where it's coming from and fix it or call a professional to help out. Being prepared to defend your home's plumbing system against a sudden burst pipe can save you thousands of dollars in damage. Think of these quick, easy fixes as plumbing first aid — they slow or stop a leak long enough to give you time to enlist the services of a qualified plumber during business hours.

TIP

To temporarily stop a pinhole leak, you need to apply pressure to the opening. The solution? Wrap duct tape around the pipe. In many instances, it supplies the necessary pressure. Unfortunately, duct tape doesn't always give you enough pressure. In that case, you need to move to a more robust fix.

Another way to temporarily stop a small leak involves a C-clamp, a block of wood, and a piece of rubber. *Note:* Because the block of wood is flat (and the pipe is round), it can only create pressure along a very narrow area of the pipe.

Follow these steps:

1. Turn off the water at the main shut-off valve.

2. Place a piece of rubber over the area where the pipe is leaking.

3. Put the block of wood on top of the piece of rubber.

4. Open the C-clamp wide enough to surround the pipe, the gasket material, and the block of wood.

5. Place the stationary part of the opening of the C-clamp against the pipe (opposite the location of the leak) and the screw part of the C-clamp against the block of wood.

   Tighten the screw clamp until it's snug.

A sleeve clamp stops everything from pinhole leaks to larger leaks. A sleeve clamp consists of two semicircular pieces of metal that, when put together, completely surround the pipe — hence, the name *sleeve*. The clamp is about 3 inches long, but you have to buy one to fit your specific pipe size — a sleeve clamp made to repair ½-inch pipe is smaller than one needed to repair ¾-inch pipe.

Other than the sleeve clamp, you only need a screwdriver. Here's how it works:

1. Wrap the damaged section of pipe with the gasket material provided.

2. Surround the gasket-wrapped pipe with the two semicircular clamps.

3. Tighten the screws that connect the two halves of the sleeve clamp.

#128
Improving Water Heater Efficiency

f your water heater is located in a garage or basement, or you don't want the heat the water heater emits into the area, install a heavy insulation blanket — R-11 or better. Doing so improves the water heater's energy efficiency and reduces the ambient heat. The R value relates to the thickness of the blanket — the higher the R value, the thicker the blanket, and the more insulating horsepower.

You can purchase a water heater insulation blanket as a kit based on the size of the heater — 30, 40, 50 gallons, and so on. The kit contains a blanket that has white vinyl on the outside and raw insulation on the inside and enough adhesive tape to finish the seams.

If you have a gas water heater, wrap the blanket all the way around and from the top to just below the controller. Don't worry if the blanket seems a bit short. Remember, the bottom of the tank is several inches above the very bottom of the water heater.

WARNING

Don't wrap the top because the insulation could catch fire from the heat being exhausted. Also, the blanket shouldn't cover the controller, the anode, or the pressure and temperature relief valve.

If you have an electric water heater, wrap the sides and the top (an electric water heater doesn't have an exhaust). But don't cover the access panels for elements; otherwise, these could overheat.

You don't need a blanket if your water heater is located where its lost heat can be felt and appreciated. Nor do you need one if you have a new water heater that's factory insulated with R-16 or better.

#129
Helping Your Furnace Work More Efficiently

The best way to ensure that your heating system is as energy efficient as it can be is to do routine maintenance. If you have an electric system, it requires virtually no maintenance. In fact, you have to do only two things: Vacuum the convectors once a month (if you have them) and pay the electricity bill.

Routine annual inspection and cleaning by a qualified, licensed contractor can keep your system running for many years without trouble. Don't be pennywise and pound-foolish. A dirty, inefficient furnace costs you ten times that much in wasted fuel. Beyond that, you can do the following:

>> **For forced-air systems:** Replace the furnace filter regularly (every month during the heating season, and every month year-round if an air-conditioning system is part of the same system) and check the ducts, which distribute warmed air to various locations throughout the house, for leaks. If you see fuzz or feel warm air coming out through the joints between duct segments, seal them with metal tape.

TIP

Although filters cost only a couple of bucks apiece, don't buy filters one at a time — get a whole case. They're cheaper by the dozen.

>> For hot-water systems: Most hot-water systems have only a single gauge, which measures three things: pressure, temperature, and altitude (the height of the water in the system). It's important to monitor the pressure. Most boilers run with only 12 to 15 pounds of pressure. The boiler can become seriously damaged and even dangerous if the pressure exceeds 30 pounds. If the pressure is abnormally high, you may have a waterlogged expansion tank that can be drained. You can drain the expansion tank yourself (use the owner's manual for information or a home-maintenance book for guidance) or call a repairperson.

You also may need to bleed the air out of the radiator. To do so, just turn the bleed valve about a quarter-turn counter-clockwise and keep the screwdriver or radiator key in the valve. If you hear a hissing sound, that's good — it's air escaping. As soon as the hissing stops and you see a dribble of water come out, close the valve.

WARNING

Don't open the valve more than is necessary; hot water will come rushing out before you can close it. At the very least, you'll make a wet mess. At the very worst, you could be scalded.

>> For steam systems: Most adjustments to your steam boiler should be performed by a pro. But you can do three important things yourself:

- **Check the steam gauge on a regular basis.** Make sure it's within the normal range. If it isn't, shut the system down immediately and call for service.

- **Check the safety valve every month.** Located on the top of the boiler, this valve vents excess pressure if the boiler goes crazy and exceeds safe levels. When the system is hot, push down on the handle to see whether steam comes out. Make sure to stand away from the outlet — the steam is boiling hot. If no steam comes out, call a serviceman to replace the valve immediately.

- **Check the water level once a month.** The water-level gauge has valves on each side. Open them both and make sure the water level is in the middle, and then close the valves. If you don't see any water, shut off the boiler, let it cool down, and add water.

#130
Saving on Your Vehicle Fuel Expenses

With rising fuel costs, increased emphasis on global warming, and the economic and political impact of dependency on fossil fuels, increasing fuel efficiency has become a major goal for federal and state governments and for most drivers, even if just to save money. The best way to avoid wasting fuel and dumping the unburned residue into the environment is to drive efficiently. But it doesn't end there: How well you maintain your vehicle has a major impact on its fuel economy because the more efficiently it operates, the less fuel it will burn and the less pollution it will add to the air. And there are other factors to consider as well.

Take a Look under the Hood

For your vehicle's best fuel economy, follow these recommendations to make sure that parts of your vehicle are in good condition and functioning properly:

>> If your air filter is dirty, you can lose one mile per gallon at 50 mph. Cleaning or replacing your air filter can cut your fuel

consumption, and if you cut it by only 10 percent, you can save an average of 77 gallons a year!

>> If your PCV valve isn't functioning properly, your engine runs less efficiently, and you may be burning and polluting your oil and the air, as well.

>> If your spark plugs are misfiring because they're dirty or improperly gapped, the problem can cost you up to 25 percent in gas mileage.

>> Consult your owner's manual for how often your vehicle needs a tune-up, and if it's overdue, have it done immediately. A simple tune-up can reduce carbon monoxide and hydrocarbon exhaust emissions by 30 to 50 percent. It also saves fuel and improves your vehicle's performance.

>> If the accessory belts that connect your fan, water pump, alternator, air conditioner, and a variety of other devices are too loose or too tight, a serious loss of efficiency can be the result. A belt should have about ½ inch of "give" and shouldn't be frayed or badly worn.

>> If a brake is poorly adjusted, it may "drag" while the vehicle is in motion. Moving the wheel against the dragging brake takes more power, which means that your brake linings and the fuel in your tank don't last as long. To check for dragging brakes, jack up each wheel and spin it. If a brake shoe or brake pad is dragging, you can feel it as you try to turn the wheel on the hub. If you have a hybrid vehicle with regenerative braking, a professional should check your brakes.

>> If you hear a rumbling sound while driving or when spinning the jacked-up wheel, your wheel bearings may be worn and may need to be replaced. The wheel bearings are in there to prevent friction, and if they're worn, it takes extra energy (think fuel) to turn the wheels and move the vehicle down the road.

Start Up without Warming Up

TIP

When you start your car in the morning, do you warm it up before you drive off? If you do, stop! Modern vehicles don't need much (if any) warm-up, and experts caution you not to indulge in lengthy warm-ups because they waste fuel, pollute the air, and increase wear on your vehicle.

Fill 'Er Up

Fuel economy involves more than altering driving techniques. How you pump gas affects your fuel consumption and can save you money as well. Keep the following points in mind the next time you fill up at a service station:

>> **In hot weather, fill up in the early morning or evening when the air is cooler and before gasoline is delivered to the station.** Like everything else, gasoline expands with heat. An increase of only 30 degrees can cause ten gallons of gas to expand by as much as four-fifths of a quart — that's as much as a bottle of whiskey! This expansion reduces its energy content, so you pay more for less when the fuel is hot.

WARNING

>> **Never overfill the tank.** When the filler hose clicks off automatically, resist the temptation to squirt in that extra little bit. An overfilled tank will run over and spill gasoline on the ground if you drive up a hill or park in the heat of the sun. Not only does this spillage waste fuel and dissolve asphalt on driveways and roadways, but the fumes also contribute substantially to air pollution.

Keep Your Side Windows Shut and the AC Turned off

Open side windows increase wind resistance, which reduces fuel efficiency. Use the interior vents or the sunroof instead. You may think that turning on the air conditioning in your vehicle is a good alternative to opening side windows, but it costs you mileage because your engine has to put out extra power to make the air conditioner work. Some air conditioners can consume an extra 2½ miles per gallon! So if you live in a fairly cool area, you may not want (or need) to use your vehicle's air conditioning at all.

Keep Your Tires Properly Inflated

Underinflated tires consume about one mile per gallon of extra gasoline. They wear out faster, too, so make sure that your tires get all they need. You can "read" your tires' treads to see whether they're properly inflated; find the proper pressure range on the sidewalls of your tires.

TIP

After a car has been driven for a while, the tires heat up and the air in them expands. Therefore, to get an accurate reading, always use your tire gauge in the morning before you drive the car, and if you need air, head to the nearest air pump and let the tires cool down before adding the proper amount of air.

#131
Adding Antifreeze

To keep the water in your car's cooling system from boiling or freezing, the water is mixed with *coolant* or *antifreeze*.

Today's engines require specially formulated coolants that are safe for aluminum components. There are long-life (sometimes called *extended life*) coolants with organic acid rust and corrosion inhibitors that promise to last for as long as five years. Automakers use some of these coolants as original fluid in new vehicle radiators made of aluminum (they can't be used in anything except aluminum radiators).

WARNING

Due to differences in Japanese, Korean, European, and American compounds, you can shorten coolant life by putting the wrong stuff in your vehicle's cooling system. So make sure that you use the automaker's recommended coolant to ensure the longest life and best protection for your vehicle.

TIP

If your cooling system is operating properly, you shouldn't have to keep adding liquid to it. But there are several situations when the coolant in your vehicle definitely should be changed:

>> If you haven't changed it in a year or in the past 20,000 miles

>> If your vehicle constantly loses liquid in the system and overheats easily

>> If you've frequently added plain water to your cooling system to the point where it's probably lowered the proportion of coolant to less than half the required 50/50 mixture

Many vehicles have a pressurized coolant recovery system called an *expansion tank* that makes opening the radiator unnecessary. These systems are considered sealed because the safety pressure cap is on the recovery reservoir rather than on the radiator. On these systems, you can check the level of liquid on the side of the plastic reservoir, and you just open the cap on the reservoir to check whether the coolant looks as though it needs changing or to add water and coolant.

You'll probably never need to open the cap on the radiator, but *if* you have to open the cap for any reason, make sure to fill the radiator to the top with a 50/50 mixture of coolant and water before replacing the cap. This addition bleeds the system by forcing any air that may have gotten into the system into the reservoir and out through its overflow pipe when the engine heats up.

Follow these basic steps when adding liquid to the coolant recovery system:

1. **Check the liquid level.**

   Look at the *outside* of the reservoir to see where the level of the liquid in it lies relative to the "MAX" and "MIN" lines embossed on the side.

2. **If the liquid level is low, add equal parts coolant and water to the reservoir.**

   Safely remove the pressure cap on the reservoir and add equal parts coolant and water until the level reaches the "MAX" line on the side of the container.

#132
Checking and Changing Your Oil

Checking and changing your oil is easy. In fact, unless your oil filter and/or oil drain plug is impossible to reach, you have good reasons to check and change your oil and oil filter yourself. It's cheaper, you know that the job's being done right, and it requires little time or effort.

Check Your Oil

Oil reduces the friction in your engine and keeps it running smoothly. You should check your oil at least once a month to make sure that there's enough oil and that it isn't contaminated.

TIP

Some European vehicles don't have an oil dipstick. If you can't find one on your vehicle, check the owner's manual for the proper way to check your oil.

To find out whether your vehicle needs oil, follow these steps:

1. **When the engine is cold (or has been off for at least ten minutes), pull out the dipstick (the one with a ring or other type of finger grip on the end of it that sticks out of the engine), and wipe it off on a clean, lint-free rag.**

   The location of the oil dipstick depends on whether your vehicle has an in-line engine (rear-wheel drive) or a transverse engine (front-wheel drive).

2. **Insert the stick back into the pipe.**

   If the dipstick gets stuck on the way in, turn it around. The pipe it fits into is curved, and the metal stick bends naturally in the direction of the curve if you put it back in the way it came out.

3. **Pull the dipstick out again and look at the film of oil on the end of the stick.**

   Note how high the oil film reaches on the dipstick and the condition of the oil and add or change the oil as needed.

TIP

   Oil turns black pretty quickly, but that doesn't affect the quality. Rub a little between your thumb and index finger; if it leaves a dirty smudge, it probably needs to be changed.

   If your oil looks clean enough but only reaches the "Add" level on the dipstick, you need to add oil. You can buy oil the next time you fill up with gas at the service station, or you can find it at auto supply stores, supermarkets, and discount stores.

   If the oil is dirty or smells of gasoline, it should be changed. You can pay a mechanic or an oil-change station to change it for you, but the task is easy and can save you a lot of money.

4. **Put the dipstick back into the pipe. You're done!**

Change Your Oil

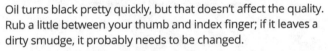

Always use a *system* when you do an oil change: *Do each part of the job in order, and don't change that order from job to job.* This may sound unduly restrictive if you like to improvise, but if you ignore this advice, you may find that you've added the new oil before replacing the oil drain plug or the oil filter. In either case, you wind up with your brand-new oil all over the ground and not enough oil in the engine to drive to the store for more. Also, the minute you replace the oil drain plug, *always* tighten it completely and — so that you won't forget it — put in the new oil immediately. (Don't laugh; people have forgotten and have ruined their engines in a couple of miles.)

Although the oil change process takes 17 steps to explain, it shouldn't take more than 15 minutes to accomplish after you buy the necessary stuff. Follow these easy steps to change your oil and oil filter:

1. **Either park on level ground or in such a way that the oil drain plug is at the lower end of the oil pan.**

2. **Before you begin work, be sure your gearshift is in Park or Neutral with the parking brake on; set out all your tools and equipment.**

   Place all the stuff you're going to use within easy reach so that you don't have to jump up and run around to the other side of the vehicle in the middle of the job.

3. **Warm up your engine for two or three minutes so that the gook gets churned up and can flow out of the engine easily.**

   You don't want the engine so hot that you burn yourself. When it's *slightly* warm, shut off the engine.

WARNING

4. **Use a work light or flashlight to look under your car.**

   You should be able to see and reach a large nut or plug located under the oil pan at the bottom of the engine.

   This is the oil drain plug. It unscrews with the aid of an adjustable wrench. If the plug is too hot to touch comfortably, let the engine cool off for a while longer.

   If you can't reach your oil drain plug easily and you still want to do this job yourself, you'll have to either crawl under your car to reach the plug or jack up the car.

5. **Push the oil-change container under the oil drain plug so that it can catch the oil.**

WARNING

   The oil may not come down vertically to start with; it may come out sideways from the direction the drain plug is facing. Allow room for that when you place the drain pan.

6. **Use your adjustable wrench to unscrew the oil drain plug until it's *almost* ready to come out.**

   Then protect your hand with the dirty rag or a disposable plastic glove and give the plug a last quick turn by hand to release it. *Pull your hand away quickly so that you don't get oil all over yourself.*

If the plug falls into the container, you can retrieve it later. The oil should drain out of your engine into the container (remember to retrieve the gasket if you're going to reuse it). While the oil drains, get out from under the vehicle and take a look under the hood.

7. **Remove the cap from the oil filler hole at the top of your engine.**

This large cap is easy to recognize: It lifts or screws right off, revealing a largish hole.

8. **Unscrew the oil filter using an oil filter wrench if you can't do it by hand.**

The oil filter looks like a tin can that's screwed onto the engine. Like most other things you find on a vehicle, the oil filter unscrews if you twist it counterclockwise. *The old filter will have oil in it, so be careful not to dump it on anything when you remove it.* If any remnants of the rubber seal from the old filter remain on your engine, scrape them off carefully, making sure they don't fall into the hole.

On some vehicles, you can easily reach the oil filter by leaning under the hood. Unfortunately, on other models the filter must be reached from under the vehicle. If your vehicle is one of these, you may have to jack the vehicle up to get at it.

9. **Empty the oil from the filter into the drain pan.**

Use a screwdriver to punch a hole in the dome of the can (which releases the pressure in the filter) and invert it in the drain pan to allow the oil to flow out. When the filter has drained *completely* (this can take as long as 12 hours), wrap it in newspaper and set it aside to take to a recycling center with your old oil.

10. **While the old oil drains out of the engine, open a new bottle of oil; dip a finger in the new oil and moisten the gasket on the top of the new oil filter.**

Then screw the new filter into the engine where the old one was.

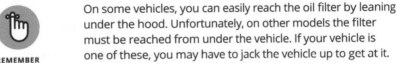

Follow directions on the filter, or turn it gently until it settles into place, and then turn it another three-quarter turn. Unless the filter manufacturer specifically recommends it or there isn't enough space to get your hand into the area, don't use an oil filter wrench to *tighten* the filter. It should fit tightly, but you don't want to crush the gasket or the filter will leak.

11. Reach under the vehicle again and use your dirty rag to wipe around the place where the oil drain plug goes.

12. Replace the oil drain plug and use an adjustable wrench to tighten it.

If your vehicle uses an oil drain plug gasket, make sure that the old one has been removed and lay a new gasket on the pan before you replace the plug.

13. After you install the oil filter and replace the oil drain plug, use a funnel — or just good aim — to pour all but one quart of fresh oil into the oil filler hole.

14. Replace the oil filler cap and run the engine for 30 to 60 seconds while you check for leaks from the oil drain plug and around the filter.

The oil pressure light on your dashboard should go out in 10 or 15 seconds (or if your vehicle has an oil pressure gauge, the needle should move off of "Low"). *Don't rev up your engine during this period.* Your oil pressure ranges from zero to low while the light is on and won't reach the proper pressure until your oil filter fills up. If the light doesn't go out, check under the vehicle and around the engine for leaks. Running the engine circulates oil into the new oil filter, and because filters hold from a half to a full quart of oil, you want to be sure that your filter is full to get an accurate reading on the oil dipstick.

15. Shut off the engine and wait five to ten minutes for the oil to settle into the oil pan.

Then remove the oil dipstick, wipe it with a clean, lint-free rag, and shove it back in. Pull it out again and check it.

Your owner's manual should tell you where the oil dipstick is on your engine.

16. Keep adding oil a little at a time and checking the stick until you reach the "Full" line on the dipstick.

17. Remove the drain pan from under the vehicle, drive around the block a couple of times, let the oil settle down again, and recheck the dipstick and the dashboard indicator.

Never keep running an engine or drive a vehicle that tells you its oil pressure is low. Because oil not only lubricates but also helps cool the engine, you can ruin your engine if you drive even a short distance with insufficient oil or with a defective oil pump.

#133
Taking Care of Your Tires

Tires don't require a great deal of maintenance, but the jobs in this section will pay off handsomely by increasing your tires' longevity, handling, and performance, as well as providing you with a more comfortable ride.

Check Tire Pressure

The single most important factor in caring for your tires is maintaining the correct inflation pressure. True, most newer vehicles have the built-in pressure-monitoring systems, but there are still many vehicles on the road without them.

TIP

If your vehicle doesn't have a pressure-monitoring system, check your tires at least once a month and before every long trip to see that they're properly inflated. Tires that are correctly inflated tend to wear properly in spite of minor weather ups and downs. *Underinflated* tires wear out faster, create excessive heat, increase fuel consumption, and make the vehicle harder to handle. *Overinflated* tires can blow out more easily, wear out faster, and make the vehicle unstable and unsafe to handle.

TIP

Check tire pressure in the morning before you start out or when you've driven less than a mile. If you drive more than that, your tires will heat up and the air will expand, so you won't get an accurate reading.

WARNING

If the weather has changed radically, it's time to check pressure again. In hot weather, the pressure in your tires rises by one pound per square inch *(psi)* of pressure for every 10 degrees Fahrenheit as the air in them heats up and expands. This can result in overinflation. Conversely, in cold weather, the pressure falls by one degree for every 10 degree drop as the cold air contracts, so your tires can end up underinflated. Therefore, if the weather gets very cold — and it looks as though it will stay that way for some time — and if you get a low reading, you may want to add a bit of air to your tires to bring the pressure back up.

Here's how you check the air pressure in your tires:

1. **Buy an accurate tire gauge at a hardware store or auto supply store.**

2. **Determine the proper air pressure for your tires by looking for the proper inflation pressure on the tire decal.**

   You can find the tire decal on one of the doors, door pillars, glove box, console, or trunk. Sometimes the tire decal specifies one pressure for the front tires and a different pressure for the rear tires.

WARNING

   Don't consult the tire's sidewall for the proper inflation pressure. The sidewall lists the *maximum* pressure that the tire is capable of handling, not the pressure that's best for performance and wear (unless you're carrying heavy loads).

3. **Remove the little cap from the tire valve that sticks out of your tire near the wheel rim.**

   You don't have to remove your wheel cover or hubcap for this step.

4. **Place the open, rounded end of the tire gauge against the valve so that the little pin in the gauge contacts the pin in the valve.**

5. **Press the gauge against the valve stem.**

   You'll hear a hissing sound as air starts to escape from the tire. At this point, a little stick will emerge from the other end of the tire gauge valve. It emerges partway almost as soon as the air starts to hiss and stops emerging almost immediately.

6. **Without pushing the stick back in, remove the gauge from the tire valve.**

7. **Look at the stick without touching it.**

   There are little numbers on it; pay attention to the last number showing. The last number is the amount of air pressure (in psi) in your tire. Does the gauge indicate the proper amount of pressure recommended on the decal?

   If the pressure seems too low, push the stick back in and press the gauge against the valve stem again. If the reading doesn't change, you need more air.

TIP

Instead of a stick, some tire gauges feature a dial on the face of the gauge that shows the air pressure, and digital tire pressure gauges are becoming increasingly common. If you have one, just check to see if the needle on the dial — or the digital readout — shows the correct psi. If it doesn't, you need to add air to the tire until the reading is correct.

8. **Repeat Steps 3 through 7 for each tire.**

   Run-flat tires and little temporary spare tires can lose pressure over time, so be sure to check them, too.

REMEMBER

9. **Add air, if necessary, by following the steps in the next section.**

Add Air to Your Tires

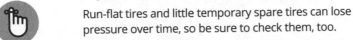

If your tires appear to be low, check the pressure according to the steps in the preceding section and note the amount that they're underinflated. Then drive to a local gas station.

TIP

Be sure to bring some change (usually quarters) with you for the air dispenser. (Forget about things being "as free as air" — at many stations it isn't!)

Follow these steps to add air to your tires:

1. **Park your vehicle so that you can reach all four tires with the air hose.**

2. **Remove the cap from the tire valve on the first tire.**

3. **Use *your* tire gauge to check the air pressure in the tire and see how much it has changed since your last reading (tests have shown that tire gauges on the air hoses at many gas stations are inaccurate).**

The pressure will have increased because driving causes the tires to heat up and the air inside them to expand. To avoid overinflating the tire, no matter what the second reading indicates, you should only add the same amount of air that the tire lacked before you drove it to the station.

4. **Use the air hose to add air in short bursts, checking the pressure after each time with *your* tire gauge.**

5. **If you add too much air, let some out by pressing the pin on the tire valve with the back of the air hose nozzle or with the little knob on the back of the rounded end of the tire gauge.**

6. **Keep checking the pressure until you get it right.**

Don't get discouraged if you have to keep adjusting the air pressure. No one hits it on the head the first time!

#134
Easily Making Other Automotive Checks and Fixes

The major goals of preventive maintenance are

» To keep your vehicle from breaking down on the road

» To catch minor problems before they become major expenses

» To prevent premature wear and tear by keeping parts from wearing each other away and by removing objects that could damage your vehicle's interior and its occupants

» To safeguard warranties and guarantees on your vehicle and its parts

The tips in the following sections tell you what you need to do to keep your vehicle running better, longer. Check out Tips #130 to #133 for additional tasks.

Do a Monthly Under-the-Hood Check

If you take 15 minutes to do an under-the-hood check, you can prevent 70 percent of the reasons your vehicle might break down on the road! At least be sure to check the following fluid levels once a month: oil, coolant, automatic transmission fluid, brake fluid, power steering fluid, and windshield washer fluid. Refill or replace these fluids as necessary.

Keep the Interior Clean

The cleaner you keep the interior of your vehicle, the longer the upholstery and carpets will remain in good condition. Remove the mats and vacuum them along with the upholstery, headliner, and carpeting when they start to get dirty or every time you wash your vehicle. Wipe up spills and get rid of stains as they occur *before* they have a chance to set and become permanent. If it's too late to prevent stains, consult a stain-removal guide for the ways to avoid making the stain bigger or permanent. Use an odor remover to keep the interior of your vehicle smelling fresh.

TIP

Keep trash and personal effects in receptacles, and keep kids' toys stashed in a box that fits snugly on the floor behind the front seat. If you have to stop short, these things can become lethal projectiles. Unsecured objects on the floor or under the driver's seat can wedge under brake and accelerator pedals.

Wash the Vehicle Frequently and Keep It Out of the Sun

Wash your vehicle once a week to protect paint and prevent rust. Work in the shade; sunlight on cleaners can ruin the finish of the paint. If water doesn't bead up on the car when it rains or when you hose it down, it needs waxing. Wax at least twice a year, in the spring and fall, to protect your car from weather extremes and preserve its finish.

Change the Filters

Changing your air, fuel, and oil filters regularly can help extend the life of your vehicle, increase its fuel efficiency, and improve its performance:

» **Air filters keep dirt out of fuel injection systems and carburetors.** Your vehicle runs on a mixture of fuel and air, so if air can't flow freely through a dirty filter, you pay the price in fuel consumption and performance. Change the filter every 20,000 miles, and more frequently if you drive in dusty areas like deserts or near construction sites.

» **Fuel filters help prevent rust and sediment from entering the engine.** Change the fuel filter at every tune-up — more often if you regularly drive with an almost-empty fuel tank. (Not a good idea!)

» **Oil filters clean the oil and remove metal and dirt that, in circulating through an engine, create friction between moving parts, damage the engine, and wear it out prematurely.** Change the oil filter every time you change your oil.

#135
Choosing an Automotive Service Facility

Several kinds of shops repair and service vehicles: dealerships, chain stores, specialists, and independents. How do you decide which is the right shop for you when your car needs more work than you can handle? Each has its drawbacks as well as its advantages. The following sections describe each of these service options so that you can choose the type that's best for you.

Of course, the type of facility you select may vary depending on the kind of specialized service your vehicle requires. If you drive a hybrid or electric vehicle, it's probably best to stick to the dealership. If you drive a traditionally powered vehicle, you may be able to depend on an experienced independent for the best deal on reliable, competent service at a good price. You may find the best buys on tires at a major chain and the best brake or transmission work done at shops that specialize in them. See Tip #136, "Finding and Evaluating an Automotive Service," for more information.

Dealerships

When they buy a new vehicle, many people assume that they have to use the dealership's service facilities, at least until the warranty period is over. Be aware that in most cases, you can have warranty service (but not repairs) done by any licensed independent mechanic as long as all the service requirements in your owner's manual are fulfilled and you've kept the invoices for service and maintenance to prove it. (There are some exceptions, so read your warranties before going elsewhere for specialized work.)

Of course, you may want to stay with the dealership that sold you the vehicle because dealerships may offer the following advantages:

>> **They often provide extra services to ensure goodwill.** These can include notification of any maintenance that's due, special sales on service and optional equipment, and so on.

>> **They usually have a variety of factory-trained specialists on the premises.** The advantage is that you may be able to have brake work, transmission work, and sometimes even bodywork done at the same place.

>> **They stock a wide variety of original parts and equipment** *(OEM)* **made specifically for your vehicle.** This not only assures you of satisfaction if parts fail, but original parts may increase the resale value of your vehicle.

>> **If you have a complaint, you're dealing with an established company that's financially able to reimburse you and that's insured to cover any major lawsuits that may result.**

However, dealerships have disadvantages to consider as well:

>> **Dealerships may be more expensive than other types of service facilities.** Independent shops usually have a lower overhead to support.

>> **The sales and service departments of a dealership often operate as separate entities.** The attitude may be, "We have more work than we can handle, so if you're not happy here, you can go somewhere else." If you feel that's the case, complain to the dealership.

>> **You probably won't receive the personalized service that you may get from an independent repair shop.** At the dealership, you generally deal with a service writer who assigns your vehicle to the next technician available when its number comes up. Of course, if you build a good relationship with the service writer, they may honor your request for a specific technician who's familiar with your vehicle and its quirks.

Chain and Department Stores

Large chain stores and department stores that have automotive service departments offer their own set of pros and cons. Some advantages include the following:

>> **They can be less expensive than dealerships.**

>> **They usually stock a wide variety of parts, many of which are made to their specifications and carry their brand name.** How these parts compare in price and quality to the original equipment supplied by the car manufacturer varies, depending on which chain you deal with.

>> **They usually provide good guarantees on parts and labor.** And if you have a complaint, they're generally motivated to keep your goodwill.

>> **Large chain stores maintain branches nationwide that honor their warranties and guarantees.** If you move or travel frequently, this feature can be very beneficial.

WARNING

Chain and department stores also have their disadvantages, including the following:

>> **They use service writers, and the work tends to be impersonal, with a new technician working on your vehicle each time.**

>> **Technicians at some chains get a commission on the parts they sell.** This may motivate them to sell you a new part instead of repairing an old one or to perform work that your vehicle may not really need.

Independents

An independent service facility can offer the best — or the worst — alternative. Consider these points:

>> **Honest, reliable, and experienced independents can provide personalized service based on high standards of excellence.** They can offer you the opportunity to communicate directly with a professional who knows you, knows your vehicle, and cares a great deal about maintaining a good reputation because most independent business comes from referrals.

>> **Many independent shops are less expensive than dealerships.** Others, especially those that service only luxury cars or high-performance sports cars, may offer the finest workmanship at relatively exorbitant rates. A cherished few provide fine workmanship at low prices — these people are probably saints disguised in greasy coveralls!

WARNING

>> **Check carefully to be sure that the shop is reliable and able to do the job.** Expertise, the ability to stay current by attending classes held by automakers (who sometimes bar independents from enrollment), the availability of specialized tools and service manuals, and the variety of parts in inventory may vary from one independent shop to another. A good independent knows where to find the proper talent, borrow the tools, and buy OEM parts at a good price. An unreliable one patches things together, uses cheap parts, and hopes for the best.

Specialists

There are two types of specialists: One type is a specialized chain store or independent facility that deals with a specific kind of repair, such as brake work, transmission work, bodywork, or muffler replacement. The other type of specialist is an independent shop that works only on specific makes or vehicles, such as Ferraris, Volvos, motorcycles, or classic cars.

Here are the pros and cons to consider:

>> **A reliable specialist can provide the experience, specialized tools, and extensive inventory that may be unavailable at a shop that handles everything in general and nothing in particular.** If you know that the trouble with your vehicle resides in a particular automotive system, you may want to look for a well-established specialist who focuses on that type of work.

>> **Some specialized chains that sell and install cheap parts may be more interested in selling new parts than in repairing old ones.** Their lifetime guarantees may keep you coming back to pay more for the labor to install those "free" replacement parts than you'd spend initially on higher-quality parts that last longer.

Check out national chains that specialize in the type of repair you need in consumer publications such as *Consumer Reports* (www.consumerreports.org) to be sure that the one you choose has a good reputation for durable parts and quality service.

#136
Finding and Evaluating a New Automotive Service

You just moved and your trusted former repair facility is too far away. Or you bought a new set of wheels, and your old shop doesn't work on that particular type of vehicle. You haven't the faintest idea of where to go when your vehicle requires service that's beyond your abilities, or where to get help in an emergency. The Internet is full of suggestions, but how can you tell which shops are reliable and which are just waiting to take advantage of you? Relax; you've come to the right place for advice.

REMEMBER

A big repair job is like major surgery: Not only do you want the best possible surgeon, but you also want to be sure that the surgery is necessary and that it's done under the best possible terms. Consumer laws in many states hold the repair facility responsible for failing to provide a written estimate, failing to notify the customer if the estimate increases radically because more problems have been uncovered, and failing to turn over parts that have been replaced when the customer has asked that they be saved. Because this may *not* be the case in your state, follow these guidelines whenever you bring your vehicle in for maintenance or repair, or to a shop you haven't patronized before:

>> **If you're dealing with a new shop or you're faced with major repairs, get at least a second opinion and an estimate of costs from another repair shop.** If there's a

big discrepancy or if it's a very costly job, get a third estimate and discard any that are much higher or lower than the others.

>> **Ask for detailed, *written* estimates and updates.** Require the shop to call you *before* they start the repairs if they find that the job will cost more than originally estimated. Beware of general statements; try to get as detailed an estimate as possible.

>> **If major work is underway, ask to be notified about what they find right after they open the vehicle up to diagnose the problem.** Will it be a simple adjustment or a major rebuild? Ask to be called if that estimate changes because the shop uncovers other problems during the course of the estimated repairs.

>> **Save yourself from paying for unnecessary R&R (which means "removal and replacement," not "rest and relaxation!").** If the technicians have to open the transmission or the cylinder head or get into the engine or any other hard-to-get-at area in order to make a repair, ask them to check the whole area for any other parts that look as though they're about to need repair or replacement. A good chunk of the cost for labor is usually associated with just taking stuff apart and putting it back together again, so if the shop has to do removal and repair only once, you save money.

>> **Don't give the shop carte blanche to replace anything they please.** Tell them that you will want to see how badly the parts are wearing before they proceed with any unauthorized work, and call around for estimates before you agree to additional major surgery if you feel that the price the shop quotes is out of line. (However, keep in mind that you'll have to pay the new shop for R&R, as well.)

>> **Ask that all the parts that are replaced be returned to you, regardless of whether the laws in your state require it.** That way you can be sure that you're getting what you pay for.

>> **Ask for credit for the core charge on any rebuildable part that's going to be replaced.** Always ask what the shop will do with your old part. If they're going to rebuild and resell it or sell it to a rebuilder, the core charge should be deducted from the price of the part that you buy to replace it.

5

Making the Most of Holidays and Other Special Events

Figure out what's most important about holidays and other special occasions and put your resources and energy there. Such events are times to celebrate and enjoy. They're also times when your budget and bank account can take a real hit. Fortunately, you don't have to do without; you just have to do a little differently.

Determine what's nonnegotiable — spending quality time with your family or giving from the heart rather than the wallet, for example — and discover that although you spend less, you give more.

#137
Entertaining on a Shoestring

D o you want to socialize with friends and family while spending as little money as possible? Here are a few ideas that are proven winners:

>> **Covered-dish dinners:** Hosts provide the main course, and guests bring side dishes and desserts. The benefits of this type of gathering are that no one has too much work to do or costs to absorb, and everyone gets to try lots of new and varied dishes. Bring the kids, hire a babysitter to watch them, or get an older child to entertain them in a separate part of the house, and the adults can visit or play cards.

>> **Wine-tasting party:** This type of get-together can be a very educational and fun experience (not to mention thrifty). Here's how it works: The host's responsibilities are to invite friends or family, lay out the rules, and provide glasses, crackers, fruit, and cheese for all. Then guests each bring a bottle of wine.

The host predetermines the rules, such as the following: Bring red wine, $10 per bottle maximum, with bottles disguised in paper bags. After all the guests have arrived, randomly number the bags, open the wine bottles, and begin the tasting. Discuss the characteristics and qualities of each wine and vote on your favorite while enjoying your snacks and the company of your friends. At the end, unveil the winning selection.

>> **Football party:** Hosts provide the theme entrée, which has something to do with the opposing team. For example, if your team is playing the Miami Dolphins, you may want to serve fish tacos. Rotate hosts with each game.

>> **Game night:** Invite two to four people over after dinner to play a dice game or another game of your choice.

>> **Movie night:** Watch a movie on a streaming service you already use so you don't spend additional money. Make popcorn or another snack. For drinks, try fresh lemonade or limeade. Freeze some and make your own Italian ice, slushy, or ice pops.

#138
Throwing a Party on a Budget

Planning a party can be just as fun as attending one. And when your planning lets you save money at the same time, well, that's icing on the cake. The simplest and most important trick is to plan ahead and put together a party budget.

REMEMBER

When you budget for your party, do so *before* you start shopping. List the items you need and estimate what you can afford to spend on each item. Keep a running total of the expenses so you know when you need to cut corners on one item because you went over on another.

Check out the following budget-saving ideas:

>> **Always shop from a detailed list.** Impulse buys are common in party planning. Those corn-shaped corncob holders would be a hit at the barbecue, but are they necessary?

>> **Use reusable tableware.** Using real dishes, utensils, and glassware can save big money.

>> **Prepare the food yourself.** Bake your own cake or serve sliced homemade snack cakes instead of ordering a personalized cake from a grocery store or bakery.

>> **Make and deliver your own invitations.** Save on postage by hand-delivering invitations to people you see regularly. Email invitations are acceptable for casual parties.

>> **Aim for a simple, balanced menu.** For a dinner party, a simple snack or appetizer, salad or soup, vegetables, and a main course followed by a simple dessert make a nice, well-rounded meal.

REMEMBER

The key to entertaining on a budget without sacrificing flair is to think *presentation*. You can make anything look special: a tray of cold cuts on a bed of curly lettuce, utensils standing in a cup tied in ribbon, napkins folded into birds.

#139
Making Inexpensive Easter Baskets

Ahh, Easter: warm spring weather, newborn bunnies, and freshly cut tulips. If only those store-bought springtime goodies, like Easter baskets for the kids and decorations for the home, weren't so expensive. But with a little creativity, you can enjoy the season frugally.

For instance, you can make your own inexpensive Easter baskets. Use wicker baskets, which last year after year, or be creative with your choice of container. Paper bags, Easter bonnets, and colorful plastic sand pails are all great options. Fill your bags or baskets with treats that you accumulate throughout the year — crayons, bubbles, sidewalk chalk, stickers, and little cookies and candies.

#140
Creating Frightfully Affordable Halloween Costumes

Halloween costumes don't have to scare the living daylights out of your budget. Even a simple homemade costume can be loads of frightening fun, especially if the children design it themselves. Make the following inexpensive costumes from things found around the house or at thrift stores.

>> **Mummy:** Attach ragged strips of cloth ripped from an old white sheet to a white T-shirt and pants. Or wrap the child lightly in surgical gauze if you find some on sale or at the dollar store.

>> **Rock star:** Throw on anything glittery or wild; things don't have to match. Spike the hair, maybe spray on a little temporary hair paint, add some oversized jewelry, a pair of dark glasses, and you're all set!

» Ladybug: Dress your child in a pair of black leggings and a plain long-sleeved black shirt. Remove the arms from a large red sweatshirt (bought at a thrift store) and pin, glue, or draw large black dots all over and a stripe down the middle of the sweatshirt. Fashion antennae with black pipe cleaners.

TIP

Shop off-season to get the best deals. Halloween decorations are cheaper right after Halloween; limit yourself to one or two new items at the end of the season and store them with your current decorations.

#141
Celebrating a Budget-Friendly Thanksgiving

Probably the single greatest expense of the Thanksgiving holiday is preparing all the food for the family and friends converging on your house. To save money, suggest that each person or family group attending the festivities bring one food item that represents their favorite part of the Thanksgiving meal. Have people tell you in advance what they're bringing, though, or you may end up with three different versions of sweet potato casserole.

TIP

Watch for sales on whole frozen turkeys throughout the year and don't hesitate to buy your holiday bird earlier in the year if you find a great price. Turkeys keep well in the freezer for several months.

You can make as many side dishes as possible ahead of time and store them in the freezer for the big day. Some good Thanksgiving items to freeze ahead are candied yams and, believe it or not, mashed potatoes. The mashed potatoes separate a bit in the freezing and thawing process, but if you stir them well as they're reheating, they recombine beautifully.

#142
Trying Creative Hanukkah and Christmas Ideas

Holiday giving and frugal living don't have to be polar opposites if you follow these easy ideas:

>> **Create homemade wrapping paper.** Make your own wrapping paper out of brown paper grocery bags, inexpensive kitchen sponges (the softer, the better), and craft paint. Cut open the paper bags and spread them flat, with the plain insides of the bags facing up. Cut the sponges into simple holiday shapes (snowmen, trees, and stars, for example), dip them into paint, and then sponge-paint randomly over the open paper bags. Tied with inexpensive brown twine, this makes a rustic and beautiful gift-wrapping idea — plus it's a fun holiday family activity, too.

>> **Find post-holiday deals.** If you like the variety and sparkle of store-bought paper, shop for it after the holidays, when it's half off or more.

»» Limit the number of decorations. A few strategically placed decorations can have a dramatic effect. A seasonal decoration on the front door, a tree in the living room, a centerpiece on the dining table, and a few fragrant candles around the house can set the mood.

»» Save on gifts. Set a limit on how much to spend on each person you're buying for. Shop early. Shop online. Purchase gifts on clearance throughout the year. If you buy gifts for extended family members, agree to a spending limit, buy a single family gift rather than individual gifts, or trade names.

#143
Hosting a Frugal Birthday Bash

osting a birthday party for your significant other or one of your children can easily become a huge financial expense. By the time you add in the cost of decorations, food, games, and party favors, you can spend hundreds of dollars. And if you hire an entertainer, look out!

The best advice on this front is, once again, to keep everything simple. Here are some examples:

>> Print out your own invitations on your computer (or send them via email).

>> Bake the birthday cake yourself rather than pay the big bucks for the local baker to do it for you.

>> Collect party favors from thrift stores or garage sales. Or make party favors out of pictures of the party guests having fun at the party. Use a camera that takes instant photos, or print photos from your smartphone, and make picture frames for the photos using cardboard decorated with ribbon.

Frugal birthday fun for a kid's party can be had for a small price if you plan ahead and get creative. Here are some ways to cut corners without skimping on the fun:

>> Have the kids do a fun activity as they're arriving at the party. Here are a couple of ideas.

- **Gift bags:** Give the kids brown paper lunch bags and let them decorate their own gift bag with crayons, markers, and stickers.

- **Festive fedoras:** Give the kids paper plates, pieces of cardboard, colorful construction paper, ribbon, and assorted odds and ends — and let them go to town making and decorating their own party hats. Even making folded paper hats out of the comic section of the newspaper can be lots of fun.

>> Bake birthday cupcakes instead of a layered cake or sheet cake; then let the kids decorate their individual cakes themselves, using sprinkles, candy, and so on. They'll actually be happier eating something they had a hand in creating. If you make a layer cake, note that kids are just as happy with candies and sprinkles on their cake as they are with their favorite cartoon characters elaborately drawn in icing.

>> Make your own party favors: homemade play dough, bubbles, even small bags with a colorful string and a handful of beads for a do-it-yourself necklace or bracelet. Cookie cutters, sunglasses, lip gloss, or nail polish from the dollar store or thrift store make great party favors, too.

>> Choose a children's picture book to read to the kids. After the story, have everyone choose a character from the story, use face paint to make each other up as that character, and then act the story out. The face painting itself makes a great party favor.

#144
Packing Up Treats on the Cheap

Homemade gifts send the message that you care enough to take the time to make something with your own two hands. Anyone would enjoy homemade gifts from the kitchen any time of year — whether you have a reason for giving or not. Give them to celebrate holidays, to mark birthdays and anniversaries, to spread cheer to someone who's not well, or for no reason at all.

TIP

Put just as much care into the way you package your gift as you do into making it in the first place. Keep a few containers, bags, or wraps on hand. They're convenient for spontaneous gift giving, so try to get in the habit of looking for these things when you're shopping. Consider the following a guided tour of places to look (you never know what unusual packaging you may be the first to discover):

>> **Craft stores:** Roam the aisles and you're sure to discover all sorts of boxes, ribbon, baskets, papers, pipe cleaners, crepe paper, twine, and raffia.

>> **Super discount stores:** Check out the toy department and see what's available in the way of buckets and such. The card departments carry cute little shopping bags. Housewares departments have napkins, mugs, and canisters.

>> **Gourmet food shops:** These shops probably have the traditional food containers, including the fancier decorative bottles and French canning jars. These items are great if they fit within your budget.

>> **Party goods stores:** Seasonal ideas are usually available in party goods stores. Wrapping paper, ribbon, tissue paper, and colorful napkins are standard items.

>> **Flea markets and related places:** Flea markets, antique stores, garage sales, and tag sales are great sources for potential containers and wrapping items. Beautiful old glass, baskets, advertising containers, linens, bowls, teacups, wine glasses, molds, and crockery are all there for the creating.

>> **Your own house:** Home is where the heart is, and it's also the starting point for finding recyclables. Reuse unusual glass water bottles (some water companies use colored bottles) by adding a cork and sealing it with paraffin. Reuse pretty tins left over from commercial cookies. Cut up old greeting cards and use them for tags or appliqués.

>> **Fabric and notions stores:** Go here if you want to wrap your gift in cloth, whether it's topping a jam jar with a square of gingham or wrapping the whole present in a fabric bundle.

>> **Stationery and card stores:** They always have the usual wrapping paper, tissue, and cards, but more and more stores are expanding their lines to carry little tote bags and tins.

>> **Garden centers and florists:** Garden shops carry all sorts of containers in varying shapes nowadays, including pots and baskets. Many garden stores also carry patio tableware in all shapes, colors, and sizes.

>> **Hardware stores:** Look in the paint department for disposable cardboard paint buckets. Empty reusable metal paint buckets are another option. In the plumbing department, buy a short section of PVC pipe to fill with individually wrapped candies or cookies and then wrap it in stiff fabric or paper like a gigantic party popper.

Everything food comes in contact with should be food safe. If you're not sure, wrap the gift in food wrap first.

REMEMBER

#145
Finding Inexpensive Gifts for Your Sweetheart

Whether it's Valentine's Day or the anniversary of your first date, here are some simple ideas for expressing your love without taking out a bank loan:

» **Bake heart-shaped food items.** Preparing a heart-shaped anything is a romantic gesture. Make heart-shaped pancakes for breakfast, heart-shaped crispy rice treats for a snack, or a heart-shaped pizza for dinner. You can also use a heart-shaped cookie cutter to cut the crust off sandwiches. How romantic — heart-shaped PBJs for that special someone!

» **Make a "100 Reasons Why I Love You" List.** Write out a list of 100 reasons why you love your dear one. Do they remember your birthday? Do they wash the dishes regularly? Do they maintain the yard's appearance? Anything and everything can become an item on this list. Have some of the reasons be funny, some just plain silly, and some sentimental and romantic. Just make them all true! If you can't bring yourself to be creative enough to do 100 reasons, you can at least come up with 20 reasons, right? Ten? Oh, c'mon!

» **Share romantic greeting cards.** Sometimes money's so tight, even the expense of a nice card for Valentine's Day may be out of the question. Making cards for each other is simple and inexpensive. Use a card-making program on your computer or draw your own cards on scraps of paper. If drawing your own designs is beyond your artistic abilities, glue on magazine clippings, pressed flowers, dried leaves, photos, ticket stubs, or any other meaningful or romantic items.

TIP

Plan a fun date for just the two of you and visit the local card shop at the mall. Or go to your favorite quirky gift shop with the unusual cards. Browse through the romantic greeting card racks and read aloud the cards that you would want to give each other. Laugh at the funny ones, gaze lovingly at each other over the sentimental ones, and blush visibly over the embarrassing joke cards.

>> **Bring chocolate.** Give chocolates to your honey. And not just a plain ol' candy heart from the bargain bin at the grocery store. Go out of your way to visit that special little gift shop downtown with the handmade specialty candy selection. Even a single, elegantly wrapped, hand-dipped almond-flavored bonbon makes a heartfelt gift and shows that you're paying attention when your loved one sighs over the chocolate counter at the expensive department store.

>> **Leave love notes in unexpected places.** Write "I love you!" in the fog on the bathroom mirror while your sweetie's in the shower. Pack a love note in their lunch or briefcase. Set one on the car seat while your honey is at work. A note is a tangible way to remind your loved one of your devotion.

>> **Make a scroll of love.** To make your scroll, use either a receipt roll from an office supply store or a paper roll from a printing calculator. Start at the loose end of the roll and then write down romantic quotes, loving thoughts, or any number of favorite feelings you want to share with your loved one. Take your time. You can make your writings an ongoing project while you watch television. Or keep it next to your computer so you can jot down ideas while you're browsing online. You want to keep this project a secret, so make sure you work on it when your love isn't around.

When you're finished, wrap each end of the scroll around a dowel cut to size, and then, when you give it as a gift, plan on reading through it together with your dearly beloved. Don't forget to bring a box of tissue if your honey's a sop for the emotional stuff.

#146
Checking Out Frugal Gift Ideas for Any Occasion

The majority of most people's holiday expenses go for gifts. Giving to others is definitely a wonderful and important part of the holiday season, but is going to the store and paying top dollar for household clutter really the answer?

Here are some gift ideas to help you think creatively about the holidays or any other gift-giving occasion (sometimes giving gifts is really a matter of creativity versus cash):

» **Make a personalized calendar.** Creating your own personalized calendar can be as simple as buying a store-bought calendar and writing important family days to remember throughout the year, such as birthdays, anniversaries, and so on. Or buy a blank calendar and decorate the entire calendar yourself. These calendars usually come with a top section that you can decorate with photos or mementos, just like a scrapbook page. Add the important family dates to the calendar, and then when the year's over, the recipient can cut off the calendar section and keep the scrapbook pages together as a memory book.

You can also design a personalized calendar on your computer's desktop publishing program. Rather than photos or artwork at the top of each calendar page, how about a simple layout design with favorite family recipes, quotations, and so forth?

>> **Put together favorite family recipes.** Many families pass down favorite recipes almost like treasured family heirlooms. Request that family members send you a couple of their favorite recipes, and maybe even a sentence or two about the recipe, its history or origin, any traditions surrounding the recipe, or even funny family stories. Then put together and print your own cookbook. (Even if you have the booklets professionally copied and bound, it's still a relatively inexpensive gift.)

TIP

If you don't have access to a computer, handwritten recipes put onto index cards are an inexpensive gift as well. Put the recipes together in a nice recipe box found during your garage sale travels or on sale at the kitchen supply store. Or buy an inexpensive plain card file box at the office supply store and decorate it with paint or stickers. Recipes make for especially nice gifts for young adults going out on their own or for a newly married couple.

>> **Give a coffee mug or teacup along with a tasty treat.** In a pretty, tasteful, or humorous coffee mug, include a selection of small bags of coffee mix or favorite coffee beans, spiced cider mix, a selection of gourmet teas, a pretty silver-plated spoon found at a thrift store, or other favorite tea time or coffee break treats. Wrap in cellophane and tie with a pretty ribbon. You can even make this gift into a tea-for-two basket by including two teacups and saucers, a variety of gourmet teabags, a box of scone or muffin mix, and a small jar of jam or lemon curd. You can often find inexpensive, "like-new" baskets at thrift stores and garage sales.

>> **Hand-decorate glass ornaments.** Buy a set of inexpensive clear glass ball ornaments at your local craft store. Remove the hanging wires and, using various colors of craft paint, pour a few drops of the paint into the balls. Swirl the balls around gently to make lines and designs with the various colors. When the inside of the balls are covered fully with paint, place the balls upside down on paper towels. Allow the ornaments to dry completely before reattaching the hanging wires. Hand-decorated glass ornaments make great gifts for grandparents, teachers, neighbors, and children's friends. If you see clear glass ornaments on sale after Christmas, you can stock up for next year's gift-giving at a great discount.

#147
Making Great Gift Baskets

Good for you — you took time away from a busy schedule to do something really nice for someone. You made a gift from the kitchen, which is always a winning recipe. But maybe you want to be a little more grandiose. Consider the possibilities of a gift basket — a one-of-a-kind present that speaks louder than words. Be serious. Be silly. Be inventive. But above all, have fun. Here are some ideas for gift baskets that will get your creative juices flowing:

>> **Midnight Fridge Raid:** Have a friend who insists on staying up to watch their favorite streaming service? Bake a pan of granola bars or another treat and stash them in an old cookie jar from a flea market or garage sale.

>> **Young at Heart:** Is someone approaching an "older than they'd like to admit" birthday? Give a gift of chocolate sauces, a set of ice cream dishes, and an ice-cream scoop. Rekindle the indulgence of youth.

>> **Dashing through the Snow:** Do you know an avid cross-country skier, a snow bunny, a parent who watches

ice-skating practice, or anyone else who may need their internal temperature raised a few notches? Give your cold comrade some soup mix along with a thermos and a lap blanket. That will warm body and soul.

>> **Home on the Range:** Looking for a little something for your resident grill master? Everyone seems to be an expert when it comes to grilling, but even if your intended recipient can't roast a hotdog, try giving a bottle of steak sauce, a flame-proof barbecue mitt, and a set of steak knives.

#148
Cutting Costs with a Birthday Box

TIP

One helpful thing you can do to cut down on the cost of gifts for your kids' friends is to keep a Birthday Box. Fill the Birthday Box with gift items (such as toys, books, and clothes) and assorted birthday cards, wrapping paper pieces, and gift bags you purchase throughout the year during clearance sales. You can also add in things you find new and still in the original wrapping at thrift stores and garage sales. When party invitations arrive in the mail, all your family has to do is go "shopping" in the closet, rather than making an expensive trip to the mall or toy store or shopping online.

#149

Exploring Alternative Gift Ideas

Rather than buying more items to clutter up families' and friends' homes, many people are starting to give alternative gifts that are more in keeping with their personal priorities and the spirit of each season. Be careful of the feelings of others, though. Some people would rather receive a cheap and tacky store-bought knickknack than a gift acknowledgment from a charity. Know your friends and family so that you can lovingly give a gift from your heart to theirs that they appreciate.

Some alternative gift ideas include the following:

>> Donate your time, energy, or resources to a charity in your friend's name. Then drop him a nice note telling them that you donated your time as their gift. Be sure you're donating to a cause your friend or family member believes in and cares about.

>> Organize a canned food, clothing, or toy drive in your neighborhood, school, or place of worship. Send a note to the gift recipient telling them you've donated your time in this way.

» Write a long, heartfelt letter to your friends and family members.

» Give a gift of time: Visit a shut-in, check in regularly on your elderly neighbor, spend time baking with your nephew, take your niece to the park.

» Put together a homemade coupon book of personalized jobs you'll do for the recipient: Mow the lawn, give a back rub, go shopping, and so on.

#150

Looking at Gifts for Bridal and Baby Showers

Bridal and baby showers don't need to be huge events with sit-down luncheons and white tablecloths. As with any party, the simpler, the better.

TIP

If any of the guests like to quilt (and it seems like every group has at least one avid quilter these days), making a quilt together can create a memorable keepsake for the new bride or new mom. Give each guest a square section of the quilt fabric and have them decorate it in a way that's meaningful. Make sure everyone signs their name with a fabric pen on their square. Sew on buttons, bows, ribbons, beads, or whatever strikes your fancy. If any of your guests don't feel at all artistic, they can simply use a fabric pen and write a favorite quote or verse. Someone else can add a small decorative flourish to the square later, if needed. You really need to plan this project ahead of time so that the person who sews the quilt together has enough time to collect the finished squares from the guests. Perhaps include the squares in the invitation with instructions for mailing the squares to the quilter when the guests are finished decorating them.

You can also have each guest bring a page telling the guest of honor how special they are or offering a few words of wisdom for the bride- or mom-to-be. Tell your guests to feel free to share funny stories or goofy advice, too. The pages can either be simple letters or intricately decorated scrapbook pages. Have someone bind them all together into a memory book.

6

Staying Afloat If the Boat Starts to Sink

Recognize that making ends meet can be more challenging than ever in a time when prices keep going up and incomes seem to keep going down. If a crisis happens — a major medical problem or a job loss, for example — the situation just gets worse.

Act if you're feeling overwhelmed with debt or are facing the real possibility of losing your home or having to declare bankruptcy.

Find advice on how to put your credit back in good standing and navigate your way through major financial catastrophes.

#151

Spotting Signs of Financial Trouble

WARNING

The early warning signs of financial trouble can be as obvious as a lost job, a layoff, or a huge medical bill, or as secretive as an addiction. In either case, you and your partner (if you have one) should remain on the lookout for these warning signs and work together to build a strong financial foundation that can protect you from foreclosure and other financial crises:

>> **Stick to a budget.** Make sure you have at least as much money coming in as is flowing out each month. If you have a partner, you both should agree, upfront, on how much to spend and what to spend it on. When partners are off spending money on their own pet luxuries, problems often arise.

>> **Pay your bills.** When the bills arrive, prioritize them and pay them as soon as possible so they don't stack up. If you have a partner, pay your bills together. Blaming them for over-spending is easy when you don't know how much it costs to heat your house or feed your family. You both need to be aware of where the money's going so you can hold your-selves, and one another, accountable.

» **Audit your books.** Add up all the money you spend each week on nonessentials and try to trim the fat. If you're teaming up with someone, determine how much you're responsible for and how much they're responsible for. This shouldn't be a blame game, but it can open your eyes to any potential spending problems that could leave the checking account short when it comes time to make the mortgage or rent payment.

» **Watch for addictive behavior.** Any addiction can be a problem, including alcohol, drugs, or the Internet. Anything that takes time, energy, and resources away from a paying job and your family (if you're supporting a family) could cause financial problems. Identify addictions early and nip them in the bud.

#152
Avoiding Credit Pitfalls

WARNING

Whether you're new to credit or you're a credit veteran, you need to be careful of counterproductive actions. Some examples of things to avoid if at all possible are payday lenders, refund–anticipation loans, check cashers, credit repair companies, and debt settlers:

>> You won't go blind from using a *payday lender* once for an emergency, but the very concept of this type of high-interest loan is flawed. If you have no savings, you're living paycheck to paycheck, and an emergency expense comes up, does getting a payday loan make sense? You have to pay back a short-term (two weeks or so) loan on your next payday. But all that money is already committed, so how can you pay it back? Chances are you'll need more than one loan and end up owing lots of money in interest charges.

>> *Refund-anticipation loans* are another potentially counterproductive borrowing product. These loans accelerate an e-filed tax refund by a very short period for a very large fee when calculated as an annual percentage rate (APR). Plus, if your refund is held up or reduced, you owe more money on the loan than you expected.

>> *Check cashers* perform a valid but expensive function for people with no bank accounts who need to cash checks. Instead, get a bank account so you have a place to begin saving and stop paying for unnecessary check cashing.

>> *Credit repair companies* have a horrid reputation. Legislation called the Credit Repair Organizations Act has tried to limit the damage caused by fraudulent actions that some companies advise to rig the credit-reporting system. If you're thinking of credit repair companies, think again.

>> *Debt settlers* can put you into an adversarial process in which you can get caught in the middle of a financial and legal tug-of-war with potentially devastating consequences.

#153
Getting Copies of Your Credit Report and Scores

Credit information collected about you is contained in your credit reports from the three major credit bureaus (Equifax, Experian, and TransUnion). Getting copies of those reports and reviewing the information in them is as easy as it is important, and doing so shows you exactly what most people or programs evaluating your credit see. Credit scores are also a part of the credit-reporting picture, although they aren't part of credit reports.

Your Credit Report

To obtain your one free credit report from each of the three major credit bureaus each year, simply visit the website www .annualcreditreport.com. Or, if you prefer, you can request copies by phone or mail:

Annual Credit Report Request Service

P.O. Box 105281

Atlanta, GA 30348-5281

877-322-8228

You need to fill out a request form if you use the mail to get your free copies from the central source.

Many different websites with similar-sounding names have cropped up since the central source for free credit reports was established. These sites advertise free credit reports, but the fine print is that your free report costs you something because you must purchase another product or service to receive it. You shouldn't have to purchase anything to get your free copies. If the site requires you to provide payment information, you're on the wrong site.

Note that your credit score isn't provided with your free annual credit reports when you use www.annualcreditreport.com. You'll be "offered an opportunity" to purchase your score after you get your free report. Credit scores are available free from a number of sources as well (see the next section).

To request a report directly from the credit bureaus, you can get things started with a phone call, a visit to the bureau's website, or through the mail. Here's the contact information for the three major credit-reporting bureaus:

>> **Equifax,** P.O. Box 740241, Atlanta, GA 30374; 800-685-1111; www.equifax.com

>> **Experian,** P.O. Box 2104, Allen, TX 75013-2104; 888-397-3742; www.experian.com

>> **TransUnion,** 2 Baldwin Place, P.O. Box 1000, Chester, PA 19022; 800-888-4213; www.transunion.com

Your Credit Score

Getting your hands on your credit reports is pretty straightforward. You only have three of them and you can request them all from the same website. Getting copies of your credit scores isn't as straightforward. Your *credit score* is a tool used in most credit reviews to objectively analyze the information from your credit report. When a lender orders your credit report, it often also orders a credit score, which helps predict the chances that you won't be able to pay a new loan as agreed.

The two best-known credit scoring companies are FICO and Vantage-Score. They developed the credit scores most commonly used by lenders today. FICO is the best-known name in credit scores. VantageScore is its largest competitor, although less well known. Four of the top five financial institutions, all credit card issuers, and two of the top five auto lenders use VantageScores for lending decisions. The most common scores from both companies range from 300 to 850.

Don't get hung up on a number. Be as good as you can be, but don't get excited and yell at the cat over a score of 820 instead of 850. The most important thing is to know what your *lenders* know about your credit score and what's in the credit report they look at. On this topic, you want to be on the same page.

The main points to keep in mind regarding credit scores are as follows:

>> Your score is different for each credit bureau report, if only because each bureau has slightly different data about you in its files.

>> Be sure you know which score you're getting: a FICO score, a VantageScore, or a proprietary score from the service providing it.

>> You can only improve your credit score by improving your credit history, not the other way around. If you take care of your credit report, your credit scores will take care of themselves.

>> About 5 percent of credit reports have errors that would result in a score change of 25 points or more according to the Federal Trade Commission (FTC). Having errors in your report can be enough to cause you to be declined or pay higher interest rates. That's why it's important to check your report regularly. Dispute errors and outdated items to ensure your credit score accurately reflects your creditworthiness.

The Fair Access to Credit Scores Act that was bundled into the massive Dodd–Frank Wall Street Reform and Consumer Protection Act allows you free access to your credit score if you've been denied credit or if some other "adverse action" (denial of insurance or utilities, for example) was taken as a result of your credit score. In fact, the law requires the lender or business that took adverse action to give you a score it used. You don't have to request your credit score if such an adverse action is taken based on that score; a copy of the score used to make the decision is automatically sent to you.

To get your current score, you need to order a credit report at the same time because your score is calculated based on the information in your credit report at the time you order the score.

If you want your credit score, you can get it from a number of places today for free:

>> **Your lender:** Your lender may provide a FICO score to you through its online banking app or with your billing statement.

>> **Credit Karma** (www.creditkarma.com): Download the free app, input your personal information, and get your FICO for free. You'll get offers for credit cards or other services. Just be prepared to say no.

>> **Experian** (www.experian.com): You can get your FICO score for free when you enroll in its basic monitoring service or sign up with its mobile app. You'll also get offers for credit cards and other services.

>> **Equifax** (www.equifax.com): Enrollment in its service at the time of writing is $19.95 a month.

>> **myFICO.com** (800-319-4433; www.myfico.com): Enrollment in its basic service is $19.95 a month at the time of this writing.

>> **TransUnion** (www.transunion.com): You can get the VantageScore through its online service, which is $24.95 a month as of this writing.

REMEMBER

The number you get will almost never match the one your lender gets exactly. That's okay. When you receive your score, you should also receive an explanation of what the number means in terms of risk. If the score says you're a good risk, your lender's score will as well. What's important is to know what the number means within its scale, not that it matches the score your lender has. You should also get a list of risk factors (also called *reason statements*) that explain what in your credit report most affected the number. Although the numbers may differ, the risk factors tend to be very consistent. Address them, and all your scores will improve.

WARNING

When you're ordering scores, most sites try to get you to sign up for a credit-monitoring service. Be sure you understand what you're agreeing to before you do. You should be able to get your one-time credit report and a score without signing up for a long-term service, but monitoring services may have advantages, too. Just be sure you read the fine print and know what's in it for you before you sign up.

#154
Checking Your Credit Report

Learning what's in your credit report (see Tip #153, "Getting Copies of Your Credit Report and Scores") really isn't hard, although the things you read and hear can make it sound nearly impossible. But it does take a little time, some patience, and occasionally persistence.

You should watch for potential problems that may indicate you're a victim of identity theft, that information on your report has been confused with someone else, or in relatively rare instances, that mistakes have been made that could cause your application to be declined or pay higher interest rates. Despite common claims, errors in credit reports that would significantly change your credit scores are pretty unusual. The FTC found that only about 5 percent of credit reports had errors that would result in a drop in credit scores that would affect lending decisions.

You probably won't find meaningful errors, but it's still very important to check your reports, just in case you do. Your credit history is used to make an increasingly large number of decisions about your future, financial and otherwise, from lending to insurance to employment. You want to keep a close eye on your credit reports to make sure they're in good shape and ready to work for you when you need them.

TIP

To begin, arm yourself with the information in your credit reports (one from each of the three major credit bureaus), as well as your credit score from FICO, VantageScore, a lender, or a credit bureau. Along with the credit score, make sure you get a list of the risk factors that go with it. The *risk factors* give you specific information about what's having the most impact on your score from your credit report. The risk factors tell you exactly what to look for in your report to work on.

As you study your credit reports, you may be surprised by how many accounts you find. Because your report lists negative information for seven years (with the exception of Chapter 7 bankruptcy, which lasts ten years) and positive information for much longer, you could see accounts, referred to as *trade lines,* that you've forgotten about, and perhaps even some that you didn't realize you still had. Some creditors, like retail stores, don't close accounts, even if you haven't used them in years. Your task is to play credit archeologist and sift through the trade lines — current and old, if not ancient — and identify any errors and inaccuracies you find.

Here's what you should look for in particular:

>> **Verify that your name, address, birthdate, and Social Security number are correct.** Variations on your name are okay (for example, Stephen and Steve). With all the data moving through the financial reporting system, however, a Jr. or Sr. can easily be missed, or confusion over a II or III designation may occur.

REMEMBER

The variations you can find listed in your name, Social Security number, and addresses aren't "mistakes." The credit bureaus list all the variations reported to them to accurately show what your lenders are reporting. If you find variations, the credit bureaus can help you identify the sources and get them corrected.

>> **Look to see whether account activity is being reported correctly.** If you see accounts that are familiar but activity that isn't — such as a late-payment notation when you don't recall having been late — report that error to the credit bureau. An account you don't recognize may be a simple misposting of data from someone else's report, or it may be a sign of something more serious, like identity theft. Contact the bureau and find out.

>> **Look out for accounts from banks or stores with which you've never done business.** In the most serious cases,

accounts you don't recognize could be a sign of identity theft. Or, it could be the result of someone else's account information being added to your credit report because of a misspelled name, a wrong address, or an incorrect Social Security number. Sometimes a merger or account purchase results in a new trade line showing up on your report. Store credit cards are often reported with the name of the bank that actually owns the account rather than the name of the store. Checking the back of your store card for the bank name can often solve a mystery account. Dispute the account using the instructions on your credit report if you aren't sure about it.

» **Identify and verify any accounts that show negative activity.** *Negative activity* can include anything from a missed or late payment to a charge-off or bankruptcy notation. Make sure that this negative information is really yours and is accurate. Also, some negatives are much more serious than others. For example, a 90-day delinquency is more serious than a 30-day delinquency, even though both are negative. Recent negative items are more serious than older ones.

» **Be sure that an account that moved from one source to another is listed as open only once.** Bank and store mergers can result in multiple entries for the same account. Multiple entries can make it look like you have excessive amounts of credit available. Be sure the older account entries are listed as closed or have another status indicator that shows they're no longer the active entry.

TIP

If you make a correction to your file, the change may not be reflected in your credit report right away. The dispute process can take up to 30 days, so it could be a while before the updates appear in your credit report. The good news is that most disputes are completed in 10 to 14 business days and often in just 2 to 3 days. Be sure to allow time for information to be updated if you're planning to apply for new credit. If you're already in the process of applying for a loan, ask whether your lender offers a rapid rescore product for sale. Developed by the three major credit bureaus, *rapid rescore* is essentially an unscheduled update to the information on your credit report. If a recent action (such as paying down a balance or closing a card) helps your credit score, then it can be expedited to the bureau as soon as it's made. The credit bureau can then update your file so that you can get an updated report and score in days, not weeks.

#155
Disputing Inaccurate Info on Your Credit Report

You can't legally remove accurate and timely info from your credit report, whether it's good or bad. But the law does allow you to request an investigation of any information in your file that you believe is outdated, inaccurate, or incomplete. You're not charged for this investigation, it won't hurt your credit scores, and you can do it yourself at no cost.

REMEMBER

Inaccurate data serves no purpose for anyone in the credit chain. The credit bureaus and lenders want the information in your reports to be accurate, just as you do. Accurate information helps lenders say yes to your application, which is what they really want to do — it's how they make money!

The Dispute Process

The process for disputing and correcting inaccurate information is simple. Your role is to check your credit reports at least once a year and before making a major credit purchase. If you see information that looks unfamiliar or wrong, you file a dispute with the credit bureau in question.

After you notify a bureau of a disputed item, the bureau contacts the source that placed the data in your report. That source has 30 days to respond. If the source can't verify the data within the time allowed — because the information never existed, the info can't be found, or the dispute processing person doesn't hit the Send button — the bureau must remove the information from your report. If, on the other hand, the information is verified, it stays on your report. In either case, you're notified in writing of any actions or nonactions that occur as a result of your dispute.

If you disagree with the findings, you can contact the company that placed the erroneous information yourself and try to get it changed. Be sure to ask how the investigation was conducted and who was contacted. You also have the right to add a statement to your report or to a specific trade line saying why you disagree.

TIP

If you place a statement on your report, be sure to keep track of the time it's on the report so that it doesn't outlast the negative data it explains and cause you further problems. Today the bureaus automatically remove statements when negative information falls off, so it should happen without any action on your part. But it never hurts to check!

How to Correct All Your Credit Reports

The credit bureaus don't always have exactly the same information in their credit reports. So, if you look at your Experian credit report, see an inaccuracy, follow the dispute process, and have it corrected, you may not be out of the woods. TransUnion or Equifax may have *different* inaccurate information. Therefore, you need to get all three reports to make sure *all* your information is accurate.

If the same error appears on two or all three reports, you need to dispute it only once. If the source of the information makes a change as a result of your dispute, the source of the information has to tell the other bureaus about the change, too. But double-check anyway.

Correcting all three reports is important, because some lenders and businesses purchase the three-in-one report that includes a credit score and credit history information from each of the three bureaus. Each bureau has slightly different procedures for filing disputes, but all three allow you to dispute inaccurate or out-of-date information by phone, by mail, or online:

- **Equifax:** Call the phone number provided for disputes on your credit report, and be sure to have your ten-digit credit report confirmation number (on your report) available. You can also dispute by mail at Equifax Information Services LLC, P.O. Box 740256, Atlanta, GA 30374 (no confirmation number is required on written correspondence); or online at www.equifax.com/personal/credit-report-services/credit-dispute.

- **Experian:** You can dispute by phone by using the toll-free number on your credit report; by mail at Experian, P.O. Box 9701, Allen, TX 75013; or online at www.experian.com/dispute.

- **TransUnion:** You can dispute information by phone at 800-916-8800; by mail at TransUnion Consumer Solutions, P.O. Box 2000, Chester, PA 19022-2000 (be sure to include the completed request for investigation form found on the website); or online at www.transunion.com/credit-disputes/dispute-your-credit.

TIP

Some people recommend that you write to initiate a dispute so that you can maintain a paper trail. Today, when you dispute online, the bureaus provide confirmation throughout the process. Saving or printing the documents along the way also establishes a paper trail for future reference. Either way, be sure to document your interactions.

REMEMBER

Make sure your dispute is very clear — for example: "I was never late," "The account is not mine," or "The account is fraudulent."

The credit bureau must forward all relevant data you provide to the company that originally reported the information. When the company receives the request for verification from the credit bureau, it must investigate, review all relevant information, and report the results to the bureau.

- **If the information is found to be accurate,** the source notifies the bureau through which you disputed the information that there should be no change.

- **If the company can't verify the accuracy of the information you're disputing,** the information must be deleted from your file. The source of the information must then notify the other credit bureaus to delete the information, too.

>> **If the disputed information is incomplete,** the source of the information will tell the credit bureau to update it. For example, if you were once late in making payments but your file doesn't show that you've since caught up, the source of the information will respond to the dispute telling the bureau that the account is now current and to amend your report to show that you're now on time with your payments.

>> **If the information is being disputed as fraudulent,** the bureau will dispute it as such with the source, who will then have it deleted. If you have filed a police report or valid identity theft report, the bureaus can proactively "suppress" the fraudulent account and help you work with the source to update their records.

When the investigation is complete, the credit bureau must give you the written results and an explanation of the results or a free copy of your updated credit report if the dispute results in a change of information. (The bureau may refer to your request for an investigation as a *reinvestigation*; they're the same thing.) If an item is changed or removed, the bureau can't put the disputed information back in your report unless the company providing that information subsequently verifies its accuracy and completeness. Then the credit bureau must give you written notice that includes the name, address, and phone number of the company that provided the verification.

You can request that the bureau send notices of corrections to anyone who received your report in the past six months. If you've applied for a job, you can have a corrected copy of your report sent to anyone who received a copy during the past *two years* for employment purposes.

If you aren't satisfied with the results of your dispute, you can dispute the item directly with the creditor. In fact, the FACT Act requires creditors to initiate a dispute with the credit bureaus directly if you ask them to. Be sure to provide copies of all the information you have. You also have the right to include a 100-word statement of the dispute in your report and in future reports. Depending on the bureau's rules, this statement can stay on your report indefinitely, so don't forget about it! When it's no longer relevant, contact the bureau to request that it be removed, if it hasn't been already. Today, such statements are usually deleted automatically, but it never hurts to check.

#156
Adding Positive Info to Your Credit Report

nsufficient information on your credit report can also cause trouble. The best way to get positive information inserted into your credit report is to pay your creditors on time and in full every month. Do so for a year or more and you'll make great strides in improving your credit history and your credit score.

TIP

Called a *thin file* in the industry, a file that contains very little information may not be able to be scored. To get around this problem, you may be able to request that a FICO XD score be used. An *XD score* uses information from alternative databases (such as National Consumer Telecom and Utilities Exchange for cell-phone landline and cable records along with LexisNexis for public record and property data) to get enough data to form a valid score. Most recently, FICO announced its UltraFICO score, which lets you include your checking and savings account history help your traditional credit score. You can read more at www.fico.com/en/products/ultrafico-score.

Add Utility and Cellphone Payments to Your Report

Utility and cellphone companies don't report positive information, but Experian has introduced a service called Experian Boost, which lets you have your positive cellphone and utility payments added to your Experian credit report. The service is permission based, so if you change your mind, you can ask them to stop. You can read more about it at www.experian.com/boost.

REMEMBER

Experian Boost only reports the utility and cellphone payments on your Experian credit report. They won't show up on the reports from other credit bureaus.

Open New Credit Accounts

Another way to get positive information into your data file is to open new credit accounts. Opening types of accounts that aren't already on your credit report is particularly helpful. For example, you may have several credit cards, so you could add an installment account, which can enhance your "type of credit used" profile.

WARNING

Be careful when using this tactic to improve your credit score. You may do more harm than good if you open an account with a large amount of available credit, which is likely to push your available credit over the limit of what lenders find acceptable. Also, do so well in advance of applying for a loan because opening a new account may have a short-term negative effect on your score.

REMEMBER

Don't get carried away with this strategy. Applying for and opening a lot of new accounts in a short period of time is a sign of risk that can *hurt* your credit score. If you're not sure what to do, get a credit score and read the risk factors that go with it. Those factors will tell you if you need to open a new account or just pay down existing debts.

#157
Taking the First Steps to Dig Out of Credit Card Debt

The most important step toward digging your way out of debt is acknowledging the problem and realizing you need to actively do something about it. If any of the following statements are true in your life, consumer debt is a problem for you (also see Tip #158):

>> You have little or no savings and are at your limit on most of your credit cards.

>> You juggle bills each month, deciding which ones to pay and which need to wait until the next payday, even if it means paying after the bill's due date and incurring subsequent late fees.

>> You've taken at least one cash advance from a credit card account or other line of credit to make payments on other debts.

>> Your debt load (including car payments but not including your mortgage) exceeds 20 percent of your income. Most budgets can reasonably handle a 10 to 15 percent debt load, but more than that is excessive.

Identifying the problem is the first step to digging out of debt. The second step is often difficult for hard-core credit card junkies: cut up your credit cards. Yep, pull out the scissors and start snipping.

Some credit providers can't officially close the account until you've paid in full, but consider it closed to your usage. Do not, under any circumstances, use a credit card until your debts are paid in full. If you're deeply in debt, this can take several years. But after you're out from under the burden of excessive debt, the relief you experience more than makes up for the inconvenience of going without credit for a long stretch of time.

Make paying off your debt a high priority or you may face a major debt-related problem such as utility shut-off notices or even a personal bankruptcy in the not-so-distant future.

#158
Gauging Your Need for Help with Credit Situations

To help decide whether outside assistance with credit is right for you, ask yourself — and include your partner if you're not in this alone — a few simple questions:

>> **Are you stressed out?** You know you need to get some help when

- You screen your calls to avoid creditors.

- You argue with your partner about money or credit.

- Your sleep is interrupted because of financial worries, and you don't look forward to greeting the day in the morning.

>> **Are you (or you and your partner) being pulled in multiple directions regarding possible solutions?** You may be unsure about which approach to use:

- Increasing income to support your current bills and future goals.

- Decreasing expenses to bring your lifestyle in line with your present income.
- Getting a loan to pay off debt or reduce payments.
- Filing for bankruptcy.

>> **Are you dealing with multiple creditors or multiple problems?** You probably can use outside help if

- More than two or three collectors or creditors have you on speed dial.
- You have many problems (financial, employment, medical, and/or relationship) creating stress in your life at the same time.

>> **Are you more than one month late on your mortgage payment?** No matter what else is going on, you need to see a counselor now! A delay or the runaround from your servicer can cost you

- Thousands of dollars.
- Your credit.
- Your home.

>> **Are you thinking that bankruptcy may not be so bad for your credit?** Get professional, nonprofit counseling before you decide; otherwise, you may not know

- Whether bankruptcy will solve your problems or make them worse.
- Whether other alternatives exist that may be less damaging to your credit.

>> **Are you new to credit or to the United States and can't seem to break Into the financial mainstream, but don't know what to do next?** You'll benefit from help if

- You don't understand how credit works.
- You need to establish credit.
- You want to get started on your own version of the American Dream as soon as possible.

#159
Taking Debt Situations into Your Own Hands

The following sections outline three credit situations that you can probably resolve without much help.

To solve any credit/debt problem, you need to

REMEMBER

>> Identify the cause of the problem and resolve to fix it.

>> Know how much money you have to work with.

>> Act quickly.

Credit Cards

If you can't make this month's credit card payment, or if you've missed a payment already, you need to act. As long as you know what you can afford and you don't mind explaining your situation over the phone, you can get quick results.

Here's what to do: Call the toll-free customer service number and explain who you are, what happened, and how you want to handle the situation. If you need a break from making payments, say so. If you can make up the missed payments over the next month or two, offer. Just ensure that you can make good on your offer. Be sure to ask the customer service representative not to report your account as late to the bureaus. This decision is up to the credit card company; often, the company is willing to go along with the request as long as you keep your end of the bargain.

If you're polite and proactive and you contact the credit card company before the company contacts you, this approach establishes you as a good customer who needs and deserves special consideration — much better than a customer who is behind in payments, doesn't call, and may be a collection risk.

WARNING

Be careful about asking that a payment be stretched out for more than a month or two. If you need three months to catch up, you may get it — or even qualify for a longer hardship program — but the creditor may close your account, which hurts your credit. Also, don't be surprised if the company asks you to pay more than you think you can. The company doesn't know the details of your situation. Do *not* agree to anything you don't think you can deliver. Saying that something isn't possible and explaining why is much better than caving in but not being able to follow through. Ask to talk to a supervisor — they may have more authority to bend the rules.

Mortgages

If you're behind on your mortgage payment, but you're within the grace period allowed in your mortgage loan documents (typically 10 to 15 days from your contractual due date) and you have the money to make up the shortfall, send it in. If you're past the grace period, what you need to do to catch up depends on the state in which you live.

Say you haven't yet made your payment of $1,000 from last month. This month you can send in only $500 extra with your $1,000 payment. So you're short $500, right? Wrong. You may be behind the full $2,000 if the bank doesn't accept either payment because you didn't catch up in full. Or the bank may apply the extra $500 to this month's principal payment rather than to last month's deficit. The gist is, if you aren't far behind and you can catch up in one shot, do it. Otherwise, don't delay — get help.

WARNING

Mortgage lenders count delinquency occurrences differently than credit card issuers. As soon as you're one day beyond the grace period, mortgage lenders consider you late, back to the original, contractual, non-grace due date. After you're 90 days late from the contractual due date (not the grace period), all the rules change, and you're in serious danger of a foreclosure! Also, be mindful that some banks have shorter grace periods for mortgage holders who don't have bank accounts with them.

Student Loans

Getting some breathing room on a student loan isn't difficult if you have a qualifying reason for being unable to pay. Unemployment, a low-paying job, illness, a return to school — any of these reasons may qualify you for a short-term waiver, but only if you give the lender a call before you get into a default situation. Student loan people usually cooperate as long as they think you're playing it straight with them.

REMEMBER

If you don't think that you have enough money to catch up on your payments, you may have an alternative: The money may be hidden in your financial budget clutter. The first step in addressing a financial problem is to maximize your income and minimize your expenses. A spending plan (or budget) helps you with that. Only a real spending plan that accounts for at least 90 percent of your income and expenses will help; rough guesses don't yield the results you need.

#160
Working with a Credit Counseling Agency

legitimate, certified credit counselor may offer just the help you need to get a handle on your financial problems. A nonprofit credit counseling agency serves as an objective party to help you see your financial situation without emotion and fear clouding your vision. In addition, a trained and certified counselor may be able to offer you some credit education, personalized budgeting advice, and a custom-tailored plan to get you out of debt — all for nothing or next to nothing.

Debts Credit Counseling Can Help With

Although credit counseling can help in a variety of circumstances, it's essential in five situations. So if you find yourself dealing with any of the following scenarios, get some outside advice pronto, before matters get further out of hand:

>> **Mortgage default:** The rules are complex, the dates are often inflexible, and the servicers are often paper pushers who waste your time until a foreclosure is imminent. Many credit counselors, but not all, are certified mortgage

counselors who can get to the right people faster than you and can lead you through a complex process based on a lot of experience and special access to decision makers.

>> **Multiple bill collectors:** You can handle one or two collectors, but when you get to five, ten, or even more, conflicting demands can be impossible to balance.

>> **Joint credit problems:** Credit problems are exacerbated when you share them with someone who doesn't see things the way you do. An outside, dispassionate point of view can make all the difference.

>> **Debts that are backed by assets:** Loans for cars, houses, and boats are all secured by assets. If you don't or can't pay, the lender can repossess and sell your car, home, or boat. If you don't pay your credit card bill, the lender doesn't have any collateral that it can take, because it has no security beyond your word and your willingness to pay as agreed. As a general rule, the more security lenders have, the less willing they are to work with you to solve what they see as your problem.

>> **Bankruptcy:** You must get credit counseling before you can file for bankruptcy. Be sure to pick a good agency that does a lot of this stuff. The agency should be fast, efficient, and cost-effective, or you may later run into problems and delays.

In all these situations, you stand to benefit from talking to a professional who can help you with experience, resources, and a clear and unbiased outside view of your situation that you can't get when you're stuck in the middle.

How to Find a Great Credit Counseling Agency

Here are some things to look for in a quality credit counseling organization:

>> 501(c)(3) tax-exempt status

>> Accreditation by a national independent third-party accrediting organization, especially the Council on Accreditation

>> A willingness to spend at least 45 to 60 minutes with you, and more if needed — and for free

>> A willingness to offer help the way you're most comfortable receiving it — in person, by phone, or via the Internet

TIP

Here are a couple of organizations that can help you with your credit counseling needs:

>> **The National Foundation for Credit Counseling:** www.nfcc.org; 800-388-2227

>> **BALANCE:** www.balancepro.org; 888-777-7526

#161
Creating a Debt Management Plan

For about 25 percent of those who turn to credit counselors, more than advice is prescribed. In these cases, in addition to an action plan, a debt management plan is recommended. A *debt management plan* (sometimes called a *debt repayment plan*) requires that the agency act as an intermediary, handling both communications and payments on your behalf for a small monthly fee. This plan includes revised payments that

>> Are acceptable to all your creditors

>> Leave you enough money to handle your living expenses

>> Generally get you out of debt in two to five years

Debt management plans are an alternative to bankruptcy and often go by other names, such as a *workout plan, debt consolidation,* or an *interest-rate-reduction plan.* A debt management plan offers all these benefits and perhaps a lot more.

Here's how it works: When creditors realize that you can't meet the original terms of your credit card or other loan agreements, they also realize that they're better off working with you through your credit counselor. Under a debt management plan, your creditors are likely to be open to a number of solutions that are to your advantage, including

>> Stretching out your payments so that the combination of *principal* (the amount you originally borrowed) and interest pays off your balance in 60 months or less

>> Changing your monthly payment to an amount you can afford to pay

>> Reducing your interest rate and/or any fees associated with your loan

>> Refraining from hounding you day and night with collection calls

Why would creditors be willing to do these things for you? Because if they don't, and you really can't make the payments, they'll spend a lot more money on collections than they'd give you in concessions. Plus, if you file for bankruptcy, your creditors may *never* get their money.

REMEMBER

The critical point here is that the creditor has to believe you can't make the payments as agreed. But how does the creditor believe that without staking out your home? The creditor generally takes the word of the nonprofit credit counseling agency you go to for help. Still, being lenders, creditors check your credit report from time to time while you're on a debt management plan to make sure that you haven't opened new lines of credit.

WARNING

Sounds like a good deal: lower interest rates and smaller payments. Well, a debt management plan isn't a free lunch. The minuses may include

>> A potentially negative impact on your credit report, depending on how your creditors report your credit counseling account (although just being in a debt management plan doesn't affect your credit score)

>> Restricted access to credit during the term of the plan

>> Difficulty changing credit counseling agencies after you begin a debt management plan

REMEMBER

The bottom line is this: If you're in debt crisis or you're concerned that you may be getting close to it, a debt management plan from a good credit counseling agency may be a solution. If you're just shopping for an interest-rate reduction or a consolidation-loan alternative, a debt management plan may *not* be in your best interest.

#162
Talking to Creditors to Work Out a Solution

Communicating effectively isn't always easy, and many people don't even know where to begin. If you're not sure where to start, keep reading. When dealing with creditors, communication can be even more difficult because of the associated guilt, anger, and other emotions; basically, your emotions can set you up for conflict and communication breakdown.

From your perspective, the situation looks like this: You're a responsible adult who has been a good customer for a long time. A series of unfortunate, unexpected, and undeserved events has descended upon you like a plague. You've tried for months to overcome your payment problems before asking for help. You can't seem to catch up. You're at the end of your rope, dangling at the edge of a cliff. But with some help, you know that you can pull yourself out.

From the customer service rep's point of view, the scenario looks like this: You made a promise and broke it. Everyone else is required to pay their bills on time, so why shouldn't you? You may be overspending and living beyond your means. You need to catch up on your payments as fast as possible. If you don't come through, the collector's job performance and business will suffer, and if the collector gets fired, they'll be unable to pay their own bills.

REMEMBER

See how two people can see the same scenario so differently? It can be very hard to see things from a different perspective, but you'll be more successful in getting the outcome you want if you're able to see the situation from the other side. For whatever reason, you haven't been able to keep all the promises you made. That doesn't mean you aren't a good person. Always remember: The issue is about money and numbers for the collector; it's not personal. But from a financial perspective, it does indicate that doing business with you may be risky.

So now it's *your* job to explain why the creditor should accommodate you. Is resolution possible here? Yes — if you do your homework, offer a solution, and follow through on your promises. Where do you start? What do you say? To minimize negative perceptions, be proactive from the start and follow the steps outlined here.

Contact Your Creditor Promptly

Putting off unpleasant tasks is human nature. However, when requesting assistance from your creditors, the earlier you make the request, the better. From the creditor's point of view, three types of customers exist:

>> Good customers who pay as agreed

>> Good customers with temporary problems who are willing to work things out

>> Bad customers who won't pay what they owe without being "encouraged," if at all

You'd like to be the first type of customer, but sometimes bad things happen to good people and you slip into the second group. What's really important, however, is not finding yourself lumped into the third group.

TIP

The best time to let your creditors know that you're in trouble is as soon as *you* know and have a solution to offer. Don't wait until you've missed a payment if possible — or one payment at most — on that credit card or auto loan. Don't wait for the phone to ring or a letter to come and *then* give your story. Get in touch *before* the payment is late if you know you aren't going to be able to make it. By taking charge early, you give yourself a much greater chance that negative information won't find its way onto your credit report, where it could haunt you for years!

Explain Your Situation

You may choose to contact customer service by phone, in writing, via email, or through the creditor's website. In some cases, you may even communicate through an intermediary like an attorney or a credit counselor. Whatever method you use, you need to explain your situation as clearly, effectively, and objectively as possible. Do everything you can to take your emotions out of it. Assure the creditor that, despite your temporary difficulties, you intend to get back on financial track as quickly as possible.

But what do you want to say? What can you do to increase your chances of getting the help you need and deserve? Here are some elements to communicate (using a phone conversation as an example):

>> **Introduce yourself and ask for the person's name.** Why? Because doing so adds a human dimension to the dialogue and may help personalize your call. Don't say "you" or "you people." Write the name down because you're probably stressed out and may forget it easily. Plus, when you call again, you'll have a name to refer to.

>> **Begin the conversation on a positive note.** Say something nice about the company and your relationship with it. For example, "I've been a customer for years, and I've always had great products/service from you."

>> **Briefly (in a minute or so) present the facts.** And just the facts. For example, you lost your job, you have no savings, and you have only unemployment insurance for income. Skip the gory details and the emotional commentary.

Offer a Solution

After you've succinctly laid out the situation, propose a solution that works for you — *before* you turn control of the conversation over to the customer service representative. Your goal is to make it as easy as possible for the rep to agree to what you need, and the best way is just to ask for what you need! This is a critical and very positive step in the communication process.

The customer service rep may actually be pleased that you've come up with a workable plan. Doing so not only increases the chance that you'll get what you want but may also shorten the call if the rep can agree to your request, thereby making the rep look like a productive employee. Plus, by keeping more control over the outcome, you have a much better chance of getting a repayment plan that actually works for you. (You may even be able to negotiate a concession or two in your favor; see Tip #163, "Negotiating a Payback Arrangement with Collectors.")

TIP

Whatever your proposed plan, be sure to cover these bases:

» **Assure the rep that you're already taking steps to resolve the problem** *now*.

» **Offer a realistic estimate of how long you need to rectify the situation.** Not "soon" or "I don't know."

» **Propose a specific payment amount and plan that you can manage.** Don't ask the creditor to suggest an amount. You won't like the answer.

» **Offer specifics.** Avoid saying, "I can't afford the $300-a-month payment right now. You're going to have to accept less." That's not a plan. Instead, say, "I need to reduce the monthly payment to $150 for the next four months. I could even pay $75 twice a month. Then, in four months, I believe I can return to $300, which only extends the length of the loan by two months." Now *that's* a plan. It shows that you're sensitive to the creditor's situation and that you're making a fair effort to make good.

» **Don't overpromise.** You may feel intimidated or embarrassed, and it's only natural to want to give the creditor what the creditor wants. Don't be surprised if the creditor pushes back and asks for more. Be firm and don't budge on your offer, if possible. In the end, though, remember that the creditor won't be happy if you promise a certain payment and fail to deliver. If you get stuck, ask to speak to a manager, who may be able to approve your offer.

Cover All the Bases

REMEMBER

After you propose your plan and agree to terms, ask for a letter outlining the new agreement to be mailed or emailed to you so that there's no chance for a misunderstanding. If that doesn't seem to be forthcoming from your contact or if you don't receive written documentation of the new terms within a few days, follow up, stating the agreement in writing. Always make sure that any agreement you reach with the collection agency is put in writing.

#163
Negotiating a Payback Arrangement with Collectors

The best way to deal with the collection process is to face your debts head on and as quickly as possible. Debts don't improve with age, and they certainly don't go away if you ignore them. In fact, as debts age, they get bigger, uglier, and harder to pay. Unresolved debts also have an uncanny knack for resurfacing when you're least prepared to deal with them.

When you and the collector agree that all the particulars of the debt are legitimate, it's time for you to make an offer to resolve the obligation, whether the cause of the delinquency was an unintended error or unfortunate circumstances. You can make an offer to repay the amount over a period of time. Say you owe $1,000. If you offer to pay $50 per pay period for the next 20 weeks, that plan may be acceptable. Or you can offer to pay $25 per pay period until your next raise in three months, at which time you'll pay $75 per pay period. Offering the amount you're able to pay is always better than waiting for the collector to demand a certain amount.

You want to convey your concern and reassure the collector that you're sincere in your commitment to pay. But that doesn't mean you shouldn't try to negotiate some concessions. For example, you may ask the collector to

>> **Keep the matter between the two of you.** If, for example, you're able to pay off your obligation and you're only 30 to 60 days past due, ask the collector not to report your oversight to the credit bureaus. When the collection is still with the creditor's in-house collection division, your chances of it not being reported to the credit bureaus are better. When the debt is so late that it has been sold or transferred to a third-party collector, they'll be less likely to agree not to report it. Taking care of the unpaid debt early is always better if you can.

>> **Lighten the late fees.** It doesn't hurt to ask if they'll waive any late fees. Be sure to tell them that, if they do, you'll be happy to get off the phone so you can pay the bill online or run to the post office to mail your check. Most — but not all — will agree if they're getting the balance due without delay.

>> **Reduce your interest rate.** Think it's not the ideal time to try to get a better interest rate? Actually, it is. The collector wants what's called a *promise to pay* from you to resolve your situation. So ask for a break on the interest rate in order to help you pay the debt faster. On a delinquent credit card account, for example, you may be looking at a 30 percent default interest rate. The lender knows that adding this much to a strained budget increases the chance of a longer and more costly default or even a bankruptcy if you feel you have no way out. Lenders are often willing to help if you're sincere.

TIP

If you're under extreme financial duress, go a step further and ask if they have a hardship program. You may have to meet some qualifications, but if you do, your interest rate may drop dramatically, perhaps even to zero, and may lower your payments for six months to a year.

#164
Avoiding Debt Settlement

Debt settlement isn't the same as credit counseling or a debt management plan. It's sometimes advertised as a way to save money, but it can be one of the most expensive methods of all! In a debt settlement plan, you pay money to a company that holds your money without making any payments until the creditor stops hounding you and supposedly is ready to take less than the face value of the debt.

WARNING

This course of action *severely* damages your credit for years to come. If that's not enough to scare you off, consider this: Often, if you actually get to a settlement, the amount the creditor forgives actually becomes taxable income to you! You guessed it: The IRS wants you to pay taxes on the forgiven amount, which can add up to thousands of dollars due on April 15 to Uncle Sam. And those agents at the IRS don't go away! Even if you later decide to go the bankruptcy route, the IRS still gets its money.

Debt settlement is an unsavory, confrontational business. Don't do it! If you must, use a qualified attorney whom you know to negotiate on your behalf.

#165
Keeping Credit Under Control While Unemployed

The job market fluctuates just as the stock market does. The economy has good years and bad years. During bad years, you may find yourself laid off or downsized. During good years, you may decide that the time is right to change jobs on your own and for good reasons (higher pay, for example).

The reality is that you can expect that your employer will make the decision to say farewell to you at least once in your career. The event will arrive at the least advantageous time possible. The following sections help you through this almost inevitable fact of modern life — temporary unemployment.

REMEMBER

Employment information isn't regularly reported as part of your credit report. The credit bureaus don't keep track of where you work or what you earn. So any unemployment impact doesn't show up on your credit record unless you fail to make your payments on time, exceed your credit limits, or do something silly, like opening a lot of credit lines just in case you need them.

Prepare Your Credit for the Worst-Case Scenario

The following suggestions help you protect your credit in case of unemployment:

» **Start an emergency savings account if you don't have one already.** Fund it regularly so it grows to between six months' and a year's worth of living expenses (not income — your expenses should be less than your income). Six months to a year is how long you're likely to be unemployed if you're caught by surprise.

» **Keep one or two credit cards or lines of credit open.** Many employers view your credit report when hiring, so you want your report to look its best even if you're unemployed. To do so, continue to pay your bills on time and keep your credit card balance at less than 50 percent of available credit if possible.

If you've established savings and you have some available credit, you have two tools to help get you through this time without damaging your credit or your employment prospects. You can put together a new plan that includes finding a new job and a budget that works while you do so. Keep reading for the full scoop.

WARNING

Stay away from using cash advances on your credit cards! Spending money this way is much more costly than simply using the credit card to pay for items. Cash advances incur an extra fee, usually have a much higher interest rate than purchases, and often have a lower limit than your credit limit.

Refigure the Family Budget

With your reduced resources, cutting back your spending to only basic needs is essential. Begin by sitting down with your family and discussing the situation and the need to reduce expenses temporarily. Don't be embarrassed in front of the kids. This situation is an important lesson in reality for them. And you can show them how adults face difficult issues and win.

TIP

If your severance is being paid out over time or you haven't yet received it, ask your employer to raise your tax deductions to the maximum allowed. The IRS wants a report of anyone with more than ten deductions, so you should generally ask for ten (after all, you don't want the IRS looking at you unnecessarily). This strategy results in more cash flowing through to you now when you need it. Yes, you may owe some taxes on this money in April (though your deductible job-hunting expenses and reduced earnings for the year may offset that). But you want to maximize today's income at the possible expense of tomorrow's demands.

TIP

If you're overwhelmed and think you can benefit from some professional perspective or guidance, go to an accredited credit counselor. You can get information on credit counselors and where to find them in Tip #160, "Working with a Credit Counseling Agency."

Protect Your Credit Lines

The downside to using your lines of credit for your basic living expenses while unemployed is that you *may* do some damage to your credit. Here are some tips for protecting your credit status while you leverage your available credit to help you get through this challenging time:

> » **Keep balances at less than 50 percent of your available credit limit.** If it becomes necessary, spread your credit use over several accounts to keep your balance on each card at less than 50 percent. For example, rather than have a $2,000 balance on one card and a zero balance on three other cards, consider spreading the amount over all four cards equally, with each balance at $500.

> » **Make all payments on time.** Note that 35 percent of your credit score has to do with whether you make payments on time.

> » **Pay the car loan first.** A car can be repossessed in as little as two weeks. Then how will you get to work when you do find a job?

> » **Pay your mortgage a very close second.** Not all bills are created equal, and your mortgage is the most unequal of all.

Partial payments don't work, and falling behind 90 days begins a very-difficult-to-stop foreclosure process.

REMEMBER

Don't contact your creditor unless you *know* you're going to miss a payment. If you just *think* you may miss a payment, it's none of their business. If you *know*, however, telling the creditor before it happens is important. Why? Because you'll have more options if you do.

TIP

If you have any income, ask for a *hardship program* — a special repayment arrangement that may be offered to a good customer in need of some extra help. Such programs tend to last for no more than three to six months. Most creditors have them, but the hardship has to be real and imminent, and you have to ask for it.

#166
Consolidating Debts

I f you have credit card debt, a second mortgage, or other loans in addition to your first mortgage, debt consolidation can take a chunk out of your monthly expenses, freeing up money to cover other bills.

Discover Consolidation Options

Consider exploring the following options for consolidating debt:

>> Refinance your mortgage.

>> Take out a home equity loan.

>> Take out a home equity line of credit.

When you're already having trouble paying your bills, you may have damaged credit, which makes obtaining the loan you need to consolidate your debt that much more difficult. If that's the case, look at other means of consolidating, like getting one of these types of loans:

>> An *unsecured loan* allows you to pay off the old debt and make one monthly payment to the bank.

>> A *secured loan* requires that you put up some form of collateral so the bank has something it can take from you and sell to cover the debt.

Which is best — a secured or unsecured loan? That depends on your situation. Discuss your options with a qualified loan officer or mortgage broker in your area.

REMEMBER

When you borrow money, read and fully understand the documents before signing them. Know what the provisions are, when payments are due, what happens to surplus funds if collateral is sold for more than is required to pay off the loan, and so on. Have an attorney review the document and advise you of any potential issues before you sign.

Compare the Costs of Loans

Consolidating debt with a loan you pay too much for isn't a smart move when your goal is to lower payments and reduce what you owe. You can select from hundreds of loan types, but the bottom line is how much the loan costs in the long run.

The best way to compare loans is to determine the total cost of each loan over the life of the loan:

1. **Add up the fees charged to process the loan, including the loan origination fee, points, and closing costs.**

2. **Multiply the monthly payment by the number of months it will take you to pay off the loan in full.**

3. **Add the amounts from Steps 1 and 2 to determine the total cost of the loan.**

4. **Subtract the total amount you expect to pay toward principal over the life of the loan.**

   Ask the bank for an amortization worksheet for each loan to see how much principal you'll have paid at the time you expect to sell the house and pay off the loan.

The result is the total cost of the loan. Simply choose the loan that costs the least over the life of the loan.

#167
Taking Control When Foreclosure Looms

As soon as you begin to sense that your financial situation has taken a turn for the worse, you and the rest of your household need to work together to keep the problem from getting worse. Picture yourself in a boat that's taking on water. Before you start bailing out the water, find the holes and plug them.

Freeze Your Finances

When foreclosure strikes, the first order of business is to get a handle on your finances. Do whatever possible to keep more cash flowing in than flowing out — boost income with overtime or a second job, slash unnecessary expenses, and sock away as much money as possible. If you have children, trimming the fat is more stressful because you may fall into the trap of thinking you're depriving your children or letting them down. Keep in mind that the one thing your kids want and need most is *you*, not the stuff you buy them.

Prioritize Your Bills

Part of the process of stabilizing your current situation is prioritizing your bills. So when you're facing foreclosure, pay your bills in this order:

» Property taxes

» Secured debts

» Homeowner's insurance

» Utility and grocery bills

» Unsecured debts

Know Who to Contact

Your most valuable assets in foreclosure are people who can assist you, so draw up a list of people you can lean on. Your list may include the following:

» Friends and relatives

» Bank representative

» Real estate agent (*Note:* Selling the home is often the best option in foreclosure cases.)

» Register of deeds

» Sheriff

» Bankruptcy attorney

» Foreclosure attorney

Gather Important Documents

Before you get too far into the foreclosure fight, gather important documents and other materials you'll be called upon to deliver at some point in the process. The most important of these legal documents:

» Mortgage, deed of trust (if you purchased your home through a bank), or contract for deed (if the seller provided financing)

- >> Note, promissory note, or contract (your promise to pay the loan in full)
- >> Modifications to the mortgage or promissory note
- >> Deed
- >> Correspondence
- >> Notice of default
- >> Sheriff's or trustee's deed
- >> Canceled checks
- >> Bank statements
- >> Listing agreement
- >> Current appraisal
- >> Phone logs

#168
Drafting a Plan of Attack to Offset Foreclosure

f you're facing possible foreclosure, you need a plan. Are you going to try to save your home? Do you want to sell it to get out from under the burden? Does it make sense to simply live in the home as long as possible and then bail out before the sheriff comes to evict you? Following are some options:

REMEMBER

>> **Filing for bankruptcy:** This is a costly option. Consult with a reputable bankruptcy attorney in your area before making any final decisions.

>> **Reinstating your mortgage:** If you think you'll be unable to pay off the loan in addition to making your mortgage payments, reinstatement may not be the ideal solution for you.

>> **Arranging for a redemption:** Here, you have to come up with a chunk of money to pay off the entire loan, plus any qualifying interest, expenses, and attorney fees that have stacked up as a result of the foreclosure.

>> **Haggling for a forbearance:** A *forbearance agreement* is similar to reinstating, but you don't have to pay a lump sum all at once.

» Negotiating a mortgage modification: Your bank tweaks your mortgage. The adjustments can include anything stated in the mortgage, including the interest rate and *term* (how long you have to pay off the loan).

» Refinancing your home with another lender: Be wary of shady loan originators who may try to take advantage of you by selling you a loan (one with a very high interest rate or an adjustable-rate mortgage [ARM] with a low teaser rate that's likely to rise suddenly) that'll put you in worse shape months or years down the road.

» Living off your home with a reverse mortgage: With a *reverse mortgage,* you receive monthly payments (tax free) from the mortgage holder instead of having to make monthly payments. Reverse mortgages are typically designed for older homeowners who have plenty of equity in their homes and need to draw on that equity to cover living expenses.

» Selling the house: For a huge majority of people facing foreclosure, selling the home and moving to more affordable accommodations is the absolute best option.

» Deeding the house to your bank in lieu of foreclosure: When offering a deed in lieu of foreclosure, make sure the bank provides you with a formal release of all obligations for repaying the debt. Otherwise, the bank may be able to file for a deficiency judgment if the house sells for less than what you owe on it; you're then responsible for paying the difference.

» Selling the house to an investor: If you can't possibly afford to rehab your home to bring it up to market standards and then sell it for a profit, an investor may be able to.

» Moving out and leaving the keys: You can't sell your home even to an investor, the bank won't accept a deed in lieu of foreclosure, and you have no other options. What do you do? Your best option may be to live in your home for as long as the law allows and save your money for the eventual move. In areas that have a lengthy redemption period, you can squirrel away a lot of cash over the course of several months.

In deciding how to proceed, weigh your options rationally:

1. Lay all options on the table, no matter how unrealistic they may seem right now.

2. Arrange the options in order, from the ones that sound most attractive to the ones that sound least attractive.

3. Move to the bottom any options that are likely to land you back in the same place you are now (or worse).

4. Get on the same page as your spouse or partner; the execution of your plan will be most effective if you present a united front.

#169
Understanding Types of Bankruptcy

Filing for bankruptcy is a very serious decision for which you need to be armed with all the information you can find. Why? Because for all the problems a bankruptcy solves, it can create many more if you make a mistake.

In basic terms, the reason for filing bankruptcy is to seek the protection of the court from your creditors. It's that simple. If you can't pay what you owe on your own, now or in the foreseeable future, call in the judge, and the judge will handle your collectors.

The courts allow many different types of bankruptcy, identified as chapters with numbers. The variety of options reflects the variety of solutions needed for different situations.

Among all the various chapters, two are most commonly used by consumers who find themselves unable to come to agreement with or to meet contractual payments with their creditors:

>> **Chapter 7:** Also known as *liquidation,* this is the most popular form of bankruptcy. It may require you to give up some assets (the liquidation part), but it gets you out of almost all your liabilities.

>> Chapter 13: Often referred to as *wage-earner bankruptcy,* this form of bankruptcy allows you to keep most of your assets and pay back what the judge rules you can over a period of time, usually three to five years, under court supervision and protection.

REMEMBER

Regardless of which chapter you file, make sure that bankruptcy will truly solve your problems — the problems you have today, the problems you'll have tomorrow, and the complications of dealing with the financial, employment, and insurance systems in the future. Both Chapter 7 and Chapter 13 bankruptcies have eligibility requirements, which is covered in the following sections.

Qualifying for Chapter 7

If qualified, under a Chapter 7, you receive relief from virtually all your debts, with a few exceptions, and you get it fast — like the same day (unlike a Chapter 13, which may take up to five years before you get a discharge).

The first hurdle in moving forward with Chapter 7 bankruptcy is meeting the *means test.* If you have too many means (that is, too much money), you can't declare Chapter 7. And the courts won't take your word for it; you have to *prove* that your income really is what you say it is. If your income over the last six months is above the applicable median for your state of residence, you can't file for Chapter 7.

TIP

To find out whether your income is above the median in your state of residence, go to the U.S. Census website: www.census.gov/search-results.html?searchType=web&cssp=SERP&q=median income by state. See www.legalconsumer.com/bankruptcy/means-test for a good means-test calculator, which includes the latest revised means tests forms while excluding any CARES Act payments from monthly income.

If your income is above the median, don't give up just yet. Next, you want to determine whether you have excess monthly income of more than $166.66 to pay $10,000 of debt over five years. So what counts as excess income? To find out, you have to use the spending guidelines approved by the IRS. Allowable expenses are shown at www.justice.gov/ust/eo/bapcpa/20200501/bci_data/ median_income_table.htm. An updated chart with the allowable expenses for each state can be found under the heading "Median Family Income Based on State/Territory and Family Size." The IRS guidelines may be very tight for you.

Using the IRS allowable expenses as a guide, if you *fail* the means test, the best you can do is to file under Chapter 13.

If you have less excess monthly income than the magic number of $166.66 after IRS expense allowances, you may proceed to the next hurdle: Do you have an extra $100 a month over the next 60 months? And will that $6,000 account for at least 25 percent of your debt? If the answer to both questions is no, you can pass go and file for Chapter 7. If not, you likely go directly to Chapter 13.

At some point during the six months before you file for bankruptcy, you have to receive counseling and get a certificate from a court-approved nonprofit credit counselor. Credit counseling costs are on a sliding fee scale. They're free if your income is below 150 percent of the poverty level for your family size. Otherwise, up to $50 is considered reasonable.

Qualifying for Chapter 13

The strict guidelines to qualify for filing a Chapter 7 bankruptcy mean that some people qualify only to file Chapter 13. The requirements for counseling and proof of income are the same for both types of bankruptcy. Although you must take the same means test, the outcome leads to different results.

Chapter 13 differs from Chapter 7 in that, after establishing your income and deducting allowable expenses, you must use the remainder of your excess monthly income to repay your debt. *Excess* is defined by subtracting the IRS allowable expenses from your income.

Just as with Chapter 7, those filing for Chapter 13 bankruptcy must establish that their family income is either below or above the median for their state. If your total income is above the state median, your excess income gets disposed of (paid to your bankruptcy trustee, who forwards it to your creditors) for the next five years, unless you can show that you can pay off 100 percent of the debt in less than 60 months. If your total income is below the state median, your excess income may be paid to your creditors over the next three years. The rest of the debt that you owe to your creditors goes unpaid, and no interest accrues on any of the accounts involved. You also want to understand any tax implications as creditors forgive that debt.

#170
Avoiding Bankruptcy

You don't need to file bankruptcy to solve a trivial financial problem or when a more targeted remedy is available. Although you shouldn't view bankruptcy as a last-ditch solution, you probably shouldn't make it your first consideration either. If you can get out of trouble without filing, that's wonderful! In fact, you may want to consider the following solutions before deciding that bankruptcy is the way out:

Make a Budget

If you can get your financial house in order through discipline and careful budgeting, go for it. The key to realistic budgeting is establishing a reasonable time frame for immediate and long-term goals and adopting a positive attitude that focuses not on what you're giving up but rather on what you're achieving.

Allow Your Family to Bail You Out

If a parent or other family member offers to save your hide, accepting that generosity is tempting. Allowing your family to bail you out may be a wise alternative to bankruptcy, but only if your Guardian Angel

>> Is ready, willing, and able to help.

>> Can pay your debts without suffering financial hardship themselves.

>> Can truly solve your problem, not just postpone an inevitable bankruptcy.

Sell Your Assets

If you own assets that you'd lose to a bankruptcy trustee, you may want to consider selling your stuff to pay your debts. If that doesn't raise enough money to pay *all* your debts, it at least helps whittle down your debt load. Consider selling your *nonexempt* assets — those that a creditor can get — not *exempt assets*, those that are off-limits to creditors.

REMEMBER

Every state has laws that make certain essential assets exempt or off-limits to creditors, regardless of whether you file bankruptcy. Don't let anyone bully you into selling exempt assets, which in most cases are off-limits even if you don't file for bankruptcy. Most states allow you to keep homesteads up to a specified value, pensions, basic household furnishings, and a modest vehicle.

Transfer Credit Card Balances

Although trading high interest rates for lower rates is worth checking out, credit-card balance transfers seldom are effective. A *balance transfer* actually is a new loan, with the proceeds going to pay debts that should be pretty far down on your list of priorities. Furthermore, whenever you transfer a balance and then end up in bankruptcy, you may be facing an allegation of fraud, and your creditors may fight to prevent the debts you owe them from being wiped out.

Restructure Home Mortgages

You may be able to free up some cash by restructuring your home mortgage. Basically, you can do this in two ways: arranging a mortgage workout agreement and refinancing.

WARNING

Taking a home-equity loan doesn't reduce the amount of your mortgage debt. With a home-equity loan, you essentially unbuy your house and then buy it back again. For a variety of reasons, home-equity loans aren't a good idea when you're in financial straits. The most important argument against a home-equity loan is that it creates a lien on your home that survives bankruptcy. Say that after sucking all the equity out of your home to pay your credit card bills, you still end up in bankruptcy. What you've done is needlessly put your house on the line. The credit card debts were unsecured and would've probably been eliminated in bankruptcy. But the value of your house secures the home-equity loan.

#171
Choosing Which Bills to Pay When You File for Bankruptcy

When you can't pay everyone, you need to invest your money where it does the most good or avoids the gravest of problems. Dribbling out money to the most aggressive collectors without an overall plan is a mistake. The payments at the top of your priority list (in order) should be the following:

>> Rent, or mortgage, if you intend to keep your house
>> Utilities
>> Essential vehicle
>> Fines, if nonpayment would land you in jail
>> Child support and alimony
>> Income taxes
>> Possibly student loans

A note about paying child support and alimony: The consequences for neglecting those obligations are serious, possibly even criminally serious if you're jailed for contempt of court. And many judges have adopted a zero-tolerance approach toward deadbeat parents.

It's no accident that credit cards, loans from finance companies, and medical bills don't make the cut in this list. That's because before creditors in these industries can ever cause you any real trouble, they have some hurdles to jump over. Before they can take any of your property, they must sue you and obtain a judgment. Besides, these kinds of debts can be wiped out if you end up in bankruptcy. In addition, if bankruptcy is in your future, you shouldn't repay loans to close friends or family members or loans that these people cosigned for. If you file bankruptcy within one year of making these types of payments, the trustee can get the money back.

#172
Negotiating with Creditors to Avoid Bankruptcy

Attempting a nonbankruptcy solution is worth the effort. If you can find someone who actually has the authority to negotiate, you may be able to cut a deal that works to everyone's satisfaction. You're more likely to succeed if your creditor is a small organization, but if your creditor is a large institution, the task will be more difficult.

Workout Agreements

Traditionally, a nonbankruptcy *workout agreement* — where a debtor reaches a negotiated solution with creditors — falls into one of three categories:

>> Composition arrangements, where all creditors agree to accept less than full settlement of the debts

>> Extension agreements, which merely extend the term for repayment in full

>> Combination agreements, where debts are reduced and paid over an extended time period

WARNING

The problem with these plans is that all your creditors must go along with it, and so, the more creditors you have, the harder it is to get them to agree. In addition, you'll probably need a lawyer to negotiate settlement agreements, and the legal fees may be exorbitant, if not prohibitive.

Workout agreements are more useful when you have valuable nonexempt assets that are worth enough to pay your debts, but you need some time to sell without having to juggle creditors. In consumer cases, rarely does a debtor have enough assets to pay his debts.

WARNING

Strange as it may seem, whenever a creditor writes off a debt outside of the bankruptcy context, the amount of the write-off is taxable income to the borrower unless he was insolvent (owed debts exceeding the value of his assets) when the debt was kissed off. If you're in this situation, consider filing Form 982 with your tax return. You can get it at www.irs.gov/pub/irs-pdf/f982.pdf.

A Threat of Bankruptcy

If you're genuinely considering bankruptcy, unsecured creditors may agree to settle for a pittance simply because when you do actually file, they'd receive nothing.

Assume that you borrowed $50,000 to start a business, which never got off the ground. There's no way you can repay this debt, and all you own is a modest home, mortgaged to the hilt, an old car, and a pension. If you file bankruptcy, the lender won't receive one red cent. If you offer the creditor the money that you'd otherwise spend on filing bankruptcy, about $1,000, they should (if they're thinking rationally) agree to take the money and write off the debt. A thousand dollars is still better than nothing. And you avoid having to file bankruptcy.

REMEMBER

The success of this kind of strategy depends on convincing your creditor that you're truly prepared to file bankruptcy. The best way to accomplish that is to hire a well-known bankruptcy specialist to handle the negotiation. That way, the creditor knows that you're serious. But don't ever bluff or threaten bankruptcy unless you're truly prepared to turn in that direction.

#173
Handling IRS Debts

An IRS debt can be one of the easiest debt situations to deal with. First, the IRS knows that *you* know who's in control, so the IRS doesn't need to intimidate you with strong-arm tactics to get your attention. Second, the IRS isn't chasing down its own money — it's chasing down taxpayer money. And third, IRS employees don't get a bonus for collecting a debt. You can probably negotiate a reasonable repayment plan with the IRS that you can manage over time.

TIP

Download IRS Form 9465 at www.irs.gov/pub/irs-pdf/f9465.pdf, fill it out, and send it in. The form isn't hard to complete, so don't wait too long before you act.

If you have an accountant, bring them along when you meet with the IRS. Your accountant may be able to calmly explain why you shouldn't owe taxes on some income or why you should get certain deductions. Like lawyers in courts, accountants have their own language and rules. Having a professional with you can give you an advantage.

WARNING

IRS debts just keep growing with age. If you delay too long, the IRS will pull any tax refunds you have coming and direct the money into the Treasury until the debt is paid. As they say, the tax man always gets his money.

REMEMBER

The credit bureaus don't include tax liens anymore — paid or not. However, other companies do collect tax lien information. Businesses check those reports, too. To make sure they don't hurt you in the future, keep good records of payments and discharges, and, if appropriate, the property records at your local town hall. Make sure that the records are updated, or you may not be able to sell your home because it has a big fat lien on it that shouldn't be there.

The Part of Tens

Get tips on how to boost your savings and cut back on your spending without reducing your quality of living. Use them as an opportunity to evaluate what's really important to you so you can get your spending habits in sync with your values.

Find advice on how to survive financial emergencies — because everyone faces financial crises at one time or another.

#174
Ten Ways to Trim the Money Tree

» **Determine which expenses you can eliminate without affecting your quality of life.** For example, are you actually using all the features of your mobile phone plan? Is that expensive data plan worth the cost?

» **Eat out no more than once a week.** A family of four can easily spend $30 at a very inexpensive restaurant. You can make that same meal, or a much better one, at home for about one-third of the cost.

» **Plant and maintain a small vegetable and herb garden.** A small garden with a few tomato plants, some green beans, basil, and oregano doesn't take up much space. In fact, you can plant all these items in pots on your deck, patio, or balcony. By growing some of your own vegetables and herbs, you save money on your grocery bills, and you and your family benefit from homegrown fun and flavor.

» **Cook a giant feast on weekends, enjoy one large meal for the family, and freeze the leftovers in individual containers.** Now you have homemade, ready-to-heat meals for a fraction of the cost of quality processed frozen foods.

>> **Sell items you don't use or need, and purchase quality secondhand items.** Check out eBay (www.ebay.com) and Craigslist (www.craigslist.org). If you have a Facebook account, you can also check out Facebook Marketplace. You can sell your extra stuff that you no longer use and buy great used stuff that you need, all for a fraction of what these items cost new.

>> **Buy merchandise when it's going out of season.** Buy next year's winter coat or swimsuit when the prices are dirt cheap instead of at the beginning of the season, when the items aren't on sale. And when you're shopping for clothes, buy wash-and-wear clothes rather than dry-clean only.

>> **Become a do-it-yourselfer.** If you currently hire someone to mow, clean, or provide other domestic services, explore how much money you could save by doing these projects yourself. And if you're a parent, by being a do-it-yourselfer, you also educate and empower your children to carry on this self-sufficient lifestyle.

>> **Use resources in your community.** Before you plunk down your hard-earned money to join a gym or for various types of entertainment and activities, consider what your community has to offer — usually at little or no cost. Consider communities centers and swimming pools, town and county libraries, and local parks and jogging trails, among other options.

>> **Automate your monthly payments.** Set up automatic monthly payments directly out of your checking account to pay all your regular monthly expenses. For example, you can contact your utility companies, sign up for their average monthly payment plans, and have those bills automatically deducted from your bank account. Having these expenses automatically withdrawn from your checking account means that you never have to worry about writing checks, purchasing stamps, or incurring late fees, saving you both time and money.

>> **Take full advantage of your employer's matching contribution.** Contribute the maximum amount that your employer will match in your retirement plan at work. You're basically receiving free money from your company! The more your employer kicks in, the less you have to.

#175
Ten Ways to Handle Financial Emergencies

>> **Plan ahead.** Build a savings cushion of six months of living expenses and make sure you have adequate insurance. Leave room in your monthly budget for surprises. Focus on the plan, and results will follow.

>> **Pay yourself first.** Put savings away as soon as you get paid. If you can, have it taken from your check and directly deposited into your savings account before you ever see it.

>> **Reduce tax deductions.** If you get more than $600 a year back in refunds, you'd be better off having that money on a month-to-month basis, earning the interest yourself.

>> **Earn more money.** Get a second job, work overtime, or ask for that long overdue raise.

>> **Sell some assets.** Whether you sell your grand piano on eBay or gather your clutter and hold a garage sale, you just may be able to offset some or all of your emergency costs by turning your possessions into ready cash.

>> **Borrow against your home.** If you own a home, have built up equity, and can afford an additional monthly payment, a home-equity line of credit may be just the ticket. Interest

payments are incurred only if you draw on the line of credit, and they may be tax deductible.

» **Borrow from friends and relatives.** Just make sure you put the terms of the loan in writing, establish a regular payment schedule, and pay interest as you would with a traditional loan.

» **Defer retirement contributions.** If you're regularly contributing to a retirement plan, temporarily funnel the money toward emergency expenses instead.

» **Seek professional help.** If you see no other way out of your financial crisis, call in the professionals at a credit-counseling agency.

» **Declare bankruptcy.** Filing for bankruptcy is a legitimate way to handle a financial emergency if nothing else succeeds.

Index

More For Dummies Titles to Keep You Living Well When Times Are Tough

401(k)s & IRAs For Dummies by Ted Benna with Brenda Newmann (John Wiley & Sons, Inc.)

529 & Other College Savings Plans For Dummies, by Margaret A. Munro, EA (John Wiley & Sons, Inc.)

Auto Repair For Dummies, 2nd Edition, by Deanna Sclar (John Wiley & Sons, Inc.)

Canning & Preserving For Dummies, 3rd Edition, by Amelia Jeanroy with Karen Ward (John Wiley & Sons, Inc.)

Careers For Dummies by Marty Nemko, PhD (John Wiley & Sons, Inc.)

Credit Repair Kit For Dummies, 5th Edition, by Melyssa Barrett, Steve Bucci, and Rod Griffin (John Wiley & Sons, Inc.)

Foreclosure Self-Defense For Dummies by Ralph R. Roberts, Lois Maljak, and Paul Doroh with Joe Kraynak (John Wiley & Sons, Inc.)

Free $ for College For Dummies by David Rosen and Caryn Mladen (John Wiley & Sons, Inc.)

Frugal Living For Dummies by Deborah Taylor-Hough (John Wiley & Sons, Inc.)

Gifts from the Kitchen For Dummies by Andrea Swenson (John Wiley & Sons, Inc.)

Haircutting For Dummies, 2nd Edition, by Jeryl E. Spear (John Wiley & Sons, Inc.)

Home-Based Business For Dummies, 3rd Edition, by Paul Edwards, Sarah Edwards, and Peter Economy (John Wiley & Sons, Inc.)

Home Maintenance For Dummies, 2nd Edition, by James Carey and Morris Carey (John Wiley & Sons, Inc.)

Instant Pot Cookbook For Dummies by Wendy Jo Peterson, MS, RDN, and Elizabeth Shaw, MS, RDN, CLT, CPT

Insurance For Dummies, 2nd Edition, by Jack Hungelmann (John Wiley & Sons, Inc.)

Personal Bankruptcy Laws For Dummies by James P. Caher and John M. Caher (John Wiley & Sons, Inc.)

Personal Finance Workbook For Dummies, 2nd Edition, by Sheryl Garrett (John Wiley & Sons, Inc.)

Reconstructing Clothes For Dummies by Miranda Caroligne Burns (John Wiley & Sons, Inc.)

Resumes For Dummies, 8th Edition, by Laura DeCarlo (John Wiley & Sons, Inc.)

Side Hustles For Dummies by Alan Simon (John Wiley & Sons, Inc.)

Stress Management For Dummies, 2nd Edition, by Allen Elkin, PhD (John Wiley & Sons, Inc.)

Telecommuting For Dummies by Minda Zetlin (John Wiley & Sons, Inc.)

Working from Home For Dummies by Tara Powers, MS, et al. (John Wiley & Sons, Inc.)

Publisher's Acknowledgments

Senior Acquisitions Editor:
Tracy Boggier

Senior Managing Editor:
Kristie Pyles

Compilation Editor:
Georgette Beatty

Project Editor and Copy Editor:
Chad R. Sievers

Production Editor:
Mohammed Zafar Ali

Cover Image: © PanuShot/ Shutterstock